Teaching Theory

Teaching the New English

Published in association with the English Subject Centre
Director: Ben Knights

Teaching the New English is an innovative series concerned with the teaching of the English degree in universities in the UK and elsewhere. The series addresses new and developing areas of the curriculum as well as more traditional areas that are reformning in new contexts. Although the Series is grounded in intellectual and theoretical concepts of the curriculum, it is concerned with the practicalities of classroom teaching. The volumes will be invaluable for new and more experienced teachers alike.

Titles include:

Gail Ashton and Louise Sylvester (*editors*)
TEACHING CHAUCER

Richard Bradford (*editor*)
TEACHING THEORY

Charles Butler (*editor*)
TEACHING CHILDREN'S FICTION

Robert Eaglestone and Barry Langford (*editors*)
TEACHING HOLOCAUST LITERATURE AND FILM

Michael Hanrahan and Deborah L. Madsen (*editors*)
TEACHING, TECHNOLOGY, TEXTUALITY
Approaches to New Media and the New English

David Higgins and Sharon Ruston
TEACHING ROMANTICISM

Andrew Hiscock and Lisa Hopkins (*editors*)
TEACHING SHAKESPEARE AND EARLY MODERN DRAMATISTS

Peter Middleton and Nicky Marsh (*editors*)
TEACHING MODERNIST POETRY

Andrew Maunder and Jennifer Phegley (*editors*)
TEACHING NINETEENTH-CENTURY FICTION

Anna Powell and Andrew Smith (*editors*)
TEACHING THE GOTHIC

Gina Wisker (*editor*)
TEACHING AFRICAN AMERICAN WOMEN'S WRITING

Teaching the New English Series Standing Order
ISBN 978–1–4039–4441–2 Hardback 978–1–4039–4442–9 Paperback
(*outside North America only*)

You can receive future titles in this series as they are published by placing a standing order. Please contact your bookseller or, in case of difficulty, write to us at the address below with your name and address, the title of the series and the ISBN quoted above.

Customer Services Department, Macmillan Distribution Ltd, Houndmills, Basingstoke, Hampshire RG21 6XS, England

Teaching Theory

Edited by

Richard Bradford
Research Professor of English, University of Ulster, UK

palgrave
macmillan

First published 2011 by
PALGRAVE MACMILLAN

Palgrave Macmillan in the UK is an imprint of Macmillan Publishers Limited,
registered in England, company number 785998, of Houndmills, Basingstoke,
Hampshire RG21 6XS.

Palgrave Macmillan in the US is a division of St Martin's Press LLC,
175 Fifth Avenue, New York, NY 10010.

Palgrave Macmillan is the global academic imprint of the above companies
and has companies and representatives throughout the world.

Palgrave® and Macmillan® are registered trademarks in the United States,
the United Kingdom, Europe and other countries.

ISBN 978–0–230–52073–8   hardback
ISBN 978–0–230–52074–5   paperback

This book is printed on paper suitable for recycling and made from fully
managed and sustained forest sources. Logging, pulping and manufacturing
processes are expected to conform to the environmental regulations of the
country of origin.

A catalogue record for this book is available from the British Library.

A catalog record for this book is available from the Library of Congress.

10   9   8   7   6   5   4   3   2   1
20   19   18   17   16   15   14   13   12   11

Printed and bound in Great Britain by
CPI Antony Rowe, Chippenham and Eastbourne

Contents

Series Preface

One of many exciting achievements of the early years of the English Subject Centre was the agreement with Palgrave Macmillan to initiate the series "Teaching the New English." The intention of the then Director, Professor Philip Martin, was to create a series of short and accessible books which would take widely-taught curriculum fields (or, as in the case of learning technologies, approaches to the whole curriculum) and articulate the connections between scholarly knowledge and the demands of teaching.

Since its inception, "English" has been committed to what we know by the portmanteau phrase "learning and teaching." Yet, by and large, university teachers of English – in Britain at all events – find it hard to make their tacit pedagogic knowledge conscious, or to raise it to a level where it might be critiqued, shared, or developed. In the experience of the English Subject Centre, colleagues find it relatively easy to talk about curriculum and resources, but far harder to talk about the success or failure of seminars, how to vary forms of assessment, or to make imaginative use of Virtual learning Environments. Too often this reticence means falling back on received assumptions about student learning, about teaching, or about forms of assessment. At the same time, colleagues are often suspicious of the insights and methods arising from generic educational research. The challenge for the English group of disciplines is therefore to articulate ways in which our own subject knowledge and ways of talking might themselves refresh debates about pedagogy. The implicit invitation of this series is to take fields of knowledge and survey them through a pedagogic lens. Research and scholarship, and teaching and learning are part of the same process, not two separate domains.

"Teachers," people used to say, "are born not made." There may, after all, be some tenuous truth in this: there may be generosities of spirit (or, alternatively, drives for didactic control) laid down in earliest childhood. But why should we assume that even "born" teachers (or novelists, or nurses, or veterinary surgeons) do not need to learn the skills of their trade? Amateurishness about teaching has far more to do with university claims to status, than with evidence aboul how people learn. There is a craft to shaping and promoting learning. This series of books is dedicated to the development of the craft of teaching within English Studies.

Ben Knights
Teaching the New English *Series Editor*
Director, English Subject Centre
Higher Education Academy

The English Subject Centre

Founded in 2000, the English Subject Centre (which is based at Royal Holloway University of London) is part of the subject network of the Higher Education Academy. Its purpose is to develop learning and teaching across the English disciplines in UK Higher Education. To this end it engages in research and publication (web and print), hosts events and conferences, sponsors projects, and engages in day-to-day dialogue with its subject communities.
http://www.english.heacademy.ac.uk

Notes on Contributors

Richard Bradford is Research Professor of English at the University of Ulster. Previously he has taught in the Universities of Oxford, Wales and Trinity College Dublin and has been Visiting Lecturer in the Universities of Warsaw and Budapest. He has published twenty-one books, most recently *The Novel Now* (2007), *First Boredom, Then Fear. The Life of Philip Larkin* (2005) and *The Life of a Long Distance Writer. The Biography of Alan Sillitoe* (2008). His authorised biography of Martin Amis will appear in 2011 and his *Poetry: The Ultimate Guide* was published in 2010.

Katherine Byrne is a Lecturer in English at the University of Ulster, where she teaches nineteenth-century fiction and critical theory. She has a PhD from the University of East Anglia, and has published articles on nineteenth-century literature and medicine. Her book, on the representation of tuberculosis in Victorian literature and culture, will be published next year.

Madelena Gonzalez is Professor of English Literature at the University of Avignon. Her latest publications include: *Fiction After the Fatwa: Salman Rushdie and the Charm of Catastrophe*, *Translating Identity and the Identity of Translation* and *Théâtre des minorités: Mises en scène de la marge à l'époque contemporaine*. She has published widely on contemporary literature and culture and is currently editing a collection of articles on genre in the contemporary novel, as well as a second volume on Minority Theatre, in English this time.

Andrew Hadfield is Professor of English at the University of Sussex. He was educated at the Universities of Leeds and Ulster, and previously taught at the University of Wales, Aberystwyth, Leeds, and Columbia University. He has published a number of books, including *Literature, Politics and National Identity: From Reformation to Renaissance* (1994), *Literature, Travel and Colonial Writing in the English Renaissance, 1545–1625* (1998, paperback 2007), and *Shakespeare and Republicanism* (2005, paperback, 2008). He has also edited, with Raymond Gillespie, *The History of the Irish Book: Vol. III: The Irish Book in English, 1550–1800* (2006). He is editor of *Renaissance Studies* and is currently writing a biography of Edmund Spenser.

Andrew James is a lecturer at Chikushi Women's University in Japan, where he has lived and worked for the past sixteen years. He holds a BA in English literature from Queen's University in Canada, an MA in English literature from Mississippi State University, and an MA in TESL/TEFL from the University of Birmingham in England. He is currently completing his PhD part-time at the University of Ulster in Northern Ireland on the development of Kingsley Amis's narrative voice. His recent publications include essays on Amis in *Englishness Revisited* (2009) and *Life Writing* (2009, Palgrave Macmillan).

Jill Le Bihan is Lecturer in English at Sheffield Hallam University. She specialises in Feminist Theory, Psychoanalysis, Contemporary Women's Writing and 19th Century Fiction, and has published widely in journals and volumes of essays. Her most recent work in print focuses on popular film and fiction and Feminist Theory.

Vincent B. Leitch, George Lynn Cross Research Professor, holds the Paul and Carol Daube Sutton Chair in English at the University of Oklahoma, where he teaches criticism and theory. He is author of *Deconstructive Criticism* (1983), *American Literary Criticism from the 1930s to the 1980s* (1988; 2nd edition, 2009), *Cultural Criticism, Literary Theory, Poststructuralism* (1992), *Postmodernism – Local Effects, Global Flows* (1996), *Theory Matters* (2003), and *Living with Theory* (2008). He serves as the General Editor of the *Norton Anthology of Theory and Criticism* (2001; 2nd edn, 2010).

Neil Murphy has previously taught at the University of Ulster and the American University of Beirut and is currently Associate Professor of contemporary literature at NTU, Singapore. He is the author of several books on Irish fiction and contemporary literature, and has published numerous articles and book chapters on contemporary Irish fiction, postmodernism, and theories of reading. His collection of essays on Aidan Higgins' work is forthcoming.

Stephen Shapiro teaches in the Department of English and Comparative Literary Studies at Warwick University. He is author of *How To Read Marx's Capital* and the co-editor of the *How to Read Theory* series. His *The Culture and Commerce of the Early American Novel: Reading the Atlantic World-system* received Honourable Mention for the British Association of American Studies Prize for best book in American Studies published during 2008.

Leona Toker is Professor in the English Department of the Hebrew University of Jerusalem. She is the author of *Nabokov: The Mystery of Literary Structures* (1989), *Eloquent Reticence: Withholding Information in Fictional Narrative* (1993), *Return from the Archipelago: Narratives of Gulag Survivors* (2000), *Towards the Ethics of Form in Fiction: Narratives of Cultural Remission* (forthcoming), and articles on English, American, and Russian literature. She is the editor of *Commitment in Reflection: Essays in Literature and Moral Philosophy* (1994) and co-editor of *Rereading Texts/Rethinking Critical Presuppositions: Essays in Honour of H.M. Daleski* (1996). At present she is Editor of *Partial Answers: A Journal of Literature and the History of Ideas*, a semiannual periodical published by the Johns Hopkins University Press.

Chronology

1937   Christopher Caudwell, *Illusion and Reality*
        L.C. Knights, *Drama and Society in the Age of Jonson*

1938   Cleanth Brooks and Robert Penn Warren, *Understanding Poetry*

1939   *Kenyon Review* founded by John Crowe Ransom

1940   Mikhail Bakhtin, *Rabelais and his World*

1941   John Crowe Ransom, *The New Criticism*

1943   Cleanth Brooks and Robert Penn Warren, *Understanding Fiction*

1946   W.K. Wimsatt and Monroe C. Beardsley, 'The Intentional
        Fallacy'
        Erich Auerbach, *Mimesis*
        Chicago Review founded

1947   Ivor Winters *In Defence of Reason*
        Northrop Frye, *Fearful Symmetry*

1948   W.K. Wimsatt and Monroe C. Beardsley, 'The Affective Fallacy'
        F.R. Leavis, *The Great Tradition*
        Leo Spitzer, *Linguistics and Literary History*

1949   Cleanth Brooks, *The Well Wrought Urn*
        Claude Levi-Strauss, *The Elementary Structure of Kinship*
        René Wellek and Robert Penn Warren, *Theory of Literature*

1950   Lionel Trilling, *The Liberal Imagination*

1951   Marshall McLuhan, *The Mechanical Bride: Folklore of Industrial
        Man*
        William Empson, *The Structure of Complex Words*
        Essays in Criticism founded

1952   F.R. Leavis, *The Common Pursuit*
        Donald Davie, *Purity of Diction in English Verse*

1953   R.S. Crane, *The Languages of Criticism and the Structure of Poetry*
        Roland Barthes, *Writing Degree Zero*

1966   Johns Hopkins University International Symposium, 'The Languages of Criticism and the Sciences of Man' at which major European theorists (notably Todorov, Goldmann, Barthes and Derrida) introduced their ideas to a predominantly US audience.
Pierre Macherey, *A Theory of Literary Production*
Susan Sontag, *Against Interpretation*
David Lodge, *The Language of Fiction*

1967   Jacques Derrida, *Of Grammatology*
Jacques Derrida, *Speech and Phenomena*
Jacques Derrida, *Writing and Difference*
Stanley Fish, *Surprised by Sin*
E.D. Hirsch, *Validity in Interpretation*

1968   Roland Barthes, 'The Death of the Author'
Norman Holland, *The Dynamics of Literary Response*

1969   Kate Millett, *Sexual Politics*
F.R. Leavis, *Literature in our Time*
Michel Foucault, 'What is an Author?'
Michel Foucault, *The Archaeology of Knowledge*

1970   Geoffrey Hartman, *Beyond Formalism*
Roland Barthes, *S/Z*
Raymond Williams, *The English Novel From Dickens to Lawrence*
Tzvetan Todorov, *The Fantastic. A Structural Approach to a Literary Genre*

1971   Paul de Man, *Blindness and Insight*
Frederic Jameson, *Marxism and Form*
Diacritics founded
Tzvetan Todorov, *The Poetics of Prose*

1972   Stanley Fish, *Self-Consuming Artefacts*
Frederic Jameson, *The Prison House of Language*
Jacques Derrida, *Positions*
Jacques Derrida, *Disseminations*
Jacques Derrida, *Margins of Philosophy*
Wolfgang Iser, 'The Reading Process: A Phenomenological Approach'

1973   *TLS* devotes large parts of two issues to the 'new' phe-
        nomenon of Semiotics, with articles by Eco, Todorov and
        Kristeva.
        Harold Bloom, *The Anxiety of Influence*
        Raymond Williams, *The Country and the City*
        Roland Barthes, 'Textual Analysis of a Tale by Poe'
        Jean Baudrillard, *The Mirror of Production*

1974   Julia Kristeva, 'The Ethics of Linguistics'
        Jean-Francois Lyotard, *Libidinal Economy*
        Luce Irigaray, *Speculum of The Other Woman*
        Christopher Ricks, *Keats and Embarrassment*
        Critical Inquiry founded

1975   Jonathan Culler, *Structuralist Poetics*
        Harold Bloom, *A Map of Misreading*
        Edward Said, *Beginnings*
        Héléne Cixous, 'The Newly Born Woman'

1976   Terry Eagleton, *Criticism and Ideology*
        E.D. Hirsch, *The Aims of Interpretation*

1977   Elaine Showalter, *A Literature of Their Own*
        Raymond Williams, *Marxism and Literature*
        David Lodge, *The Modes of Modern Writing*
        J. Hillis Miller, 'The Critic as Host'

1978   Edward Said, *Orientalism*
        Colin McCabe, *James Joyce and the Revolution of the Word*
        Michael Riffaterre, *Semiotics of Poetry*

1979   Jean-Francois Lyotard, *The Postmodern Condition*
        Susan Gubar and Sandra Gilbert, *The Madwoman in the Attic*
        Harold Bloom, Paul de Man, Jacques Derrida, Geoffrey
        Hartman, J. Hillis Miller, *Deconstruction and Criticism*
        Paul de Man, *Allegories of Reading*
        Raymond Williams, *Politics and Letters*
        Mary Jacobus (ed.), *Women Writing and Writing about
        Women*
        Feminist Review founded

1980   Jean Beaudrillard, *Simulacra and Simulations*
        Barbara Johnson, *The Critical Difference*
        Stephen Greenblatt, *Renaissance Self Fashioning*
        Geoffrey Hartman, *Criticism in The Wilderness*
        Stanley Fish, *Is There a Text in This Class?*
        Frank Lentricchia, *After the New Criticism*

1981   Frederic Jameson, *The Political Unconscious*
        Geoffrey Hartman, *Saving the Text*
        Press coverage of the 'MacCabe Affair' involving Cambridge
        University's 1980 decision not to make permanent Colin
        MacCabe's temporary lectureship.

1982   Jonathan Culler, *On Deconstruction*
        J. Hillis Miller, *Fiction and Repetition*
        Harold Bloom, *Agon*
        Paul de Man, 'The Resistance to Theory'

1983   Terry Eagleton, *Literary Theory*
        Edward Said, *The Word, the Text and the Critic*
        Jerome McGann, *The Romantic Ideology*

1984   Paul de Man, *The Rhetoric of Romanticism*
        Jonathan Dollimore, *Radical Tragedy*
        Raymond Williams, *Writing in Society*
        Henry Louis Gates (ed.), *Black Literature and Literary Theory*

1985   Elaine Showalter (ed.), *The New Feminist Criticism*
        Jonathan Dollimore and Alan Sinfield, *Political Shakespeare*
        Jerome McGann, *The Beauty of Inflections*
        Toril Moi, *Sexual/Textual Politics*
        Gayatri Chakravorty Spivak, 'Can the Subaltern Speak?'
        Eve K. Sedgwick, *Between Men: English literature and male
        Homosexual Desire*

1986   Paul de Man, *The Resistance to Theory*
        J. Hillis Miller's MLA presidential Address: 'The Triumph of
        Theory, the Resistance to Reading, and the Question of the
        Material Base'
        Textual Practice founded

1987   Barbara Johnson, *A World of Difference*
        Discovery of pro-Nazi, anti-Semitic articles written by Paul de
        Man in Belgium during the 1940s.
        J. Hillis Miller, *The Ethics of Reading*
        Gayatri Chakravorty Spivak, 'The Post-colonial Critic'

1988   Stephen Greenblatt, *Shakespearian Negotiations*
        Sandra Gilbert and Susan Gubar, *No Man's Land*.
        Genders founded

1989   Stanley Fish, *Doing What Comes Naturally*
        Jerome McGann, *Towards a Literature of Knowledge*

1990   Terry Eagleton, *Ideology of the Aesthetic*
        Gayatri Chakravorty Spivak, *The Post-Colonial Critic*
        Elaine Showalter, *Sexual Anarchy*
        Judith Butler, *Gender Trouble*

1991   Stephen Greenblatt, *Learning to Curse*
        Frederic Jameson, *Postmodernism*
        J. Hillis Miller, *Theory Now and Then*
        A.J. Greimas, *The Semiotics of Passion*

1993   Edward Said, *Culture and Imperialism*
        Eve Sedgwick, *Tendencies*

1994   Harold Bloom, *The Western Canon*
        Karl Kroebar, *Ecological Literary Criticism*
        Homi K. Bhaba, *The Location of Culture*

1995   Lawrence Buell, *The Environmental Imagination*
        Kate Soper, *What is Nature? Culture, Politics and the Non
        Human*
        Terry Gifford, *Green Voices: Understanding Contemporary Nature
        Poetry*
        Jeffrey Weeks, *Invented Moralities. Sexual Values in an Age of
        Uncertainty*

1996   Alan Sokal's 'Transgressing the Boundaries: Towards a Transformative Hermeneutics of Quantum Theory', a spoof post-modern/poststructuralist engagement with science accepted by the journal *Social Text*. His exposure of the weaknesses of Theory was covered later in his 1998 book *Intellectual Impostures*.
         E.D. Hirsch, *The Schools We Need and Why We Don't Have Them*
         Edward Said, *Peace and Its Discontents*

1997   Eve K. Sedgwick, *Novel Gazing: Queer Readings in Fiction*
         Judith Butler, *Excitable Speech: A Politics of the Performance*
         Stuart Hall, *Cultural Representations and Signifying Practices*

1998   Frederic Jameson, *Brecht and Method*
         Malcolm Bowie, *Proust Among the Stars*

1999   PMLA Forum on 'Literatures of the Environment' (Ecocriticism)
         David Scott Kastan, *Shakespeare after Theory*
         Stanley Fish, *The Trouble with Principle*
         Geoffrey Hartman, *A Critic's Journey: Literary Reflections, 1958–1998*
         Gayatri Chakravorty Spivak, *A Critique of Postcolonial Reason*

2000   Tzvetan Todorov, *Hope and Memory: Lessons from the 20th Century*
         Isobel Armstrong, *The Radical Aesthetic*

2001   Lawrence Buell, *Writing for an Endangered Planet*
         J. Hillis Miller, *Speech Acts in Literature*
         Terry Eagleton, *The Truth About the Irish*
         Slavoj Žižek, *On Belief*

2002   Jacques Derrida, *Acts of Religion*
         Slavoj Žižek, *Welcome to the Desert of the Real*
         Valentine Cunningham, *Reading After Theory*

2003   Eve K. Sedgwick, *Touching Feeling: Affect, Pedagogy, Performativity*
         Julia Kristeva, *Hannah Arendt*
         Terry Eagleton, *After Theory*
         M. Payne and J. Schad (eds), *Life. After. Theory*

Introduction: The History and Present Condition of Theory – A Brief Account

Richard Bradford

This volume can claim a special status within the 'Teaching the New English' series because its subject is not a branch of the literary canon. It is a way of writing about, or frequently not about, literature. Theory has obtained and maintained a unique status in literary studies. It is neither literature nor in a conventional sense literary criticism, but something that can be both practised and studied in its own right.

An exact and reliable history of how Theory arrived in universities and set up home in English degree programmes would require a full-length, scrupulously researched monograph but I will proffer some observations, based largely upon fact.

Formalism, the mother or father of structuralism, had taken root in Continental European institutions during the early to mid-20th century and it was not regarded as a particularly incongruous presence. Most literature-based degree courses were closely allied with linguistics and the expansion Westward of the linguistics-based sub-discipline of Formalism was a natural progression. In France, during the 1950s and especially the 1960s, the techniques of Claude Lévi-Straus, allegedly the first Structuralist, were annexed by writers and academics as much set upon dismantling as analysing cultural apparatuses, and Barthes was, of course, the best known of these non-conformists. By the end of the 1960s poststructuralism was abroad with its high priest, Jacques Derrida, forging ahead with such icons to abstruseness as *Of Grammatology*. We should never cease to remind ourselves that Literary or Critical Theory had at this advanced stage in its process of gestation become a misnomer. Theory would certainly have groundbreaking repercussions for routine habits of critical analysis and for standard conceptions of literature, but Theory did not service literary criticism; quite the opposite. Criticism and literature were but two of the numerous topics consumed

1

by this intellectual behemoth: its 'subject' was everything. Consult any guidebook to Theory or any list of lectures, coursework and exam titles on a university Theory module and you will encounter subdivisions, disciplinary legacies, whose relationships with the old fashioned, rather unsteady, idea of purely literary studies are marginal to say the least. They seem to owe more of an allegiance to fields as diverse as political science, sociology, psychology, philosophy and history. But as Theory buffs are aware the miscellany is misleading. Marxism, Psychoanalysis, Feminist Theory, to name but three, may trace their origins to different progenitors, intellectual traditions and historical moments but since the 1960s each has integrated, without losing their essential character, with the super-discipline that evolved from Saussurian linguistics through Structuralism and Poststructuralism and into the ongoing, curious – though apparently not atrophied – condition of After Theory.

I mention the interdisciplinary character of Theory because this primarily was the cause of the enormous number of disputes, most still unsettled, that greeted its arrival in Britain, Ireland and the United States. It is, for many, a familiar tale but one that merits a revisit. A number of Central and Eastern European eminences had found positions in US Ivy League institutions in the 1940s and 1950s – notably René Wellek and Roman Jakobson – and they adapted themselves to the US version of Europe's commitment to the science of language and sometimes provided a rigorous superstructure for attempts by the so-called new Critics to arrive at some definition of literature. In short they assimilated and did not significantly influence the prevailing nostrums in the English-speaking world on how its literature should be venerated, analysed and taught. Then suddenly – and no one has as yet provided a convincing explanation for this – Theory arrived *en masse*. Its influence began to be felt in the UK and the US at the turn of the 1960s and I will venture a thesis on why its was welcomed by a small but very influential group of academics and treated with fear, loathing and antipathy by so many more. For such American eminences as J. Hillis Miller, who in only two years went from second generation New Critic to US Deconstructionist-in-Chief, Theory offered transformation. True, Derrida was not a conventional literary critic but his writings offered literature a special status among the various sub-discourses of language. Literature by its nature explores the self-contradictory nature of language and challenges language's claim upon representational authenticity. Thus, literature was no longer seen as a recreational dilettantist activity; it now incorporated a means of undermining the complacencies of philosophy or history. At the other end of the spectrum, indeed the Atlantic, many UK literature academics, often those who had gone from school to career during the 1960s, wanted a disciplinary schemata for their radical political affiliations. Hence we have the so-called 'classic' introduction to Theory, Terry Eagleton's *Literary Theory* (1983). It is a witty, persuasive book yet at the same time as we follow him through his lucid explanations of the various sub-classifications of Theory we detect something like the child searching through a mammoth pile of Christmas presents, impatient for the one he really wants: Marxism.

Eagleton's book discloses, unwittingly, a feature of the UK and US experience of Theory that is rarely acknowledged. Like many other catch-all guides it provides a tour of Theory which is roughly chronological and in this respect it uncovers a dilemma. Formalism and New Criticism were roughly contemporaneous though certainly not collaborative, despite nurturing similar objectives. Formalism, however, mutated into Structuralism and the rigid analytical methodologies of the latter prompted the more rebellious experimental aspects of its successor, poststructuralism. Most Theory guides adopt the same format and the implied evaluative judgements as Eagleton's, with Theory claiming a lineage back through Poststructuralism, Structuralism and Formalism, and, circa the 1970s, coming to occupy the intellectual territories once dominated by the New Critics and their less disciplined yet idealistic peers such as F.R. Leavis. And one should note that the majority of modules on Theory, particularly those which attempt a comprehensive coverage of it, also model themselves upon the format of the guidebooks. Generally speaking, Theoretical subcategories such as Marxism, Feminism and Psychoanalysis feature after the core discussions on New Criticism, Formalism *et al.* but not because they are seen as their descendents or by-products; rather because this complicated interrelationship is far too contentious and amorphous for students to properly comprehend. This is not a failing on the part of the guides' authors and module planners: it is only now with the benefit of hindsight and a good deal of experience that academics themselves have properly begun to understand how the various strands of Theory progressed and interwove from the mid-1960s to the mid-1990s.

As I have already indicated the aspects of Theory which took hold in the most prestigious US institutions during the 1960s and 1970s were of the same species of highbrow intellectual detachment as American New Criticism. Deconstruction and other strands of Poststructuralism arrived without their antecedent baggage of Formalism and Structuralism as an immensely challenging exercise in the metaphysics of literary engagement. They projected academic criticism far beyond the routines of explication to a level of discrimination that equalled philosophy. And despite the controversy that would eventually surround the alleged Nazi allegiances of Paul de Man, they were in their US manifestation largely apolitical.

In the UK the effect of Theory was quite different. Most of those initially drawn to it were young academics who during the 1960s had as undergraduates and research students been closely involved in left-wing politics and feminism. John Barrell (Sussex), Catherine Belsey and Terence Hawkes (Cardiff), Nicole Ward Jouve (York), Lisa Jardine and Jacqueline Rose (Queen Mary and Westfield, London), Janet Todd (East Anglia), the late Anthony Easthope (Manchester Metropolitan), Sandra Harris (Newcastle Trent), Frances Mansakker (Glamorgan), Peter Widdowson (Middlesex) the late Raman Selden (Sunderland) and of course Terry Eagleton (Oxford) all during the 1970s became advocates of Theory and began to publish student targeted books and set up what were then unprecedented courses in their own institutions. The British heritage of, say, Marxist criticism had involved the empiricist work of figures such as E.P. Thompson, Richard Hoggart and, pre-eminently, Raymond Williams, concentrating upon how an author's background and circumstances influenced their representations of class and social structure. The methodology of French theorists, such as Althusser, provided a far more radical interpretation of Marxian notions of the text and subjectivity, based upon Poststructuralist formulations. Similary, French thinkers such as Helene Cixous and Julia Kristeva, whose work was also grounded in the disparate, but for the British very revolutionary, post-Saussurian concepts of discourse and identity become the primary influences for a more confident brand of Feminist Theory.

The arrival of Theory in the UK and the US was a fascinating phenomenon, one that has yet to be properly documented but which nonetheless has had significant influence upon the ways in which these new ideas were implemented in university curricula. It is notable, for example, that in the UK there have been very few figures who over the past forty years can claim the rank of originating Theorists, by which I mean that while a large number have advocated and adapted to their own critical and ideological principles the essential characteristics of ideas formulated in Continental Europe, few if any stand out as genuine innovators. Consult the burgeoning number of Theory reference guides and the only British names that feature prominently are Empson, Leavis, Richards and others who established their reputations prior to the influx of Theory. (See, for example Malpas and Wake, 2006.) In the US things have taken a different course. Before its espousal by major American academic critics deconstruction was only peripherally connected with literary interpretation. It was, in Continental Europe, a multidisciplinary vortex involving philosophy, linguistics, and the broader field of cultural studies and history. Only when it entered the smithy of craftsmen such as Hillis Miller, de Man, Hartman, and Bloom was it fashioned as the intellectually fearsome challenge to the governing yet atrophied protocols of traditional criticism. Derrida might have fathered deconstruction but its literary critical manifestation was born and raised in the USA. Similarly Stanley Fish appropriated and fully reconfigured European ideas on hermeneutics and receptive Theory; as did Judith Butler with concepts of gender difference and sexual orientation.

For academics this retinue of beachheads and excitements was energising, compelling and, professionally, very propitious. For undergraduates of the 1970s and 1980s and 1990s all of this barely registered. Instead they were faced with a hierarchy of Theoretical trademarks; the chronology of Formalism-and-after became also a programme of intellectual usurpation. Consider, for example, the observations by two eminent British Theorists, Jonathan Dollimore and Alan Sinfield in 1987 when Theory was becoming fully established in university teaching.

> Before LTP, teachers were political in the union, feminist groups or whatever; but to politicise your teaching, for many of us, seemed somehow improper, ... LTP afforded both the language and the confidence to 'come out' specifically in teaching as a socialist/feminist/gay/unilateralist (p.12)

They go on to stress that Structuralism/Semiotics/Poststructuralism offered them the means of channelling their own political and ideological commitments into courses that had before been scrupulously literary in format and content. The LTP (Literature Teaching Politics) was formed in the early 1980s, mostly by radically inclined academics in the then Polytechnics, as a forum with no rigid agenda but it developed into an intercampus focus group which concentrated on how the left-leaning ideological principles of most of its members could be harnessed to the somewhat chaotic influx of Theoretical paradigms: everything from the earliest findings of the Moscow Linguistic Circle (circa 1915) to the contemporaneous writings of Derrida seemed to be arriving at the same time. The group's members were concerned less with research and writing than with adapting, radicalising the curriculum and devising new strategies for teaching. Similar groups from around the same period included the feminist, women-only forum NETWORK: Oxford English Limited (OEL, which ran conferences on how the solidly conservative bastion of the Oxford syllabus might be breached by new options on women's writing and Theory); the Marxist Feminist Literature Collective; and the Association of Cultural Studies. Like LTP all were preoccupied mainly with the incorporation of Theory into the teaching fabric of Higher Education. All manner of myths and legends surround the alleged antipathy to this. The famous early career of Colin MacCabe, allegedly witch-hunted out of Cambridge in 1984 and forced to live on a dismal Professorial salary in Glasgow, sticks in the mind. The press was fascinated, presenting MacCabe as a 'Structuralist' without explaining or, evidently, understanding the meaning of the term. (He was, essentially, a cultural materialist cum poststructuralist.) Seven years later the same, largely broadsheet, media were equally enthralled by the promotion of Terry Eagleton to the Warton Professorship of English at Oxford. Even the generally left-wing *Guardian* and *Observer* seemed mildly affronted by the prospect of a self-proclaimed anti-establishment intellectual as one of the old school hierarchy. Typically, James Wood in the *Guardian*: 'After the Marxist meals come the bourgeois banquets, after the long knives come the fish knives' (*Guardian* 23 May 1991), as if Eagleton had never eaten at High Table before.

Between MacCabe's departure from Cambridge and Eagleton's promotion at Oxford had Theory, with the assistance of LTP and OEL activities, triumphed over the academic orthodoxy? Speaking from my own experience of middle-ranking English Departments and, vicariously, Oxford, the answer is, not really. Theory courses were present in most UK English departments by the end of the 1980s but their position within the curriculum was that of a supplement, albeit in most cases an obligatory supplement, to the all-presiding recipe of literary history, the traditional canon of authors and texts and an orthodox attendance upon standard genre distinctions.

As will have become clear from my very brief account of the history and odyssey of Theory its arrival in the UK and the US was largely a matter for academics alone, and even in that regard only those who were inclined to take notice of such things. The publication of Culler's *Structuralist Poetics* (1975) was a landmark in that the book was the first comprehensive explanation of the nature and history of the cornerstone of Theory. I have no knowledge of the exchanges that attended its commissioning by Routledge but common sense indicates that the publishers were convinced that such a book would fill a gap in the market. It is a strange hybrid and in some respects unique because it does not fall into the category of the unapologetically highbrow critical monograph; for one thing it was the first full-length study of methods, techniques and customs of analysis rather than of the objects analysed. At the same time while it is uncompromisingly demanding in its manner it cannot disguise its function as explanatory guide for the uninitiated. I doubt that its projected audience were undergraduates, even the most exceptional; because at the time most students had never heard of Theory. No, its intended readers were academics, particularly those who had heard rumours of this new, challenging counter-discipline but knew little of what it meant or involved. David Lodge's Philip Swallow comes to mind.

However, two years later Routledge launched the New Accents series. Its editor Terence Hawkes had persuaded them that there was indeed a market for student targeted guides to Theory and over the next fifteen years the series developed as the standard bearer for accessible introductions to the procedures and principles of Theory. All this seemed to indicate that Theory had become entrenched within the undergraduate programme and required reliable manuals, but I wonder about this. I know that in some universities in the early 1980s – Cardiff, for example, home of Hawkes – Theorists were busily attempting to integrate their particular enthusiasms with the student curriculum, with varying degrees of success. As stated above Theory was generally admitted as a supplement to traditional degree structures and I know of six middle-ranking, respectable university English departments where in the mid-1980s Theory simply did not exist, and I suspect that these were by no means exceptions. I wonder then if the explosion of expository accounts of Theory during the late 1970s and early 1980s was a brilliantly contrived sleight of hand; it seemed to reflect an endemic state of change but was in truth its vanguard. If such publications were indeed designed to provide the momentum for teaching Theory their success is now self-evident. Over the past twenty years every English department has seen the appointment of academics either enthused by Theory or experienced, open-minded or desperate enough to be press-ganged into teaching it. The question of how exactly Theory should be integrated with, or possibly replace, orthodox programmes of a degree course still, however, remains unanswered. The Theory Wars, so-called, might have reached a state of attrition – in that debate continues but no one has any expectation of defeating or winning-over their opponents – but when scrutinising their history and legacy one becomes aware that very few if any of the protagonists have taken time to consider the day-to-day activities of the humble lecturer and the now much less humble, fee-paying, undergraduate.

And here we encounter a harsh unwonted contradiction. Theory became part of the academic establishment at around the same time that Universities in the UK underwent their most radical period of transformation since the beginning of non-Oxbridge post-war expansion. The introduction of fees was irreversible and amounted effectively to privatisation. I recall some mumblings of discontent from the union and other affiliated groups and individuals but very little to compare with the threats of 'industrial action' that routinely attend salary negotiations. It is beyond dispute that when fees arrived the vast majority of established and junior academics associated with Theory and Literary Studies were those who had spent much of their careers advocating the twin-track benefits of intellectual enlightenment and political radicalism that Theory would bring. It is odd then that these same individuals should allow their congregation to be cast into the maw of capitalism – in practice, long-term debt – in return for being allowed to continue to teach them to think subversively. To some my line on this might seem immoderately tendentious but no one can deny that the situation in which we find ourselves today, whatever its cause, bears an extraordinary resemblance to that of almost a century ago when English battled to establish its credentials as an academic discipline. Then the unease, felt as much by the new English Dons themselves as their detractors, arose from two principal questions: why 'study' English Literature at university when most moderately intelligent individuals could be expected to understand and appreciate it without instruction?; would the treatment of poems, plays and, God forbid, novels, as works of art, even appendices to intellectual enquiry, vulgarise respectable disciplines such as Classics and Philosophy? The key issue was relevance and it has returned with a vengeance, complicated considerably by the institutionalisation in the curriculum of Theory alongside the Canon of major texts. The New Critics and their less easily classifiable contemporaries toiled for more than five decades during the mid-20th century to create an acceptable legend for English Studies, to answer the embarrassing questions raised at its inception. They attempt, with varying degrees of success, to 'define' literature as an aesthetic genre, a phenomenon worthy of intellectual scrutiny and some, famously Leavis, went further and averred that its intensive study would bring ethical, even moral improvement: literature is good for each of us and for society. Ironically the branch of Literary Studies with which the Canonical Texts now share centre stage in University Curricula, Theory, has employed its considerable, multifaceted resources to demolish all of the premises upon which these early claims were founded. Any attempt to specify the definitive features of literature is now overruled by a consensus which accepts without question the findings of every anti-intrinsicalist from Reception Theorists to Marxists. And an academic today who would base their module on Shakespeare or 19th- Century verse upon the notion that each text possesses some key to moral advancement would probably be recommended for anti-delusional therapy. Theorists and Theory have arrived. The latter is part of the circuitry of modules that make up degrees in English, the former key elements of the post-1980s personnel, the post-Theory generation. But their arrival has brought with it an inherent contradiction, one that we seem reluctant even to attempt to resolve for reasons that virtually all of us privately accept but which none, for reasons by turns understandable and pitiable, are willing to address. The reason that we are constantly being scrutinised – 're-evaluated' or whatever term will next be coined – is that degrees, or to be more accurate selling degrees, is now a business and it is deemed necessary to protect ourselves against complaints from the customer. Hence, problems which might twenty years ago have been seized upon as an inspiration for academic dynamism – the fascinating irresolvable contradictions of English; text versus Theory; aesthetics versus ideology; relevance versus significance – are now swept under the carpet. Why? Because it is feared that few students – and for that matter few parents – would wish to invest a vast amount of cash in spending three or four years studying a discipline which cannot make up its mind what it is. Its relevance for a career in the real world is as a consequence questionable. This volume does not, cannot, provide an all-encompassing solution to this problem. That would involve the commissioning of several single-authored polemics, and even then, in a world of government diktat, it is unlikely that even the most thoroughly argued and persuasive thesis would result in practical change. However, the chapters below do reflect the complexity and diversity of the state of things, some focussing upon the day-to-day problems of teaching specific modules, others examining the principles and theses that underlie teaching practice, and some encompassing experience, anecdote, hypothesis and deeply felt polemic.

As I have indicated the history of Theory and its effect upon academics in the UK and US stands in perverse relation to the pragmatics of teaching it, from the basic first year introduction to the more sophisticated elective modules of the second and third years. On the one hand the enormously complex spectrum of affiliations and attachments spawned among academics during the heyday of Theory is still a matter for debate and something that we do not properly comprehend.

At the same time, however, the practicalities of explaining what Theory, in its different manifestations, actually involves, precludes a thorough provision for students of how many debates regarding the validity of Theory rage on while others have become habituated as accepted routines. In short we can explain what Theory is but in doing so we leave out the puzzling dynamic of its advocates and detractors, its different effects in the UK and US and the present sense of a debate that is multifaceted, often atrophied, yet certainly not concluded. As academics we face a situation comparable to the farcical yet disturbing image of the dog eating its own tail. Imagine an assembly of anxious, perhaps even enthusiastic first years, being instructed by a coterie of amiable lecturers on what faces them for the subsequent three years. The big questions of why the degree course is structured as it is and how they might benefit from its architecture cannot of course be avoided. Should we be honest and offer our new charges a brisk account of the discipline with which they have landed themselves, at considerable expense, roughly as I have above? I.e., that two utterly discordant antithetical Schools of opinion on what English is and how it should be written about and studied have spent the past forty years in a state of irreconcilable conflict, reached an absurd compromise and papered over the cracks. And you, dear fee-payer, might over the next few years begin to encounter some of the bizarre inconsistencies that inform this 'subject', might indeed begin to doubt its intellectual credibility let alone its monetary value as a preparation for the world beyond the university.

There is no practical solution to this in that the only way in which undergraduates can become conversant with this strange diversity within the profession is by becoming a postgraduate or an academic themselves. To attempt to introduce them to it alongside a thorough grounding in its particulars would be an absurd and impracticable policy. This volume most certainly does not propose such an interface but the dichotomy does I contend justify an inconstancy – an enlightening inconstancy – of themes and perspectives. Some chapters, notably Byrne's, Gonzalez's and Le Bihan's, are concerned primarily with the pragmatics of teaching. Others such as my own and Shapiro's are less easy to categorise, noting as they do parallels and irresolvable discontinuities between the academic world of Theory and the exigencies of the seminar and lecture room. Toker advocates the teaching and significance of formalism; its benefits, she avers, are self-explanatory. If we study English literature we need to understand what it is – a traditional and convincingly argued view point. James returns us to the pragmatics with a piece on the ever-burgeoning industry of Theory Guides while

Leitch and Hadfield blend powerfully argued polemic with sagacious assessments of what can, even should, be done with Theory in universities. Murphy's chapter seems ostensibly the least suitable for a volume concerned predominantly with the minutiae and opportunities of pedagogic practice, but read it closely and you will find that his dissection of the tensions and contradictions of Postcolonial Theory are relevant to anyone attempting to explain this vast multifaceted topic to students.

Vincent Leitch addresses six key questions concerning Theory teaching now. How does and should Theory factor into the curriculum of the university literature major? What are the main goals for teaching Theory? In what ways should one respond to opponents of Theory and its teaching at institutions of higher education? What is the relationship between literary and critical theory and cultural studies? What role does poststructuralism currently play in the teaching of Theory? What is the future of Theory in higher education?

Leitch takes the long view, looks at the key issues that attend the status of Theory in university teaching; in his appendix he also shows how a number of these broader themes taper into the practicalities of teaching. My own chapter is similarly discursive yet one might surmise from its title that nihilistic or terminal would be more apt descriptions. The title, however, refers not to the chapter itself but to an exercise in shock tactics employed to arouse in students opinions and responses that lie beyond the somewhat anaesthetised routines of formal seminar exchanges

Leona Toker's main point is that (1) in the early stages of the academic teaching of literature it is important to place the emphasis on close text analysis – for instance, along the lines of descriptive poetics and the New Critical focus on the text itself – but that (2) eventually this methodology becomes unsatisfactory. The training in narratological analysis (she deals mainly with prose narratives) helps the students to unlearn message-hunting, intentionality and similar pitfalls; it can also help them to avoid bending the text for ideological purposes. Eventually, however, the text has to be returned to its various contexts – historical, political, ideological, etc. In her opinion the most useful basis for doing so without relinquishing close intrinsic analysis could be constructed from Jan Mukařovský's theory of the multifunctionality of a work of art and Benjamin Hrushovski's influential distinction between Internal and External Fields of reference. The two approaches can unite in a broader theoretical base, the semiological triad of syntactics (Internal Field of references), semantics (External Field of Reference) and pragmatics (author-text and text-reader interface). She demonstrates the applicability of these distinctions to the deployment of motifs and character portrayal in Dicken's *Our Mutual Friend* and Jane Austen's *Mansfield Park*.

Andrew James contends that the greatest change in guides over the last twenty years is in their tone, that they have become more opinionated and topical. If one assumes that a guide is necessary in Theory courses, perspective is a key factor in the selection process. Perspective should not be confused with neutrality, but should be understood as a frame to help students shape their existing knowledge of criticism and Theory with suggestions about how to expand that knowledge. The purpose of his study is twofold: to analyse the merits and demerits of the recent crop of Theory guides and to consider how guides have changed over the last few decades. Reference has been made to some of the most relevant textual legacies and he has focused on seven texts, each of which has something different to recommend it, and concentrated specifically on the perspective, stated or otherwise, of each.

Shapiro argues that literary theory has to be taught in ways that reveal its authors' motives in replying to other authors. Otherwise, he contends, criticism's terms and concepts appear as alien at best and pedantic at worst. Using the writing of F.R. Leavis, Raymond Williams and Edward Said as an extended series of responses, Shapiro sketches a new way of teaching the debates regarding the relation of language, landscape, and literature and raises several questions. Is there an imperial national writing? Can debates about the national imaginary be conveyed to students in ways that do not either depend on identitarian responses or result in an intellectual stalemate?

Andrew Hadfield, who has built a considerable reputation as a literary historian, particularly of the Renaissance, offers an intriguing perspective upon the use of literary history alongside Theory. He is not professing another brand of cultural materialism; rather he avers that Theory is now in danger of becoming an atrophied ritual of memorised formulae and that the ancient practice of rhetoric could be reintroduced as a means of invigorating the teaching of Theory.

Jill Le Bihan is similarly dismayed by the decline in the state of Theory in the classroom over the past 15 years. In her experience acts of resistance by sceptical students – welcome in themselves – have been replaced by a blend of exigency and indifference; fees and job prospects mean that interest is focussed upon decent marks rather than intellectual stimulation. In her chapter she focuses upon what, for her, are still the exciting and engaging elements of Theory – mainly related to

Feminism – and indicates how such enthusiasms can be bestowed upon her students.

Katherine Byrne's and Madelena Gonzalez's pieces read almost as a dialogue between the UK and France. Byrne makes clear her particular objectives and ideals and bases these firmly in a detailed account of her day-to-day experiences of teaching students, marking their work and integrating their experience of a Theory module with the rest of their degree. Gonzalez offers a similarly down-to-earth report on her experiences of teaching a Theory module in the University of Avignon. The most obvious difference is that while Byrne makes no mention of Theory teaching as being anything other than entirely assimilated as a key element of the culture and degree structure of her Ulster English department, in France an academic's affiliations to a particular doctrinal formula or theorist is capable of generating bitter interpersonal tensions. Gonzalez goes on to explain how she copes with this in teaching her own course and reflects on how Theory is taught in a nation that, for most, is still regarded as its home.

Neil Murphy's chapter can in places seem slightly incongruous in a volume whose remit is pedagogic practice in that he gives particular attention to the stultified, inflexible nature of Postcolonial Theory as perceived by those working within it as academic specialists. However, it should be noted that his prefatory remarks establish the context in which his fascinating subsequent analysis should be interpreted. By 'Reading' he means the recipe of texts cemented by guidebooks, reading lists, curricula and, crucially, the mindset of Postcolonial Theorists themselves. In short Postcolonialism, at least in his view, suffers from a particularly severe double bind with teaching being held in check by writing and vice versa.

References

Culler, Jonathan (1975) *Structuralist Poetics: Structuralism, Linguistics and the Study of Literature*. London: Routledge.

Dollimore, Jonathan and Sinfield, Alan (1987) ' "Are we talking about literature": a history of LTP', *Literature Teaching Politics Journal*, 6, p.12.

Eagleton, Terry (1983) *Literary Theory: An Introduction*. Oxford: Blackwell.

Malpas, S. And Wake, P. (eds) (2006) *The Routledge Companion to Critical Theory*. London: Routledge.

1
Teaching Theory

Vincent B. Leitch

Contemporary context

The teaching of contemporary literary and cultural theory particularly in the American university has been explicitly and increasingly caught up in politics. It was during the 1980s that conservative attacks like William Bennett's *To Reclaim a Legacy* and Allan Bloom's notorious *The Closing of the American Mind* began to defend vigorously the canon of great works against the purported corrupting influences both of popular culture and of nihilistic, usually foreign, theory. While this strand of the culture wars has ebbed and flowed over the decades, it continues into the new century, for example, with the publication of David Horowitz's *The Professors: The 101 Most Dangerous Academics in America* (2006). This work names names, and it speculates there are tens of thousands of "dangerous professors." Most are melodramatically associated with "ideological fields like women's studies, African American studies, gay and lesbian studies, postcolonial studies, queer studies, whiteness studies, and cultural studies" (p. xxv). What is wrong with such recent theory, according to this paleoconservative view, is not only that it corrupts the young and undermines patriotism, but that it questions traditional notions of scholarly disinterest, objectivity, and neutrality as well as standards of good professional methodology, conduct, and integrity.

When I started to teach theory in the 1970s, it was entangled with politics, although at that time it had much more of an internal configuration than the external framing of the later culture wars. Politics then took various and sundry forms such as Marxism versus formalism, radical versus liberal feminism, pan-African versus nationalist black aesthetics, literary structuralism versus contending extrinsically-oriented criticisms, left versus right poststructuralism. Even though these theoretical

14

camps were not disconnected from worldly politics, they often staged their disputes intramurally, appearing socially disengaged and isolated behind ivy-covered walls. This condition led to many calls during the 1980s and 1990s for the rebirth of the public intellectual, a figure for actively engaging with the world and especially for responding to the mounting conservative attacks against theory and the corruption of the university.

It was in this *fin-de-siècle* context that critical pedagogy, which derived from Paolo Freire's *Pedagogy of the Oppressed* and the broad New Left, gained a wide audience, as did the fair-minded liberal tactic of "teaching the conflicts" ably advocated by Gerald Graff. Foremost among the conflicts of the time were the debates, still going today, surrounding multiculturalism. These invariably took up the conditions of black, brown, red, and yellow people; the related diasporas, colonialisms, imperialisms; and the need for new accounts of minorities constructed from below and from the margins.

But no sketch of the context for teaching theory and literary and cultural studies today could be complete without emphasizing the situation of academic labor. I am referring to the restructuring of the professoriate notably in the US since the 1970s, which involves the overproduction of PhDs, the doubling of the time to earn the PhD degree (currently nine years following the BA), the increasing use of cheap and insecure (non-tenured) casual labor, and the growing number of unionization drives by graduate students and faculty. All this forms part of the framework for theory teaching in these times (Leitch, "Work Theory").

Six concerns of theory teaching now

In this chapter I address six key questions concerning theory teaching today. How does and should theory factor into the curriculum of the university literature major? What are the main goals for teaching theory? In what ways should one respond to opponents of theory and its teaching at institutions of higher education? What is the relationship between literary and critical theory and cultural studies? What role does poststructuralism currently play in the teaching of theory? What is the future of theory in higher education?

1. Curriculum

How does and should theory factor into the curriculum of the university literature major today? Most North American literature students are required to complete one or two introductory theory courses during their sequence of eight to ten courses. At my institution, a typical large US state university, undergraduate students take both Introduction to Critical Reading and Writing and Introduction to Literary and Cultural Studies. They can supplement these two with optional offerings. One that I regularly teach, for example, is Issues in Cultural Studies. There are numerous anthologies, readers, guidebooks, and glossaries for all such theory courses, whether beginning or advanced, to help faculty and students (Leitch, Selected Bibliography, *Norton Anthology* 2001, 2010). I expect something resembling this institutionalization of theory to continue into the foreseeable future. In this way students gain necessary knowledge of the premises and practices of literary formalism, psychoanalysis, feminism, poststructuralism, Marxism, new historicism, etc. as well as awareness of the history of thinking about literature from Plato and Aristotle to Bourdieu and Butler.

What is less obvious and perhaps more important is the incalculable theory teaching that happens in the other courses taken by literature majors, ranging from ancient and Medieval literature up to the present. I have in mind, for instance, the new feminist and queer perspectives on Shakespeare and Renaissance drama; critiques of modernization relating to eighteenth- and nineteenth-century-fiction; the emergence of globalized Anglophone literatures and postcolonial theories; the relevance of the deconstruction of the human subject and the rise of contemporary cyberpunk and electronic literature. But I also have in mind the close reading of the lyric poem in the old ingrained early postwar formalist manner and the still more venerable commonsense historicization and moralization of literary settings, characters, themes, and authors. Such unprogrammed encounters with theory in every classroom and in all reading and writing assignments constitute a second front of theory teaching in the always-important informal curriculum. My point here is that in the multitude of syllabi, one-off course packs, and impromptu as well as planned course discussions, theory shows itself more a part of the atmosphere than simply a discrete well-packaged subdiscipline or specialty contained in one or two introductory courses.

2.   Goals

About the goals of teaching theory, certain well-recognized general aims remain essential. These include teaching students to think and read critically; to write well; to master technical terms and knowledge; to grapple with canonical texts, figures, and traditions; and to contextualize materials historically. This is a matter of discipline in several senses: as a prescribed body of knowledge; as training in required skills; as good professional practice.

Grading, exams, and recommendation letters come in here. Students are required to be on time with assignments and class attendance. They are expected to exhibit good manners in the conventional social and professional senses. As everyone knows, the teaching profession is integrated into bureaucracies and ideological state apparatuses. That was made memorably clear three decades ago by Richard Ohmann's *English in America* and contemporaneous works by Bourdieu, particularly his co-authored *Reproduction in Education, Society and Culture*. Not surprisingly, professors sometimes work against the grain, uncomfortable teaching certain requirements of the reigning social order and of discipline. But there is no way to inventory the innumerable modes of resistance, often spontaneous, singular, local.

The teaching goals specific to literary theory are for me probably best summarized by exploring in the classroom the following repertoire of fundamental questions: What is literature? Who defines it? In what ways? How is it produced, disseminated, used, evaluated? What are the protocols of interpretation? How and why do the definitions, roles, and social positions of author, reader, and literary genre change? What institutions are involved in literature and literary teaching? Do past answers to such questions have currency today? For cultural theory courses or modules, we can change the word literature here to culture. At the risk of being formulaic, to theorize characteristically entails asking fundamental questions, scrutinizing answers, and seeking new, often defamiliarized, understandings, concepts, practices (see the Appendix to this chapter on theory heuristics). It takes place within but it is not limited to disciplinary frameworks.

Given the improvisational performative dimensions of classroom teaching, there exist, of course, elements of potential fun and danger, of risk, for all teaching, but perhaps more so for contemporary theory teaching with its skeptical historicist disposition, penchant for speculation, and antinomian drift. In this connection, most teachers today no doubt increasingly feel themselves part of the entertainment industry rather like standup comedians or talking heads on television. Media values during our postmodern times have seeped into numerous previously autonomous domains. Nowadays the classroom is a commercialized as well as a surveilled public space.

Full-time tenure-track faculty members are accountable at US institutions, which in turn plays a considerable role in shaping course goals. Like many workers today, professors receive regular multifaceted formal evaluation and supervision. To begin with, th American students in each course typically complete end-of-semester rating sheets, responding numerically and in prose to a dozen or more questions about teaching. The anonymous results are quantified and compared with a statistical group such as all literature or all arts and sciences professors, using standard deviations and median scores. Also there are annual evaluations of each professor's teaching, research, and service by departmental administrators and/or senior faculty. Moreover, junior faculty undergo periodic progress-to-tenure reviews as well as the tenure review itself, the latter often involving anywhere from five to twelve outside evaluators in addition to departmental colleagues. More and more senior professors face periodic post-tenure review. I had one following five years of tenured service, and every five years since. Among other things, I am required to project ahead and plan for five years and to look back and self-evaluate the past five years. This kind of extensive formal ten-year examination of the professional self is increasingly common. It is worth underlining here two conflicting modes of evaluation, reflecting contending styles of modern management (scientific and humanistic), with the quantitative in the ascendancy. Casual faculty receive less evaluation, sometimes none. But we are all on stage and accountable. It is in large part a numbers game that affects teaching.

During spring the Provost at my university requires each faculty member to hand in a one-page mini-vita recording accomplishments in teaching, research, and service for the prior calendar year. The department chair and two elected senior faculty then assign a grade in each category, ranging from zero to five, worked out to the second decimal point. So a faculty member might receive a 3.75 in teaching, 4.50 in service, and 4.10 in research. The annual evaluation sheet also lately totals up three-year rolling averages in each category plus composite averages for each year and for three years, all worked out to the second decimal point. My composite for last year was 4.50 and for the past three years 4.69. This kind of severe mathematical reduction in the interest of institutional accounting would, no doubt, give Pythagoras himself pause. It plays havoc with the self-image of would-be independent, not to mention rebel and bohemian professors. It is not just that it impacts faculty annual raises and sense of self-worth as well as future strategies for career success, but it privileges the short-term and speed-up. (Faculty had to campaign for the three-year averages.) Ten-year scholarly projects appear old-fashioned, incalculable, despite the impression of post-tenure reviews. In much postindustrial capitalist work, education included, productivity must be quantifiable, copious, rapid.

This whole apparatus of necessary and often useful accountability affects teaching goals. At various times I, like others, have tailored my teaching to discard low-scoring activities, to increase high-scoring practices, to maximize short-term returns. Such behavior is, I believe, second nature now to contemporary American professors, shaping all aspects of teaching, including theory teaching and its goals, for good and ill.

3. Opponents

How does one respond to the main opponents of theory and its teaching in institutions of higher education? There are several justifications and refutations worth highlighting. To start with, history of theory teaches the great tradition, with its foundational figures and texts from Plato's *Republic* and Aristotle's *Poetics* to Bloom's *The Anxiety of Influence*, Gilbert and Gubar's *Madwoman in the Attic*, and Said's *Culture and Imperialism*. In addition, it teaches canonical answers to perennial questions about literature and culture such as the place of censorship, the elements of genre, the dynamics of tradition and influence, the role of madness in the arts, the social mission of literary education. Theory teaches not only cultural history and literary appreciation, but critical reading and self-reflexively the historical development of critical reading. Now to the complaint, often seeming hysterical, that theory students are taken away from studying literature and the canonical texts, my experience and empirical studies undertaken by the Modern Language Association of America have demonstrated that simply is not the case (Huber). Here I would recall also what Frye in *Anatomy of Criticism* pointed out: literature majors study criticism not literature, with the latter taken up by creative writers. 'The difficulty often felt in "teaching literature" arises from the fact that it cannot be done: the criticism of literature is all that can be directly taught' (p. 11). As concerns contemporary theory, in particular, from formalism, structuralism, and new strands of psychoanalysis and Marxism to reader-response criticism, deconstruction, new historicism, postcolonial studies, and queer theory, all these movements and schools have happened and cannot be iged. Of course, they should be evaluated and criticized where necessary. Programs of literary and cultural study are obliged to teach developments in recent professional history, their roots, mechanisms, conflicts.

Angry charges of partisanship and classroom advocacy often arise in attacks upon the teaching of contemporary theory. The time-tested way to avoid such problems is to teach all schools of criticism as optional points of view and reading strategies – the so-called approaches method.

That is the way I learned theory in the s. The Marxist approach, the for-malist approach, the psychological approach – take your pick. Whatever critical methodology works is fine. The proof is in the pudding: out-comes matter uppermost. Practical criticism is what is important after all. One variation on this way of handling the issue is for the teacher to be studiously neutral, teaching what has happened and how the differ-ent methods operate. Teach the conflicts and stay out of it.

It was Robert Scholes, however, who noted in *Textual Power* that critical reading, that is, reading against the grain as distinct from both explanatory and sympathetic textual interpretation, depends on com-munal standpoint. "My point here is that criticism is always made on behalf of a group" (p. 24). One undertakes critique, Marxist, feminist, Christian, conservative, etc. as a member of a group. Everybody stands somewhere whether he or she realizes it or not. This standpoint epistemology, characteristic of our postmodern posthumanist times, challenges all calls for neutrality. It also undermines the pragmatic methodologization of critical schools and movements which transforms beliefs and perspectives into convenient flexible tools, into approaches. For example, feminist theory for many women is not one approach selected among many, but an existential perspective built out of pain-ful lived experience. Some of the best teachers are extreme in their beliefs. So advocacy yes, but indoctrination no (Graff, 1996, p. 427). Compulsory objectivity and obligatory critical disinterest, sacred cows of many a theory opponent, often mask blind spots, racial and gender privileges, nationalistic mindsets, and prejudices.

4.   Cultural and literary studies

This is a good place to address the question of the relationship between literary and cultural studies *vis-à-vis* theory. Because disciplines bear distinct and perdurable national frameworks as well as national tradi-tions, the position of cultural studies in relation to literary criticism and theory differs in Australia, Canada, the United Kingdom, the United States, etc. Consider the place of cultural studies, for instance, in the UK, which is markedly different from the US. The British his-tory famously goes back to the 1950s works of Hoggart, Williams, Hall, and the slightly later Centre for Contemporary Cultural Studies at the University of Birmingham (s--1980s). By the mid-1980s the spread of cultural studies as a breakaway distinct discipline across the UK academic world appeared an accomplished fact. This is the point at which US cultural studies begins. I have told this story elsewhere so I won't repeat it here (Leitch and Lewis). Now looking back several decades, I can summarize the most obvious differences by saying that early cultural studies in the U.K. was a school, if not a coterie, while in the US it was an amorphous movement, lacking consensus on politics as well as essential traditions. By the dawn of the twenty-first century, even though US cultural studies had seeped into many humanistic and social scientific disciplines, but in unequal and singular ways, it did not become a separate discipline. Where it is not simply cast as one methodology among others today, US cultural studies takes the form of a small wing, camp, or tendency inside traditional fields such as anthropology, communication studies, comparative literature, English, political science, and sociology. So do not go looking for departments of cultural studies on US campuses. Needless to say, the role of theory in this situation is quite complex, requiring a discipline-by-discipline account.

When, for example, I worked as a professor in the Department of English at Purdue University, it was in the late 1990s that a handful of faculty and graduate students managed to establish within that unit a graduate program in Theory and Cultural Studies (TCS). The pre-existing semiautonomous programs inside that large department included Creative Writing, English as a Second Language, English Linguistics, English Education, Literary Studies, and Rhetoric and Composition. Each offered precedents and program models for TCS. The formation of a parallel semi-autonomous TCS entailed a repackaging of existing graduate courses, including both the three long-standing graduate courses in the history of theory (Plato to Kant; Wordsworth to Eliot; Contemporary Schools and Movements) and the usual variable topics seminars in theory. In the context of such repackagings, Wollstonecraft's *A Vindication of the Rights of Woman*, Arnold's *Culture and Anarchy*, Marx's previously iged writings on commodification in *Capital*, and the Frankfurt school's works on culture (especially those by Adorno and Benjamin) gained pride of place in the history of literary theory courses. Literary theory went cultural at the close of the twentieth century. Contemporary critical theory offerings, not surprisingly, have accorded increased room to culturally oriented poststructuralists (notably Althusser, Bourdieu, Foucault) and to Birmingham scholars like Hall, Hebdige, and McRobbie. While there is a distinct cultural studies theory course imaginable and on offer here and there, cultural studies theory is usually embedded into literary and critical theory courses in English departments. In other words, cultural studies for US literary theory is commonly treated as one more school or movement like reader-response theory, new historicism, ethnic criticism, queer theory, etc. It is one among many other approaches. In the case of the TCS program, cultural studies was caught – symptomatically so – between its tendency to be a new discipline or, less ambitiously, a semi-autonomous subfield and its sacred obligations to the overarching goals of literary and rhetorical education within the US English department and discipline.

There are yet further wrinkles in this account. Cultural studies in the US is for literary and cultural theory not only a methodology or an approach as well as a recent movement, but, significantly, a paradigm. So there are at least five faces of American cultural studies: approach or method; school or movement; disciplinary wing or tendency; new discipline or department; and main paradigm of research within a department. Starting in the 1990s and up to the present, cultural studies in English departments occupies a central position as did for-malism/New Criticism from the 1940s–s and poststructuralism from the 1970s–1980s. It is the dominant model of research and scholarship in a field of contenders, only vastly more heterogeneous than its two immediate forerunners. This cultural studies consists of several dozen semi-autonomous areas of research and study such as, to repeat a stand-ard list, body studies, indigenous studies, institutional studies, media studies, popular culture studies, porn studies, subculture studies, trauma studies, whiteness studies, working-class studies, etc. While some resist incorporation, most scholars in these subfields consider themselves to be part of cultural studies. That is the ruling paradigm.

Consequently, when I teach an undergraduate course on Issues in Cultural Studies in the English department, I offer half a dozen modules on variable topics focusing upon contemporary US "literary" matters. They range from female body images in advertising discourses (body studies) and in pulp fictions (popular culture studies) to the activities of bookstores (institutional studies) to the phenomena of slam poetry (media studies) to the upsurge of white trash literature and television shows (working-class and whiteness studies). This is a kind of literary theory teaching that I could not have imagined when I started out in the 1970s as a professor of English. could I have foreseen, being under the sway of formalism then, the types of critical theories and practices brought to bear now. These include institutional analysis and ideology critique that systematically attend to the circuits of cultural production, distribution, and consumption, plus matters of race, class, gender, and national identity (all essential elements of analysis for the reigning cul-tural studies paradigm).

However odd, uncomfortable, and fleeting a situation it may be, cultural studies has recently become an orthodoxy of sorts in US English departments. At the same time it retains much of its socially critical edge and its links with antinomian critical theory. Conservative critics of cultural studies and its subdivisions, as a result, regard themselves very self-righteously as an embattled miity, a heterodoxy, defending the great tradition and objective scholarship against popular culture and the debased new postmodern discipline of cultural studies purportedly given over *in toto* to theory, multiculturalism, political correctness, and classroom advocacy (Patai and Corral). Those are main battle lines for classroom teachers in the early twenty-first century.

5. Poststructuralism today

On the question of what role poststructuralism currently plays in teaching theory, I would say without fear of contradiction that it is ubiquitous and indispensable, yet its prominence has receded since the late 1980s. Whether one is thinking of contemporary literary theory, critical theory, cultural theory, or theory in general, several handfuls of poststructuralist concepts form part of the lexicon of key terms as, for example, docile body, cultural capital, male gaze, heteroglossia, ideological state apparatus, the imaginary, floating signifier, intertextuality, deconstruction, subject-in-process, surveillance society, etc. These regularly show up in glossaries, of course. They remain productive critical and speculative instruments in the classroom. The teaching of the major figures and texts of poststructuralism has been more or less standardized by now, as a review of theory anthologies and readers reveals. There is a well-sifted recurring body of poststructuralist texts from Althusser, Barthes, Baudrillard, Bourdieu, Cixous, Deleuze, Derrida, Foucault, Irigaray, Kristeva, Lacan, etc. When I and the five editors of the *Norton Anthology of Theory and Criticism* made our poststructuralist selections, there was little difficulty in choosing teachable as well as rewarding and influential texts. The real challenge was finding new undiscovered gems such as some of the lesser-known essays of Barthes's *Mythologies* or overlooked chapters in Kristeva's *Revolution in Poetic Language*. Even though certain poststructuralists are legendarily difficult like Derrida, Lacan, and second-generation ones like Bhabha and Butler, there are nowadays ways and aids to contextualize and set up their works, making them meaningful to literature and other majors whether advanced or beginners.

Yet there are vexing problems of naturalization, recuperation, canonization, and taming, pertaining as much to postmodern poststructuralist texts as to earlier avant-garde modernist works. Just the same, there seem regularly and surprisingly to be new things to find in previous texts. I am thinking of the indigestible, the undiscovered, the unseen, the contradiction, the gap, the new context or lens, not to mention the new text. Many of Foucault's very recently published thirteen books of annual lectures have yet to be scutinized. The forty-three books of Derrida's annual seminars from 1960 to 2003 have just begun to be published and translated. I believe there are futures for poststructuralism beyond mechanical repetitions and calcifications.

For me a productive role for poststructuralism today lies not only in its inventive concepts and its continuing position as useful target and revealing scapegoat, but in its openness to external critique and self-critique. Based on my experience, a classroom teacher can interrogate the standard poststructuralist works to good effect. For instance, many poststructuralist texts overplay the suffocating seamlessness of social systems, appearing blind to resistance and alternatives. That pertains to Foucault's panoptic society, Althusser's ideological state apparatuses, Derrida's logocentrism, and Bourdieu's habitus. But within poststructuralist theory there are key texts giving voice to resistance. Here is where enter, for example, de Certeau's famous resisting practices of everyday life; Deleuze and Guattari's nomads and schizos pioneering lines of flight and deterritorializations; Cixous's disruptive *écriture féminine*; Kristeva's modernist revolution in poetic language; the creative role accorded by Said against Foucault to certain rare independent thinkers of orientalism; and Barthes's imaginative and self-indulgent writerly readers. Each of these forms of resistance against specific social institutions and oppressive practices is itself open to critique. So there is a rich body of material here for current and future theory that opens to account the strengths and weaknesses of poststructuralism.

6. The future

What, speaking very broadly, is the future of theory teaching in higher education? First and foremost, theory is an established element of programs in literary study and cultural studies not just in North America but elsewhere, to be sure. It is increasingly recognized and accredited across the arts, humanities, social sciences, and professions (particularly law). And significantly, it is studied more and more around the globe, notably in Central and Northern Europe and in East Asia. There lies a substantial future.

Sooner or later, however, theory, especially the history of theory and its teaching, must take on non-European traditions stemming from

Arabic, Chinese, Indian, Japanese, and other sources. So right there both in materials and in outreach rests another future for theory.

The dissemination of theory through innumerable academic specialties, subspecialties, areas, periods, disciplines, and national contexts continues apace. Here and there it loses its distinct identity through grafting and incorporation. The tendency for almost everyone, it seems, particularly in US literary and cultural studies, to see themselves as having and doing theory, which marks a certain annexation and weakening of its identity, can be anticipated to continue. Paradoxically, this accounts for the diminution in the job market for theorists since the high watermark of the 1980s while bearing witness to an unequivocal, though ambiguous, triumph. Since just about everyone, whether scholar of Medieval, Renaissance, Enlightenment, or modern literary culture, does theory of some sort in the US, there appears little reason to secure the services of scholars doing full-time stand-alone theory. Area and period specialists can teach theory as need be and on the side so to speak. What this comes down to is the reassertion of the powerful modern (pre-postmodern) matrix of scholarship where recognized periods and genre hierarchies set within clear and certain national contexts form the rigid infrastructure and value system of the arts and humanities. In this scenario, theory, like textual bibliography and linguistics, is a handmaiden in service to aesthetic analysis, historical investigation, cultural critique. It appears an historical anomaly on its way out. So it is that US doctoral students wanting to specialize in theory nowadays strategically adopt a secondary recognized literary area, usually contemporary American fiction or poetry, as a way to put on a traditional face in order to improve their chances in a long-overcrowded job market. For many young theorists, theory in disguise and in the backseat is the future.

Given the growing number of segments as well as fault lines running through the domain of theory, it is no surprise that it increasingly takes the form of semi-autonomous enclaves. Proliferation generates disaggregation. Overviews have become harder to draw. Since the late 1990s, it has seemed impossible to map the world of theory, with its lengthening list of "studies" areas (Leitch, 2010, ch. 14). Under such conditions, teaching is very much a matter of sampling and mixing and matching, which constitutes a certain future for theory teaching.

Professorial comportment

This is a good spot, now at the close of the discussion, to summon up the teaching body and persona performing in front of captive students.

There is, to begin with, the matter of deportment and its many implications. In my personal case I would say my daily suits and often ties, for instance, sometimes act as camouflage, conservative cover for irreverent interrogations of the status quo. I like to think so. Twelve years of Catholic school and two years in a Merchant Marine academy, all in uniform with tie, mean I don't squirm and yank at the collar. I pass comfortably. Fashion speaks. My public voice, exercised daily in order to be deep, clear, loud, and free of my "wretched" New York dialect, exudes white male authority but is softened for other effects. The message is: here stands professorial authority, confident, self-assured, yet enthusiastically, sometimes corrosively, open-minded. The doctored voice is a main instrument of teaching.

For teachers there is always the background of syllabi, mandatory course plans, sequenced modules, coverage of material, legal requirements, calls to duty as well as regimented seats, class times, expected attendance, grades, docile bodies, official records, very bright lights. The two main temptations of classroom teaching from time immemorial have been "turkey stuffing" and "cruising." I mean lecturing and dialogue, drifting, excursions into unplanned spaces. The rigid body and the body in motion. The moments of getting lost, of rifts, of roaming take place within the larger context of well-designed courses and curricula. Such moments gravitate toward questions, contradictions, paradoxes, countercurrents. In my experience it is always best to be on the lookout for these opportunities rather than leaving them to pure chance. Being raised on the South Shore of Long Island, my favorite sport has long been body surfing in the Atlantic Ocean. While there is inevitably a rhythm to the waves, the odd ones, slightly askew, often deliver the best rides, provided the prevailing currents and undercurrents line up just right. Catching a wave looks like luck, and it is, but it depends on attentiveness, judgment, opportunism, a body positioned in a certain way open to the most immediate future. Body work, I know, plays out differently for women and for minority teachers.

Anyone who has looked into "futures" on today's financial markets realizes not only that they are highly risky instruments, but that they focus on short-term performance, one year or less. You put up a little money (a small margin) and open a future position, choosing either to speculate on an increasing market or to hedge on a declining market for, say, oil, coffee, sugar, or some other asset. On any day during the term of the brief contract, you can estimate the fair value of your futures asset. (There is a standard calculation which takes into account average rate of profit, prevailing interest rates, current price of the asset in question, and the terms of your contract.) If you choose, you can close out your position at any time. In our current neoliberal capitalist milieu, an era of fast turnovers and casino sensibilities, "futures" signify quick gains made off growth or decline (Harvey, 1990 and 2005). No matter which. It goes without saying that investors do not generally produce products, rather they speculate on them. Not surprisingly, there is an academic futures market in theory, including the history of theory. That bears on our comportment.

The theory futures market is more volatile than the markets, for instance, in Renaissance or Enlightenment scholarship and teaching. In his 2002 book, *The Future of Theory*, Rabaté concludes with a list of ten growth areas shaping theory's future: material culture, technoscience, globalization studies, ethical criticism, trauma studies, new textual bibliography, chaos theory, late deconstructive hauntology, new wave ethnic studies, and translation studies (pp. 146–8). Academics, whether theorists or not, but especially up-and-coming young scholars, will calculate on any given day how the market looks for new historicism, feminist theory, poststructuralism, cultural studies, Marxism, new formalisms, postcolonial theory, etc. Intellectuals today operate in a world of markets. You can close out or open a position seemingly on any theory at any moment. Personally, I am regularly asked by students, faculty, and others about theory and cultural studies: whether to buy, sell, or hold and in just those terms. People want to know very badly what is the latest thing. Without being coy, I remain wary of my role as futures advisor for potential theory investors including bemused professional onlookers. In the latter category I have in mind colleagues, higher education journalists, humanities deans, book publishers, and journal editors. I work for them too. My final observation: there is a pressing future in theory futures. Theory teachers have to speculate about futures.

Bibliography

Abrams, M.H. *The Mirror and the Lamp: Romantic Theory and Critical Tradition.* New York: Oxford University Press, 1953.

Aronowitz, Stanley and Henry Giroux. *Postmodern Education: Politics, Culture, and Social Criticism.* Minneapolis: University of Minnesota Press, 1991.

Bennett, William. *To Reclaim a Legacy: A Report on the Humanities in Higher Education.* Washington, DC: National Endowment for the Humanities, 1984.

Bloom, Allan. *The Closing of the American Mind: How Higher Education Has Failed Democracy and Impoverished the Souls of Today's Students.* New York: Simon and Shuster, 1987.

Booker, M. Keith. *Teaching with the NORTON ANTHOLOGY OF THEORY AND CRITICISM: A Guidebook for Instructors.* New York: Norton, 2001.

Bourdieu, Pierre and Jean-Claude Passeron. *Reproduction in Education, Society and Culture.* Trans. Richard Nice. 1970; London: Sage, 1977.

Darder, Antonia, Marta Baltodano, and Rodolfo D. Torres, eds. *The Critical Pedagogy Reader*. New York: RoutledgeFalmer, 2003.

Freire, Paolo. *Pedagogy of the Oppressed*. Trans. Myra Bergman Ramos. 1968. New York: Continuum, 1982.

Frye, Northrop. *Anatomy of Criticism: Four Essays*. Princeton: Princeton University Press, 1957.

Graff, Gerald. *Beyond the Culture Wars: How Teaching the Conflicts Can Revitalize American Education*. New York: Norton, 1990.

———. "Advocacy in the Classroom – Or the Curriculum? A Response." *Advocacy in the Classroom: Problems and Possibilities*, ed. Patricia Meyer Spacks. New York: St. Martin's Press, 1996.

Harvey, David. *The Condition of Postmodernity*. Cambridge: Blackwell, 1990.

———. *A Brief History of Neoliberalism*. New York: Oxford University Press, 2005.

Horowitz, David. *The Professors: The 101 Most Dangerous Academics in America*. Washington, D.C.: Regnery, 2006.

Huber, Bettina J. "Today's Literature Classroom: Findings from the MLA's 1990 Survey of Upper-Division Courses," *Association of Departments of English Bulletin* 101 (Spring 1992): 36–60.

Leitch, Vincent B. "Postmodernism, Pedagogy, and Cultural Criticism," *Postmodernism – Local Effects, Global Flows*. Albany: State University of New York Press, 1996. Ch. 11.

———, ed. *et al. Norton Anthology of Theory and Criticism*. New York: W. W. Norton, 2001. [2nd edn, 2010.]

———. "Work Theory." *Critical Inquiry* 31.2 (Winter 2005): 286–301.

———, and Mitchell R. Lewis, "U.S. Cultural Studies," *Johns Hopkins Guide to Literary Theory and Criticism*, 2nd edn. Eds Michael Groden, Martin Kreiswirth, and Imre Szeman. Baltimore: Johns Hopkins University Press, 2005.

———, *American Literary Criticism Since the 1930s*, 2nd edn. New York: Routledge, 2010.

Ohmann, Richard. *English in America: A Radical View of the Profession*. New York: Oxford University Press, 1976.

Patai, Daphne, and Will H. Corral, eds. *Theory's Empire: An Anthology of Dissent*. New York: Columbia University Press, 2005.

Rabaté, Jean-Michel. *The Future of Theory*. Malden, MA: Blackwell, 2002.

Sadoff, Dianne F. and William Cain, eds. *Teaching Contemporary Theory to Undergraduates*. New York: Modern Language Association, 1994.

Scholes, Robert. *Textual Power: Literary Theory and the Teaching of English*. New Haven: Yale University Press, 1985.

Williams, Jeffrey J., ed. *PC Wars: Politics and Theory in the Academy*. New York: Routledge, 1995.

Wilson, John K. *The Myth of Political Correctness: The Conservative Attack on Higher Education*. Durham: Duke University Press, 1995.

Appendix: Theory Heuristics – Short Guide for Students

"Heuristics" involves the use of routine questions, texts, and frameworks to produce knowledge. One well-known heuristic device is the journalist's "Five W's," that is, the habit of asking of an object or phenomenon "who, what, where, when, and why." Another standard heuristic is the question "what might have been excluded or minimized?" Both of these all-purpose tools are useful in coming to understand contending literary and cultural theories. Here I shall touch upon a selection of general and specialized heuristic devices helpful for students in studying theory.

It is often revealing in studying a specific theory to ask hypothetically what some other disciplines might think of the theory. This can be a productive routine for generating wide-ranging knowledge and understanding. If a particular theorist argued that literature imitated life, students might ask, for example, how a biologist, sociologist, historian, psychologist, or art historian would respond. This should lead students to see that "life" needs further elaboration to take into consideration nature (biology), society (sociology), tradition (history), consciousness and the unconscious (psychology), and representation or imitation itself (art history). Other disciplines, for example, anthropology, philosophy, women's studies, or theology, might be added here to produce further understanding and refinement.

A widely used heuristic technique, of course, is "comparison and contrast." In the field of criticism and theory, it typically takes the form of finding on a given topic the similarities (comparison) and differences (contrast) between any two or more theorists—for instance, Plato and Aristotle on mimesis or on genres; or schools like Marxism, formalism, and feminism on reading or on tradition. To elaborate a bit, "reading" for many Marxists means "ideology critique," for formalists "textual explication," and for some feminists "resistance to patriarchal codes." Students might further the inquiry by exploring a range of permutations, which, in this case, could be investigations concerning the role of ideology in formalism; the presence of patriarchy in Marxism; the pertinence of explication for feminist criticism. Such comparison and contrast is often a powerful discovery mechanism for students and scholars of theory, even in the few cases where it leads to a blind alley, which is an informative endpoint.

A productive heuristic question to pose when studying aspects of theory is "what institutions and social agents are involved?" For example, it helps in understanding ancient or Renaissance theory of tragedy to know about the institutional status of the theater, of acting, of playwriting, of audience composition, of reviewing, of publishing, of financing, of censorship and control, of education, and of government's relation to the theater. Asking routinely about institutional dimensions can illuminate the dynamics of literature and culture—and theory too.

Theory courses and textbooks usually offer heuristic maps, charts, or graphic models of the field. A standard one, developed by M.H. Abrams in *The Mirror and the Lamp: Romantic Theory and the Critical Tradition* (1953) pictures the art "work" at the center of a pyramidal structure with the outer three points being occupied by the "universe" at the top and at the sides the "artist" and the "audience." Let me consider this famous map and generate some heuristics in my elaboration and critique of it. To emphasize the relations between the work and the universe, according to Abrams, is to stress mimetic theory. The links between work and artist foreground expressive theory, while those between work and audience highlight didactic and receptionist theories. Focus on the work itself stresses formalist theories, which characteristically deemphasize connections among text and universe, artist, and audience. Up until the early Romantic era, notes Abrams, literary theory dealt largely with the poem's relationship to the universe and the audience; then in the nineteenth century it added the artist; and in the twentieth century it turned to the work itself. Most theories of criticism and literature, argues Abrams, juggle these four major elements and orientations, privileging one.

In studying theory, this taxonomy and its lessons have proven highly useful, especially in illustrating basic theoretical orientations and in delineating broad historical trends. It is gospel in some classrooms. But the map has limitations. It leaves out or minimizes such major topics as language and critique, which have always been important in the history of theory and criticism, but particularly in more recent times. It lodges the work at the center of attention as though the "work" were autonomous and disconnected from constitutive linguistic and social codes as well as from the audience, artist, and universe. The map valorizes each of the four fixed points and not the unnamed circuits that link them, despite its arrows going out from the work to the three points at the edges of its triangular structure.

Perhaps the main problem today with Abrams' famous diagram is that, without being able to say so, it stops with modernism. It was drawn up before the onset of such influential theoretical movements as structuralism, poststructuralism, feminism, postcolonial theory, and cultural studies, to name just a few postmodern trends. Latter-day theory and criticism have arguably come at the end of a progression from mimesis and didacticism to expressionism to formalism to cultural critique. This progression entails complex shifts of focus from imitation of reality and its lessons and impacts to inner truths and visions to poetic techniques and their orchestrations to sociohistorical and political representations and their values. In this development none of the "old" problems disappear, rather they recede from view, undergoing reconfiguration and occupying new spaces. Thus Abrams' diagram has pertinence and heuristic value for students studying theory today, but only when its limitations are set against its strengths. This is true of all heuristics.

Note that heuristic devices can get you into trouble. Also keep in mind that conflicts and problems structure the field of theory and criticism, and that mastery of the discipline requires familiarity with such points of contention. Moreover, among the talents most prized by theorists are the abilities, first, to discover and explore problems and, second, to propose convincing and imaginative solutions.

There are several approaches regularly used in both constructing and studying the history of criticism and theory. Check any syllabus. According to my outline here, students may study (a) leading figures, or (b) key texts, or (c) significant topics and problems, or (d) important schools and movements, or (e) some combination of the above approaches. How is a syllabus organized? Each method of organization has strengths and weaknesses, which I shall touch upon here, using this frame to uncover problematics and generate heuristic protocols.

Study of major figures usually examines the careers of a relatively few "geniuses," offering productive case studies of people who over time have elaborated nuanced theories significantly shaping the field. This approach implies, however, that cultural history and value stem from gifted individuals, not minor figures or wider movements. It also tends to foreground intellectual biography, leaving social foundations and cultural history in the background. It is as though the genius springs out of nowhere. In studying theory, examine presuppositions, looking at what is privileged and what is devalued, including in syllabi and textbooks.

The study of key texts positively de-emphasizes heroic biography while opening spaces for outsiders who work in other fields but have made important contributions to theory and criticism. There are quite a number of such outsiders. Key texts in their density often communicate a great deal of information and a profound understanding of central aspects of theory. Unfortunately, this approach suggests that intellectual history consists of a string of blockbusters. Like artworks in a museum, great works of theory appear cut off from the people, places, and events that swirled about them in their time. The category itself of "great work" needs to be interrogated for the values it promotes and the institutions it depends on. Historical context is part of the history of theory.

Studying theory by examining significant topics and problems – for example, the concepts of "literature," "interpretation," "culture," or "gender" – offers the twin virtues of coherence and variety. Also it takes the spotlight off great works and major figures. The reflections of numerous authors on specific issues provide broad coverage and in-depth analysis of the field. However, it too dwells in the rarefied intellectual realm of concepts severed from sociohistorical contexts. Moreover, it privileges innovation over continuity and philosophically-oriented theory over more mundane critical routines. It portrays theory as fixated around a core of perennial problems. And it invariably promotes a "critical pluralism" in which respect for multiple points of view wins over the rigors of position taking. In studying theory, be attentive to the place accorded to the everyday and the normal in relation to the extraordinary. And keep an eye on origins and endpoints. These can be helpful heuristic protocols.

Study of schools and movements, a favorite among contemporary teachers and students, assembles within coherent boundaries numerous major and minor figures, influential texts, key problems, and institutional issues. In the latter case, it frequently takes into account such factors related to theory as the formations of new fields and projects, of publications outlets, of organizations and associations, and of support structures. Since this approach studies an array of competing schools and movements, it usefully dispenses with simple notions of historical evolution, continuity, cyclicality, devolution, or teleology. However, it excludes mavericks and independents, examining coherences and loyalties among school members, sometimes construing differences as problems or anomalies. It values new waves but devalues normative practical criticism as well as traditional scholarship. It has little or no applicability to earlier eras. And finally, it too risks disconnecting criticism and theory from political, economic, and related sociohistorical contexts.

For many theorists, part of the task of studying theory requires self-reflection, including on the theory curriculum. Theory students are implicated in this process. The mission of theory to ask questions does not stop at the covers of the book.

The contents and forms of the syllabus, your syllabus included, deserve consideration. What are the problems and limitations of a specific program of study? The ways teachers organize the syllabus, textbooks, the curriculum, and the history of criticism and theory are important matters for understanding the field.

Let me list the heuristic devices mentioned in this short guide. When studying a figure or text or problem or critical school:

– Inquire into the Five W's.
– Consider what might be excluded or minimized.
– Contrast different disciplinary viewpoints.
– Compare and contrast concepts, figures, and schools.
– Compose permutations and grafts of concepts.
– Take into account institutional factors.
– Apply M. H. Abrams' pyramid.
– Examine presuppositions.
– Assess point of view.
– Look at what is privileged and what devalued.
– Extrapolate conditions of possibility.
– Consider changes, especially recent developments.
– Look at context.
– Try to rearrange parts and elements.
– Seek out problems.
– Create solutions to problems.
– Evaluate effects.
– Locate the space allotted the everyday and the normal.
– Analyze origins and endpoints.
– Study the conflicts of the field.

It goes without saying that studying theory means asking about concepts of language, literature, interpretation, experience, society, and ideology. I can formulate this into additional heuristic protocols to be used in studying criticism and theory:

– Examine theory of language.
– Isolate theory of literature.
– Scrutinize accounts of interpretation and reading.
– Consider the definition and place of experience.
– Factor in society and culture.
– Do critique of class, gender, and race matters.

I could go on here and list further heuristics related to recurring problems in theory, but the two dozen already given provide enough material to get a student started and to enable her or him to generate further heuristics. Amongst theorists "to theorize" entails creating new heuristic procedures and routines.

2
The Resistance to History: Teaching in the Present

Andrew Hadfield

Should we actually teach theory at all? Put this way, one suspects, the question appears to be too provocative and conservative. But the problem we have all faced as literature teachers in higher education is how to fit everything into the curriculum. Something cannot be allowed in without something else being taken out. This works at the level of micro-content. For example, the rise of Virginia Woolf has been at the expense of Ezra Pound; the triumph of Seamus Heaney meant that no one studied Philip Larkin any more, especially once his reading tastes became more widely known. More significantly, the rise of theory has probably been at the expense of close reading. How many teachers, let alone students, understand prosody? Or even know what it is? Can anything be done other than to teach less theory?

The issue goes beyond the once sustained conflict of the theory wars and has become pedagogical as much as ideological. Whenever Higher Education teachers working in English Departments are gathered together, they often wonder aloud how much teaching theory has changed what they do. Many openly state that they were committed to the project of theory when they first entered the profession, but now find that it hampers rather than facilitates how they think, how they process and package the material they wish students to read, and the questions they want to ask and that they want their students to ask. It is also common for academics to ask whether certain forms of political criticism have now become outmoded as they have become absorbed into the mainstream and whether we have, in fact, lost sight of literature and should return to teaching this without a theoretical apparatus. The fear is that while a generation of readers of literary texts, trained in the inchoate but indispensable skills of New Critical close reading, were able to use their talents to open up new avenues when they turned their

33

attention to political and historical issues, forging innovative forms of political criticism, subsequent generations of students of literature, taught by the above group, who are forced to see literature as a political/ historical artefact will not have the ability to read literature as such and will only reproduce what their teachers think. Many think that the attempt to challenge the deadening effects of the dominance of a Leavisite version of literature as an object that expressed the essence of a real life it always refused to define has led nowhere and has made literature studies a pale imitation of the social sciences. We have travelled a long way from the crusading optimism of Terry Eagleton's *Literary Theory* (1983), which started off by pointing out the effects of the rise of English and ended with an impassioned appeal for political criticism. But then Eagleton himself might appear to have travelled an equally tortuous path, writing works of fiction, books on the novel, tragedy and how to read poetry and an autobiography.

Perhaps the key issue was that the teaching of literature as or in history was never really properly historicised and that it has now become another victim of a historical process. The notion that importing historical knowledge into the literature curriculum would somehow make the discipline more exciting, relevant and perpetually oppositional, seems somewhat naïve in retrospect. Hardly as foolish as the tautological assumption that great literature simply produced unique human truths, but nearly as problematic. The curse that has bedevilled political criticism is part of a wider malaise that has derailed the project of literary theory and its more apocalyptic hopes of transforming the subject and much more besides. There is probably no literature department in the United Kingdom that does not teach literary theory: often, in fact, departments that are not widely regarded as theoretical in orientation teach more theory than those that are (a greater number of students in the Department of English at Aberystwyth, where I used to teach, read more theory than many at Sussex, where I teach now, which might surprise an outside world which still regularly caricatures Sussex as a university full of academics in blue jeans spouting Foucault and Judith Butler to admiring young radicals). The very success of theory has blunted its edge so that it has become a vocabulary and a pedagogy that can be endlessly reproduced. It is little wonder that a book such as Peter Barry's guide, *Beginning Theory* (1995), has become a runaway academic bestseller, and a far more central and mainstream work than more recognisably traditional guides to literary studies. Irritation at this turn of events has spawned collections of essays that desperately seek to put the radical back into the theoretical. The opening words of the introduction to the volume, *Post-Theory: New Directions in Criticism* (1999), provide a good sense of the perceived need to revitalise a necrotic body:

> This is not the first time that Theory has been reported dead.
> This is not the first time that Theory has been reported dead.
> This is not the first time that reporting the death of Theory has been reported dead.
> This is not the first time that reporting the death of Theory has been reported dead.
> However, we believe we are the first to call for an end to reporting the death of reporting the death of Theory (McQuillan *et al.*, eds, 1999, p.1).

But, one would hope, it is the last. The showy rhetorical ploy of these opening lines is testimony in itself to the anxiety that theory might really be dead.

The point is made even more sharply if we consider the history of deconstruction, which was still a relatively exotic continental import into English in the 1980s and had the distinct and pleasurable power to shock the unconverted. Now, far more teachers have a confident grasp of deconstruction – or assume they have – enabling them to reproduce and explain the ways in which Derrida undermined logocentrism, showed how speech does not precede writing, and can wearily point out that 'il n'y a pas de hors texte' does not mean that Derrida was foolish enough to believe that writing – in its colloquial sense – defines reality and that he had failed to observe that some things are not actually words on the page. The point that needs to be made is that these elements of Derrida's thinking all date from his work in the 1960s, most particularly *Of Grammatology*, but also *Writing and Difference* and *Dissemination*. Derrida moved on and not only did he write about other subjects in his later works – friendship, justice, money, mourning, the archive – but he employed a very different vocabulary. Deconstruction is routinely criticised for its disregard of history, but Derrida's sensitivity to change is more acute than that of most writers who highlight their own commitment to history. Frederick Jameson's maxim, 'Always historicise', proclaimed in *The Political Unconscious* (1982), is fundamentally ahistorical, apparently imagining that history is the one category that does not need to be historicised, an error Derrida would never have made. Deconstruction as it is practised is invariably acutely aware of its contingent nature, and what used to be largely a critique of philosophy that pointed to the relationship between philosophy and literature, has become a series of writings that explore the overlap between literary criticism and creative writing.

Deconstruction, as it is often taught to students, dehistoricises its practice and reproduces the discourse of the late 1960s.

If we follow this logic, then the uncomfortable truth may be that we cannot really think intelligently about history without facing the fact that the ahistorical can be historical and the historical can be ahistorical, to adapt a formula that has come to characterise the now old-fashioned New Historicists. Moreover, this is something that needs to be explored as both an intellectual and a pedagogical issue. History cannot simply be represented as endless flux or it ceases to have any meaning and purpose and might just as well be abandoned (see Davies, 2006). There has to be some form of principle that connects and binds any history in order for it to have meaning, an issue that is both intellectual and pedagogic.

Departments that teach literature are faced with a problem when they abandon the shared understanding that literature expresses the highest form of human achievement, the nebulous but powerful ideological glue that bound the subject together from its inception in late Victorian England through to the waning of the powers of New and Practical Criticism in the 1970s. It is easy now to sneer at F. R. Leavis's response to René Wellek's review of *Revaluation*, when he agreed with Wellek's statement of the general critical principles that he had outlined in the book, but argued that literary analysis should never succumb to the temptation to declare its hand and so risk becoming imitation philosophy (Leavis, 1937; Wellek, 1937; Donoghue, 1992). In deliberately avoiding any statement of principle, beyond the basic argument that literature was about life and the critic was duty bound to analyse the particular work or passage in question, Leavis was resisting both theory and history, a manoeuvre that helped critics and academics imagine their discipline as a coherent whole and argue for its particular value. Indeed, as Terry Eagleton points out, Leavis was conspicuously successful: 'In the early 1920s it was desperately unclear why English was worth studying at all; by the early 1930s it had become a question of why it was worth wasting your time on anything else' (Eagleton, 1983, p.31).

In attacking the ideals of Leavis, it might be argued that English Departments have cut the ground from beneath their feet, however necessary the critique (Widdowson, 1982; Paulin, 1984). Without the belief that literature actually performs some serious cultural work of its own the subject risks breaking down into an ill-assorted collection of very different, even mutually incomprehensible subjects. There are theorists, who are often deconstructionists; creative writers, who form a distinct sub-set within a department, and either exist alone, or, more rarely, overlap with some of the theorists, many of whom are now interested in the possibilities of creative writing; period specialists, who are invariably historicists; and, perhaps, collections of philologists, linguists, English Language specialists, and Comparative Literature specialists, many of whom have migrated from besieged, dying and dead Modern Language Departments. There may, of course, be journalism and media, or even philosophy subject areas within the department. This will be familiar enough to many academics struggling to cope with institutional change and new amalgamations forced on them by ever more perilous university finances in the UK. Once change has taken place it is much easier for more to follow. Moreover, the very success of English Departments in attracting students drawn to the ideology of a subject that hardly any of its teachers support, simultaneously hampers and limits the subject that one would imagine would benefit from healthy market forces. University departments of a subject such as Art History, when they have not been forced to close through lack of student numbers, have often been extremely successful in forging an identity that explains and defines what they study and do. English Departments, in contrast, now represent and contain an amalgamation of groups and forces that make it hard to state what it is that they study or do.

A significant aspect of the problem is the role of history in explaining and defining the subject. As is often noted, most teachers of English Literature are, broadly speaking, historicists in training and inclination. They write books on subjects such as the relationship between modernist literature and technology; Victorian literature and psychology; Medieval literature and the changing role of the family; literature and slavery in the romantic period; or, even, early modern literature and travel writing. They have gradually narrowed their focus through the arduous journey from doctoral student to young professional, then look to write a second book to gain further promotion, hopefully finding a project that will gain funding from the AHRC or Leverhulme Trust and so gain them enough time to start it up or finish it off (although already such opportunities look limited as the era of big grants has come to define higher education). If they have started on the historicist route, they are unlikely to change course at this stage. A complaint frequently made by more senior English academics is that everyone is a historian these days.

Such institutional trends have also been reinforced by intellectual developments in the subject area. Although it is often pointed out that criticism was never as ahistorical as it was sometimes claimed for polemical convenience, and that New Criticism had actually been a reaction in part to the dominance of a historicist approach to literary criticism which was always an important component of literary studies, the case remains that theoretical movements such as New Historicism and Cultural Materialism did do much to revitalise a discipline that had often sought to minimise the significance of historical context. Context was often perceived as something that was necessary but which was only of use in facilitating the interpretation of literary texts. One needed to know about early modern science in order to read Donne's 'Anniversaries', or about The French Revolution when studying the Romantics. The idea that literary and non-literary texts might be read alongside each other without one privileged as foreground, the other reduced to background, was indeed revolutionary, as was the notion that literature might – indeed, should – be read in terms of its political and social significance.

In such circumstances many young scholars were eager to shake up their departments and to make a name for themselves by pointing out the elisions of historical evidence which had been allowed to smooth over the rough edges of literary history. Colonial history, in particular, had been neglected and it was easy to expose the importance of Britain's imperial past on the diverse writers who were caught up in its historical development – Edmund Spenser, Rudyard Kipling, Joseph Conrad – sas well as explore the legacy of colonial and imperial history on more recent writers throughout the world. For example, Edward Said's claim that Jane Austen's *Mansfield Park* could be read as a colonial text because the Bertram family are implicated in the West Indian slave trade, provoked outrage (Said, 1994, pp.100–16; Gellner, 1993). Equally important was a concentration on the issue of power, which inspired analysis of literary forms and their relation to dominant modes of authority, from the Stuart masque to the Modernist novel, from Medieval court poetry to twentieth-century travel writing. The writings of Michel Foucault, largely absent from general discussion now and the preserve of specialists, were everywhere in articles and teaching programmes twenty years ago, and the use of his gory description of an execution at the start of *Discipline and Punish* became a notable cliché (Foucault, 1977, pp.3–31).

However, the theoretically-inspired case that literature needed to be historicised was, if anything, too successful to sustain its momentum. As more scholars and critics became interested in history the larger generalisations outlining the use of power, colonial domination, social and sexual identity, were challenged by a greater wealth of research, which demanded that many generalisations be rethought and refined. Clearly, this was a natural and inevitable development, and shows how much contemporary critics owe to pioneering Cultural Materialist and New Historicist studies (Hadfield, 2003; Sinfield, 2006, ch. 1). Equally it is worth pointing out that the greater availability of primary sources through the internet and other computer facilities, such as Early English Books Online (EEBO), has made historically grounded research much more straightforward for those who do not have the time or the ability to consult archive materials. The period when there was an obvious split between the archive-based scholarly work of many staff at leading, traditional, established universities, and the more theoretically-inflected studies of their counterparts in more recently established institutions has receded, if not entirely disappeared.

It is easy to see why such developments are supported in the larger institutional context in which research funding is so important for universities, and the AHRC, responsible to parliament for its distribution of funding, is obliged to insist that research has a solid and substantial grounding, and that money is given only to projects that can be completed in a reasonable time. A certain amount of historical information has, therefore, found its way into undergraduate curricula. However, it is undoubtedly the case that most students in most universities want to study literature and are often resistant to attempts by their teachers to turn them into historicists. An already existing reluctance to read pre-twentieth century literature is further exaggerated, and the result is that students naturally drift towards courses that teach contemporary literature and creative writing. This places faculty and students at odds, with teachers often frustrated because students do not want to study what they want to teach. And, for many academics, teaching and research can often be separate activities which are only loosely connected. Although students get much of what they want, as teachers are – quite rightly – under pressure to design courses that are popular and satisfy student demand, there is clearly a huge structural flaw in a university system which pulls in opposite directions. Many departments, especially ones with a well-established or ageing faculty, are unbalanced, as they represent a different age when the ideal was to appoint staff who could cover everything from *Beowulf* to Virginia Woolf. What is now required is a team who place greater emphasis on the present – contemporary literature, literary theory and creative writing – and who do not see their primary task to teach the history of literature.

Any three-year degree will have a tightly packed curriculum and one change will inevitably result in the loss of another area. In terms of the literature studied, one might note, for example, that Daniel Defoe has suffered because of Aphra Behn, *Oronooko* replacing *Robinson Crusoe*, which now slots into the ever decreasing part of the degree which covers the Restoration. Writing by women is much more widely available and significantly represented in undergraduate degree courses: it is impossible now to teach eighteenth-century literature without including work by Lady Wortley Montagu, Charlotte Smith or Helen Maria Williams, which has reduced the amount of Pope and Dryden on offer. Jane Austen has become the second most important figure in English literary history. T. S. Eliot and D. H. Lawrence have certainly lost considerable ground to Virginia Woolf, now the most widely read of all modernist authors.

More radically, the increase in the amount of theory and historical material studied has inevitably reduced the amount of literature that students actually read so that survey courses have frequently been squeezed in terms of their content, especially as they are frequently the areas of a degree scheme that students enjoy least. Introductory courses and options now contain far more contextual/theoretical material, leaving less time for literary texts. Furthermore, the decline of the long vacation as a time when tutors could ask students to read long novels and narrative poems ready for the forthcoming year, and the need to account for the precise number of hours that students spend studying on individual courses, has also limited what can be set on courses. Together with the abolition of the student grant, which has all but eliminated the sale of secondary texts other than a few essential guides, and it is little wonder that, whatever the reservations of academics, the anthology has come to dominate teaching in the last two decades. Such works, whether produced by Norton, Longman, Broadview or Arnold, all contain some contextual material in line with the expectations of university teachers. Students now study extracts and selections rather than complete texts, often until they begin to study work written in the nineteenth and twentieth centuries, which further increases their preference for literature written in the past two centuries.

The resistance to history is a complicated story, one that defies easy categorisation but which cannot be ignored. Probably the most basic problem is that there is too much to study and too little time in which to do it, so that, as ever in life, hard choices have to be made. The old English curriculum was simple enough: one either studied an Oxford-based philological English degree, which required English Language and Anglo-Saxon, or a Cambridge one, which left these out but included some material placing literature in a broader cultural and intellectual context (you would read some Montaigne when you studied the Renaissance, some Darwin when reading the nineteenth-century). Students could not read all of Byron's poems, may not have got through much Trollope or Arnold Bennett, but had a clear enough map of English literary history. Now such simple choices and divisions are impossible, and there is always a struggle about the content and purpose of the English degree, which involves faculty members with very different ideas, needs and desires; university managers and administrators, eager to make sense of ever more complex systems as student numbers increase more and more rapidly, and with an acute sense of declining unit resources; and students, current and prospective, who have their own agendas, usually involving more choice, more contemporary literature, and more opportunities to produce their own creative writing. While the force exerted by the first group often pushes the curriculum in the direction of more history, the last two push it away.

What is to be done? The first and most obvious observation is that an English degree cannot simply contain everything and it is foolish to imagine that we can simply replicate what used to be done and then cram a few more things in. Many university teachers complain bitterly that students nowadays do not know what they used to know when they were students – Latin, modern languages, the wider range of English literature, proper grammar – apparently forgetting that they know other things instead – literary theory, IT skills, contemporary literature, how to write creatively (if not accurately). We must all accept that things have changed and concentrate more carefully on what we wish to preserve and what can be let go. There is a loss in abandoning compulsory Old English, a subject I would never have chosen but which benefited me greatly, but it became clear even to the most devoted Anglo-Saxonist that it could not continue when so few students were converted to the cause. Indeed, of all areas of the English curriculum, Old English and Medieval studies has probably been transformed as drastically as any other by recent developments. Whereas medieval scholars were renowned for being the most conservative in their departments, the courses taught by their contemporary counterparts enthusiastically embrace women's writing (how many courses do not contain Marjory Kempe's autobiography or Julian of Norwich's *Devotions*?), descriptions of the Peasants' Revolt and kingship rituals, literary theory and textual theories of editing, sensible strategies for attracting students, as well as a reflection of scholarly interest. The same point can, of course, be made about any period studied. Renaissance courses have to include a variety of canonical works, newly rediscovered women's writing (Mary Sidney, Mary Wroth, Ann Lok), extracts of cultural history (witchcraft, descriptions of Virginia), and critical essays on literature and early modern concepts of power.

The problems, if anything, become even more acute when designing courses on modern and contemporary literature. Apart from the sheer range of material – literary and non-literary – available in print, most teachers find it much easier to apply critical and theoretical essays to more recent literature as essays were invariably written about such literature. To take just one example: Roland Barthes' ubiquitous essay, 'The Death of the Author', a work that does so much to confuse students and render conservative academics apoplectic, was written about trends in contemporary writing. The final statement of the essay, 'the birth of the reader must be at the cost of the death of the author' (Lodge, ed., 1988, p.172), has often been read as though it were a philosophical statement and debated in class as such. However, it is clear that the real focus of this polemical essay is 'new writing', which Barthes argues has overturned traditional assumptions of the relationship between writer and reader:

> The reader is the space on which all the quotations that make up a writing are inscribed without any of them being lost; a text's unity lies not in its origin but in its destination. Yet this destination can-not any longer be personal: the reader is without history, biography, psychology; he [sic] is simply that *someone* who holds together in a single field all the traces by which the written text is constituted. Which is why it is derisory to condemn the new writing in the name of a humanism hypocritically turned champion of the reader's rights [Barthes' emphasis] (Lodge, ed., 1988, p.172).

As the phrase, 'any longer', and the last sentence make clear, Barthes' argument is a historical as well as a theoretical one. Many theoreti-cal arguments have developed out of an interaction with recent and contemporary writing, which is why the two areas of the curriculum enjoy a symbiotic relationship that makes them harder to separate and easier to develop in tandem. Given that students feel less in need of historical information when studying material that is more up-to-date, and are more keen to read history they feel they have some ability to comprehend, then the stubborn reality of the resistance to history is further evident. As many deconstructionists rightly point out, there is no straightforward division between history and poststructuralist criti-cism, deconstruction being steeped in the reality of historical processes and debate (Attridge *et al.*, eds, 1989). Nevertheless, it is symptomatic of a range of inter-related responses and confusions that a gulf is assumed to exist.

Put another way, the problems of the resistance to history and the content of the curriculum are practical ones. They also raise a cluster of pedagogical and theoretical issues. There is only so much that can be taught and if new things are introduced then old things have to be left out. When literary theory courses started to replace practical criticism courses in universities many academics were delighted that the free-floating, ahistorical analysis that had been at the heart of the Leavisite/New Criticism revolution had finally been made answerable to political, cultural and social forces. But the benefits of the change, while undoubtedly numerous, have not been without considerable costs. As many commentators have pointed out, it was naïve for many to dismiss 'Prac. Crit.' as inherently reactionary, as the study of close reading in the classroom, even if bolstered by I. A. Richards' eccentric and naïve faith in behavioural psychology, had helped to democratise literary study and turn it away from the superior form of wine tasting that David Cecil and George Saintsbury championed (at their worst...). Its disappearance from schools and university English courses has, in turn, led to justified complaints that today's students are not as good as close reading as previous generations. You win some, you lose some.

More seriously, perhaps, theory makes more work. English departments now choose to – or have to – cover a range of subjects imported from other areas: psychology (especially Freud); visual culture; philosophy; political thought; feminism and women's studies; comparative literature; cultural history, creative writing, and so on. It is little wonder that curricula are under strain even before the question of including historical material is considered. The answer must surely be that things cannot go on like this for ever.

But what would replace the miscellany of subjects, methods and material that constitute the current English degree and which makes English Departments such pluralist and vaguely defined institutions? Perhaps the truth is that we need to embrace this plurality more enthusiastically and accept that we cannot simply define an English degree in terms of its two traditional functions: teaching literary criticism and literary history. English is a relatively new subject, only just over a hundred years old, and far younger if we consider it in terms of its role as a central feature of the university portfolio. It is hard to imagine that it will remain within its traditional boundaries, especially after the bewildering changes we have witnessed in the last twenty years. The period when English was a coherent subject based on Prac. Crit., Englishness and the benevolent effect of literary culture, will, I think, come to seem a distinct phase in its development, roughly 1930–1980. That English might change should seem to many as a good thing and will be, I believe, a result of the theory revolution that has not yet reached a conclusion, and which may lead us in directions that past devotees could never have imagined.

Any revolution always looks backwards as well as forwards and my proposed vision of the future is deeply rooted in the past, suggesting that a way of countering the resistance to history is to appeal to a history to ease an obsessive love/hate relationship. University education used to be centred around the act of writing. Classical, medieval and early modern educational programmes were based on the need to teach students how to write in different styles and registers and on different subjects. Students were taught rhetoric, the art of persuasion (Vickers, 1989). They had to imitate various models of writing, learning how to produce forensic (making a legal case for or against a subject) and epideictic (attributing praise or blame) rhetoric. They learned how to structure an argument in accordance with the five basic principles of rhetorical development: invention, the ability to think of a persuasive and interesting subject; arrangement, how to organise the speech into a series of properly constituted parts; style, applying the correct register and vocabulary to the speech; memory, inserting key mnemonics for ease of delivery; and delivery, applying ways and means of ensuring that the speech made sense and could be followed by an audience. Such principles were then applied to written work when it became more widespread. Rhetoric was the key feature of an education in the humanities in the Western world and the main use of the classics; Cicero became one of the key authors because of his stress on the principles and practice of oratory, which could be imitated and taught; Ovid became important not just because he had a scandalous reputation as a poet of love and exile (although these factors helped), but because he was a fluent poet and easy to read, teach and copy; Quintilian and Demosthenes, because they were the most famous orators of the ancient world. Philip Sidney's *Apology for Poetry*, the best written and most important treatise of the English Renaissance, argues that poetry is the best form of learning because it should move its audience to behave more virtuously, an argument derived from his education in rhetoric (Sidney, 2002). The argument often strikes students as both appealing and odd, but perhaps it should just seem more familiar. Only when more and more subjects had to be crammed into the curriculum in the post-Renaissance world, was there much more emphasis on the content than on the form.

Even so, rhetoric was always a key component of any tertiary educational system until relatively recently and still survives in name in some Scottish universities, and as a subject in many North American universities, where it is an essential component of a first year English course, sometimes under the title 'composition'. Indeed, there is ever growing pressure for English universities to adopt a similar component to their English degrees as there is widespread agreement that students new to university may need more coaching in writing than has hitherto been thought necessary. The rise of theory courses and the decline of practical criticism may be seen as a further cause of this change; the desire for creative writing causes as a result.

What might classroom teaching look like if we start to introduce structural changes to English degrees as I have suggested? I would suggest that students will spend a part of their degrees – perhaps a whole strand running through the three years – learning how to write various forms: essays, book reviews, dialogues, polemical arguments, types of poetry, short stories, documentary articles, reports, and so on. They will also spend time reading works carefully and thinking how they might develop advanced reading skills that they can use when they read other works (i.e. transferable skills). It is important, and given my title and the thrust of the argument, hardly surprising that I do not see this as incompatible with a sense of historical process. One of the problems with practical criticism was that it was all too often taught as if reading were an ahistorical phenomenon and the reader left alone with the text could extract virtually all that was required. Sometimes this is actually true, and texts can be read across the ages: historicism does not mean reducing everything to its particular historical moment and claiming that unless one knows what ale James Joyce preferred we will never be able to read *Ulysses*, or what the dimensions of bedrooms in Tudor London were we will never get to grips with Donne's 'The Flea.' Rather, students need to think about what they need to know, how the past was different (when it was), how the form of texts shapes what they mean, and how we can recover meanings, if we ever can. These are debates that are not exclusive to that large and amorphous collection of works that is labelled 'theory', and can be seen as also germane to much traditional literary criticism and historiography (Lambert and Schofield, 2004). But, theoretical works certainly sharpened a reader's awareness of the reading process and these questions are central to such books as Roland Barthes's painstakingly meticulous analysis of Balzac's novella, *Sarrasine*, a critical work that no serious student of literature should fail to read before they leave university (Barthes, 1974).

One way I have tried to practise what I preach here is on a course I have taught over the years in various guises, at various institutions (Leeds, Aberystwyth, Columbia, Sussex), and at both undergraduate and postgraduate levels, its most recent incarnation being, the MA module, 'Race, Writing and Colonialism in Early Modern England' at Sussex. I try to confront students with a series of theoretical perspectives on race (now gathered together conveniently in Loomba and Burton, eds, 2007) and postcolonial theory (Bhabha, Said, Spivak, Young, collected in Ashcroft *et al.*, eds, 1995) in the opening seminar so that they have to think about how useful such work is in making us think about the past, issues of ethnic and racial difference, and whether we can apply our understanding of differences to texts written a long time ago. Then, in the second seminar, I ask them to read translations of Christopher Columbus's notebooks and letters (Columbus, 1992). We explore the text in terms of what we have read in the first week, and try to work out how Columbus saw the natives of the Caribbean, whether he regarded them as absolutely different to Europeans or people who had much in common with the voyagers/colonists. Is race the key issue that divides the peoples for Columbus? If so, what concept of race is he using? We also try to work out whether we can reconstruct what went on from the text we have and whether it opens out towards a world that we can understand or whether what happened must always remain opaque for later readers. What textual clues are provided and how can we use them? Are they reliable? When must we be sceptical about what the text tells us and when can we trust it, often in spite of what the author appears to think? Such discussions establish an important platform for us to discuss various texts (*Utopia, Othello, Tamburlaine, The Faerie Queene, The Tragedy of Miriam*), places (Ireland, the Mediterranean, Africa, the Americas) and identities (principally ethnic and religious) in the remaining weeks. The course could, of course, be taught without the input of theoretical writings. But, I would maintain, it was my reading of theory that made it possible to teach, that forced me to ask myself relevant and difficult questions, and which helps to inspire students to make connections.

Perhaps the time has come to surrender to the forces that are besieging our discipline as it is currently conceived, to move the subject forward by swimming with the tide rather than resisting it. We should recognise that we have not paid enough attention to form in education, its history and its purpose. This does not mean abandoning what most of us do, literary criticism, literary history and literary theory. Rather, it suggests that we have to accommodate them into a more flexible and broadly based curriculum, one based on teaching styles of writing and speech (after all, both students and employers often complain that universities place far too much emphasis on written not verbal skills and every now and again we try to correct this problem by introducing half-hearted measures such as oral assessment). Writing and speech should become the focus of our teaching efforts so that students learn how to produce different styles of argument, weighing up evidence carefully, reading different types of material, producing different forms of writing (essays of varying lengths, book reviews, pieces of creative writing, imitations of poems, parts of novels, journalism) and speech (traditional forensic oratory, perhaps epideictic as well, debates, formal disputations). The effect would be to make our degrees more historically grounded, as well as to satisfy student demands for a proper training, the chance to express themselves and become more actively involved in their learning (a goal that all our benchmarking statements and professional bodies share). It would also accommodate the ever increasing demand for creative writing and enable more traditional academic staff to teach it, so that universities are not forced to employ novelists and poets who simply do not want to fit into commonly understood university teaching patterns, an ever growing problem that exposes a severe structural flaw. And, of course, making writing the basis of an English degree rather than reading does not mean that we have to design courses in which students do not read anything significant or challenging. One of the tasks that students will be expected to undertake will be argument based on the intensive study of a particular period, type of writing (novel, lyric or narrative poem, and so on) or a series of theoretical arguments. Another will be the imitation of types of writing as outlined in the previous sentence, which means that current divisions of specialist subjects as they now exist will not be made redundant and our subject will not change beyond all recognition, although it will be transmuted and our knowledge applied in different ways. But that, perhaps, is the inevitable price of progress, which always exposes faultlines, one made visible in this case by the rise of theory, the resistance to the history of our subject and, paradoxically, a current research obsession with history.

References

Ashcroft, Bill, Gareth Griffiths and Helen Tiffin, eds, 1995. *The Post-Colonial Studies Reader*. London: Routledge.

Attridge, Derek, Geoff Bennington and Robert Young, eds, 1989. *Poststructuralism and the Question of History*. Cambridge: Cambridge University Press.

Barry, Peter, 1995. *Beginning Theory*. Manchester: Manchester University Press.

Barthes, Roland, 1974. *S/Z: An Essay*, trans. Richard Miller. New York: Hill and Wang.

Columbus, Christopher, 1992. *The Four Voyages of Christopher Columbus*, trans. J. M. Cohen. Harmondsworth: Penguin.

Davies, Martin L., 2006. *Historics: Why History dominates contemporary society*. Abingdon: Routledge.

Donoghue, Denis, (1992), 'The Use and Abuse of Theory', *The Modern Language Review*, Vol. 87, No. 4, xxix–xxxviii.

Eagleton, Terry, 1983. *Literary Theory: An Introduction*. Oxford: Blackwell.

Foucault, Michel, 1977. *Discipline and Punish: The Birth of the Prison*, trans. Alan Sheridan. Harmondsworth: Penguin.

Gellner, Ernst, 1993. 'The Mightier Pen? Edward Said and the Double Standards of Inside-out Colonialism' *Times Literary Supplement*, 19 Feb., pp.3–4.

Hadfield, Andrew, 2003. 'Shakespeare and Republicanism: History and Cultural Materialism', *Textual Practice* 17, 461–83.

Lambert, Peter and Philip Schofield, 2004. *Making History: An Introduction to the History and Practices of a Discipline*. London: Routledge.

Leavis, F. R., 1937. 'Literary Criticism and Philosophy: A Reply', *Scrutiny*, 6(1): 59–70.

———— 1948. *The Great Tradition: George Eliot, Henry James, Joseph Conrad*. London: Chatto & Windus.

Lodge, David, ed., 1988. *Modern Criticism and Theory: A Reader*. Harlow: Longman.

Loomba, Ania and Jonathan Burton, eds, 2007. *Race in Early Modern England: A Documentary Companion*. Basingstoke: Palgrave Macmillan.

McQuillan, Martin, Graeme MacDonald, Robin Purves and Stephen Thomson, eds, 1999. *Post-Theory: New Directions in Criticism*. Edinburgh: Edinburgh University Press, 1999.

Paulin, Tom, 1984. *Ireland and the English Crisis*. Newcastle: Bloodaxe.

Peter Widdowson, Peter, ed., 1982. *Re-Reading English*. London: Methuen.

Said, Edward Said, 1994. *Culture and Imperialism*. London: Vintage.

Sidney, Sir Philip, 2002. *An Apology for Poetry*, Robert Maslen with Geoffrey Shepherd. Manchester: Manchester University Press.

Sinfield, Alan, 2006. *Shakespeare, Authority, Sexuality: Unfinished Business in Cultural Materialism*. London: Routledge.

Vickers, Brian, 1989. *In Defence of Rhetoric*. Oxford: Clarendon Press.

Wellek, René, 1937. 'Literary Criticism and Philosophy', *Scrutiny* 5(4): 375–83.

3
The Attractions of Theory

Jill Le Bihan

I'd like to take this opportunity to talk about the change in the status and context of the academia over the last fifteen years and what this has done to the teaching of literary theory. The change is from a culture of resistance to a culture of compliance. Fifteen years ago a student stood up in a critical theory seminar I was leading and ripped the module handbook in two after a session on deconstruction. Now, our students offer a resigned 'we'll do it if it will get us a 2:1'. In my undergraduate days in the mid-1980s, theory was a radical and marginal enterprise, and its institutional reputation, as something intellectually demanding and politically subversive, was its allure. As I write today, a principal lecturer who has taught literary theory throughout her career in higher education, I find that 'Theory' follows only 'Introduction to English' courses in terms of its broad institutional adoption (Halcrow Group 2003). This means the attractions (or repulsions) of theory are really quite different.

I wish to investigate the current personal engagement, or, more likely, lack of engagement, with literary theory by undergraduates, and I will restrict the focus to an examination of the current feelings, a carefully chosen word, provoked by feminist literary theory. My reasons for selecting feminism as a theoretical area are chiefly, of course, due to my own commitment to it, both as a teacher and in terms of my own political conviction. This means that my disappointment in my failures to convince my students as to the veracity of the cause has increased, as feminism's fashions and fortunes have fallen in the last decade.

The inclusion of the discussion of the attractions of theoretical feminism within a volume on teaching theory is apposite for another reason, a reason that influences the style and methodology underpinning this essay: the way the discipline of feminist literary theory has configured itself around emotional issues, around the expression of personal experience, and around pedagogy. Jane Gallop, in her collection of essays on what she has called 'Anecdotal Theory', argues that feminism has brought about a transformation of theoretical writing through the inclusion of personal details, and she emphasizes the long tradition of the connection between the feminist movement and pedagogy:

> If the adjective 'personal', elevated to noun status, has become a central focus for pedagogical theory, it is singularly due to something called 'feminist teaching'. Feminists teaching and feminists talking about teaching have not only challenged the exclusion of the personal from the academic but have gone so far as to insist that a proper measure of learning is personal. Even a cursory glance at feminist writing on pedagogy will yield a continual and widespread affirmation of "the personal" – as content, style, and method of pedagogy (Gallop 2002: 23).

The aim of this essay is to consider both the significance of 'anecdotal theory' for contemporary literary theory and to evaluate the attractions of feminism for contemporary British undergraduates. I will suggest that engagement with literary theory remains an emotive subject, certainly for feminist teachers, but in a different way to the mid-1980s. The emotional investment of students in the Twenty-First Century is more tentative and less easy to classify.

The use of personal experience as the basis for theoretical exposition remains, for me, a feminist brought into being through poststructuralism, a dangerous game which leads to paradox and self-contradiction. Diana Fuss, in *Essentially Speaking*, debates the problems presented by the use of personal disclosure in the seminar by students to underline the authority of a particular point, and she reads it as a strategy that might be necessary for those whom the higher education experience of theory might otherwise undermine their ability to speak. But for teachers, particularly teachers of theory, it presents particular difficulties. Fuss explains:

> Experience emerges as the essential truth of the individual subject, and personal "identity" metamorphoses into knowledge. Who we are becomes what we know; ontology shades into epistemology. ... Exactly what counts as "experience", and should we defer to it in pedagogical situations? Does experience of oppression confer special jurisdiction over the right to speak about that oppression? Can we

only speak, ultimately, from the so-called "truth" of our experiences, or are all empirical ways of knowing analytically suspect? (Fuss 1990: 113).

There remains for me a tension between respecting the 'truth' of experiences offered as part of a discussion – indeed, seeing that offering as precisely one of the transformative values of poststructuralist feminism, in challenging the very possibility of an objective theoretical position, in emphasising the subjective – and acknowledging the profound philosophical problems raised by 'the personal as political', which seems to reinstate the personal outside a discursive framework.

One way of retaining the value of the personal is to understand it as a cultural or political product, rather than as a privileged authentic experience that somehow stands outside an ideological framework. Naomi Scheman, in 'Anger and the Politics of Naming', explains the persuasive ideological features that govern 'the theory of privileged access (the philosophical view that we are each the ultimate authority about our own emotions)' (1993: 27). Using the example of anger as an emotion that can be recoded according to historical, institutional or interpersonal context, she presents the critical problems with accepting that each person knows best what is going on in his or her head, and argues that the assumed right to determine one's own emotional state is:

> unequally distributed. Adults, for example, often tell children what they are and are not feeling, and what those feelings mean ("You're just overtired"). And the interpretation of women's feelings and behaviour is often appropriated by others, by husbands or lovers, or by various psychological "experts". Autonomy in this regard is less an individual achievement than a socially recognized right, and, as such, people with social power tend to have more of it (1993: 28).

In feminist consciousness-raising groups, women's depression at their restricted lives was transformed, renamed, as anger, and mobilized as a political force, argues Scheman. This is more than 'getting in touch with your true feelings', she maintains, but is an explicitly political project in which those feelings are created, but in a self-conscious way, which is cognizant of the influence of the group, and its political objectives.

Scheman's choice of an example to illustrate her explanation of how emotion might be constructed is not made arbitrarily. Anger and feminist theory run closely together. I love the opportunity that feminism offers to be angry, and thereafter to see this as something that might be explained (rather than explained away as an irrational, over-emotional contribution to a debate). I love the possibilities provided by feminism to construct polemic. Whatever my disputes might be with the particulars of their arguments, Dworkin's *Intercourse* (1988), Greer's *The Female Eunuch* (1972) and *The Whole Woman* (1999), Wolf's *Fire with Fire* (1993), even Roiphe's *The Morning After* (1994), are provocative, emotive, argumentative pieces. This is one of feminism's legacies, but one which is difficult to pass on. Anger is rarely viewed positively, and almost inevitably is viewed as something that must be cleansed from one's system, not used to poison future generations. Like a wicked stepmother rather than the earth kind, I would like to hand down the chalice, but there is no one willing to take it. And if the poisoned chalice analogy has any weight here, one must, I must, recognize the wisdom of the refusal.

When I was first teaching, I was involved in teaching on both a BA and an MA in Women's Studies. These have long since closed due to the dwindling number of applications, reflecting the lack of interest in feminism in our culture as a whole and so, I am left to teach feminist theory (at least explicitly) in a single lecture on the mandatory, final-year, Literary Theory course on an undergraduate English degree. The students come to the session with varied perspectives, of course, but the perspective that gets voiced in the seminar, the opinion the group allows, is that of an opposition to feminism, but, by and large, an opposition that is devoid of much interest or feeling. When faced with statistics about unequal pay, for instance, or low numbers of women professors in British universities, despite the vast number of female graduates, students are largely unmoved. I ask them for their personal experience of oppression and they appear to bring no experience of oppression with them. They claim never to have faced discrimination under the thumb of patriarchy; in contrast, it is feminists themselves who are often viewed as the oppressors. In a recent session, students were able to name Wollstonecraft and Greer as feminists, and although unable to name Dworkin, could articulate rather simplistically, and label as feminist, the argument that all heterosexual intercourse is rape. That was the extent of the student base of knowledge exhibited in the group. Of course, some students knew more, had read more, especially those doing dissertations on related subjects, but they were silent in a cultural group that deems feminism to be an unacceptable affiliation.

The criticisms of feminism from within its own ranks, from within the establishment of feminist academics (that it is too white, too (hetero) sexist, too poststructuralist) are not the criticisms of feminism from within the classroom; here, students argue merely that feminism is too feminist (anti-male? extreme? political? strident?). Some students, when pushed, might agree to some of the principles established by feminism, but do not wish to be considered 'hard-nosed'. When asked what they might mean by hard-nosed, the direct response I received was 'You'.

I choose to think that the students were not being deliberately insulting, but what they were recognizing was my professional persona and place in the institutional hierarchy, as quite a senior member of a department. I think they were reading feminism to mean, partly, a woman with some professional status. I think there are other more superficial, stereotyping features to them giving me this label: I am recognizably feminist, perhaps, because I have short hair and wear trousers. In fact, I embrace the notion of being feminist as part of a professional identity (see Gallop in Lurie *et al.* 2001: 687) which remains possible within an English Department in a university in a way it may not be possible in many other places outside the academy.

In 1992, as part of a training course that I was doing for teaching in Higher Education, I wrote an essay on adopting a gendered professional persona in the seminar room. As I reflect on this paper now, it allows me to conceptualize clearly the shifts in the intervening years, as well as a great deal of continuity. My own professional status has changed considerably since 1992, when I was on a short-term contract and still finishing my PhD. At the time, as evidenced in the piece, there was for me some ambivalence about poststructuralist feminist politics and how to engage feminist strategies with mixed student groups. Jane Gallop, in her own reflections on teaching feminism in the late 1980s, produces a very concise account of the debate that ruptured the sense of easy community:

> Two stories are often told about academic feminism in the 1980s. The first is that the encounter with poststructuralism called into question feminism's certainties and generalizations. The second story is that white feminism's universalizing moves were challenged as racist by Black feminists and other feminists of color. According to either story, by the end of the 1980s it became obligatory within academic feminism to recognize differences other than gender, differences between women (Gallop in Lurie *et al.*: 2001: 698).

At the point I was writing in 1992, I had begun to be distrustful of some of the abstractions of poststructuralist theory and the problems this raised for some of my students, as well as the way it appeared to disallow certain kinds of discourse of the personal, which it seemed to me feminism had fought hard to have recognized. I would like to resurrect part of my old and dusty argument at this point to try to reproduce a sense of what I thought feminist pedagogical practice might be able to achieve:

*   *   *

The practice of offering personal testimony in a theoretical context is an explicitly feminist one. It brings with it a number of contingent problems, such as embarrassment (confessing the secrets of the classroom), ambivalence (regarding the practice of navel-contemplation), the question of authenticity and truth (is it really as I describe it?), the ethical difficulty of professional responsibility (the desire not to betray one's colleagues) and the contestation of irrelevance (who's bothered about my experience anyway?). The grounds for persisting are provided in Magda Lewis's coherent argument:

> Women have found legitimation only to the extent that we have been able or willing to appropriate the male agenda, a particularly self-violating form of escape from domination which in the end turns out to be no escape at all. The price we pay for this appropriation is the disclaiming of our collective experience of oppression, an act that forfeits our voice and gives overt support to the dominant social, political and economic forms (Lewis and Simon 1986: 462).

I persist for the sake of the women in our theory groups who would like to adopt the strategy of offering personal testimony as a way of making a contribution, but who are worried about the appropriateness and safety of doing so, and consequently often remain silent. I persist for the sake of these women regarding whom a male teacher rolled his eyes when I asked how his seminar on feminism had gone. 'It was a crap class. They only talk about their husbands and the cooking. I've heard it all before.' My suggestion is that we need to find teaching techniques that can make this kind of participation appropriate to our syllabus.

I am not proposing a simplistic model of experiential testimony here, where the subject's speech is something that carries with it the weight of authentic presence as a means of direct access to objective truth. Neither am I suggesting that experience is valued unproblematically for its own sake. I do however object to an easy split being made between feminist theory and the day-to-day lived oppression of women that many anti-essentialist critics would like to make. My concern is the willingness of those with power to speak (often in the name of anti-essentialism) on behalf of those with less, the willingness of those with claims to authority to rephrase what those who make no such claims say ('what she really means is …'), and especially their willingness to make the decision as to what is and what is not relevant to a discussion, without realizing that what they are doing may be construed as an act of oppression. My concern in all this as a teacher is to try to make sense of the experiences that students choose to reconstruct in the class, and to understand them as an attempt to enter the debate (however irrelevant their words may at first seem), and to try and make a connection between the general abstractions of a theory classroom and the experiential testimony of students within that classroom (which means the rhetoric of the testimonial should come to be understood theoretically as a methodology appropriate to the seminar room).

* * *

In the early 1990s, then, I wanted to find ways of allowing students to speak feministly and still find it possible to incorporate that into the standard business of the academy. In coming home from teaching a feminist theory session in 2009, I write, in despair, of an absence of anything like experiential testimony. I complain of the students that they put nothing at risk. There is both nothing personal and nothing political to discuss in the feminist theory session. Of feminism, there is nothing to say, apart from 'we don't want it'. And if my professional persona is profoundly bound up with a feminist identity, it is very difficult not to feel the students' resistance as a personal rejection.

But there is a tension, it seems to me, between the resistance towards institutionalized patriarchy, which I would like my students to embrace, particularly in the way in which they contribute in the seminar and in the essay, and which I myself would like to be seen to embody, a tension between that and the students' wishes to comply with the requirements of the institution, and of a profoundly anti-feminist culture; but in so complying, they precisely produce a sort of resistance (to me), and it is, curiously, resistance that I am endorsing (but not that kind). In my paper of seventeen years ago, I could happily see myself as set at a tangent to the institution, as a neophyte, not yet a doctor, not yet a permanent employee. But now I embody the institution, as a principal lecturer with responsibility for leading the English programme; I am fully incorporated within the academy. Surely, in resisting me, the students are doing what I require?

In her essay 'Reading Between Bodies and Institutions', Mary Eagleton assesses the conflicts for institutionalized feminist teachers, who wish both to embody a resistance to a patriarchal economy, but who are also, from the students' point of view, representatives of the institution:

> there is a deep irony in feminist teachers bringing into the academy responses, such as the embodied, that have traditionally been

excluded, only then to render those responses subject to institutional management. So, while I encourage my students to take the risk and experiment in their writing with the affective, the intimate, the excessive, the feminine, I also pick up my red pen and confine the unquantifiable strictly within the bounds of the quantifiable by assessing and marking it (Eagleton 1998).

Increasingly, says Eagleton, we are working within a model which counts students as 'bodies', 'entities without vitality, merely impersonal units to be quantified just as "hands" used to be counted in factory systems'; these are not the 'desiring, libidinal, postmodern' bodies constructed within feminist theory, but rather 'the alienated body of a market economy' (Eagleton 1998).

Students' compliance with the institutional requirements, as 'alienated bodies', means that, despite their rejection of the professional feminism I represent, they still wish to please me. They see not the feminist but the professional, or at least, they can afford to, or are socially obliged to, spurn the feminist in a way they can't spurn the professional. After a recent class, a (young, male) student who had transferred into my group from another, was discussing an upcoming assignment and he said 'I wish I'd been in your class longer, so that I know more what kind of thing you would like me to write.' I said that I wanted him to write what *he* wanted to write, not write something to please me. But of course, in doing this, in writing 'what he wants to write', he *is* writing to please me.

The common metaphorical structure for understanding the demands created in the relationship between the woman teacher, the student and the institution, evident in much of the feminist pedagogical literature of the 1980s and 1990s, is a psychoanalytic one (see Culley *et al.* 1985, Eagleton 1998, Wallace 1999). For example, in their influential work, Margo Culley and Catherine Portuges write:

> Our students see us as something more, or certainly something other, than simply their teachers. We are, inescapably, also their mothers – necessary for comfort, but reinforcing a feared and fearful dependency if such comfort is too easily accepted (Culley and Portuges 1985: 14).

I will confess that I did want to avoid discussing this metaphor, as I remain uncomfortable with the familial models for teaching relationships. As Culley and Portuges, and many others, present it, the mother–child relationship figures a nurturant, giving woman/teacher who creates (brings into being) dependent children/students. This is based on culturally reinforced expectations of the mother–child dyad, rather than on actual experiences of maternity and infancy, or even on analytic discussions of the same, and as such serves to constrain both student and teacher within a pre-ordained structure which is often experienced as being limiting by parent and offspring alike. It denies agency to the dependent student, and traps the teacher into trying never to fail the person who relies on her. This model interprets seminar relationships according to established gender expectations, rather than reconstruing the classroom as a place where these expectations might be subverted. How might the mother–child figuration account for the relationships that 'nurturing' male tutors have with their students, for example? Are they always in drag? And what of the woman who is seen more in the role of the wicked stepmother than the Madonna, the 'hard-nosed' professional feminist?

Miriam Wallace, in 'Beyond Love and Battle: Practicing Feminist Pedagogy', interrogates but ultimately reinforces the psychoanalytic analogy as a model of the teacher-student relationship. The traditional seminar, claims Wallace, can be described as a 'battlefield' or certainly as a site of competition, the teacher struggling to attract the students' attention, the students competing with one another in debates or in hierarchies of achievement. The feminist classroom 'where the "love relationship" serves as the dominant metaphor tends, by contrast, to be self-consciously "alternative"; the teacher renounces the "master-knower" position for that of "nurturing mother" or "mentor-guide"' (Wallace 1999: 184).

Wallace goes on to argue, following Jane Tompkins and Jane Gallop, that feminist teachers should strive to displace the master-knower position but that they should 'destabilize authority from within a position of authority rather than merely disavowing authority altogether' (184). Wallace seems to be invoking the nurturing mother as a replacement for the authoritarian father in terms of the hierarchy of the teaching situation, but the difficulty might be that students have difficulty recognizing that the feminist (maternal) model has any authority. To continue through with the psychoanalytic structure that Wallace and other feminist pedagogic theorists have invoked, it becomes very difficult not to see the mother as the one without the phallic power. Jane Gallop's reading of Lacan, summoned by Wallace, argues that this is the point: that the way of destabilizing authority from within is to show that the mother does not have the phallus but nor does the father. Any understanding of such a thing, in a Lacanian framework, is illusory. But as Gallop, I'm sure, would be the first to admit, not having the phallus for the mother is not the same as not having it for the father. Destabilizing paternal authority is, or at least was, different from destabilizing maternal authority. It seems to me that, for my current students, maternal authority is none, and resisting feminism is no different to resisting patriarchy. In the most positive interpretation, students now – differently perhaps from the 1980s and 1990s when much of the theoretical discussion of feminist pedagogy was taking place – see feminism as part of an authoritarian model that they would like to resist rather than a loving maternal body to join and embrace. In a less positive interpretation, they simply see feminism as beside the point.

Wallace's solution to the problem of refusing to take up a kind of masculine authority as the master-knower is to adopt 'a kind of attentiveness associated with the analyst, an openness to what is being said but also to what is being resisted ... I have to listen, not only for what students can't yet say, but for what I can't yet hear' (184), and although I struggle to see how adopting the position of the analyst, the one who has the last word on interpretation, is a refusal of authority, the position she is suggesting might be akin to Eagleton's solution to the paradox of what a feminist teacher does with authority. Eagleton represents herself as 'groping' towards 'impersonality':

> as a way to prevent the tutor from being fixed in the position of 'the subject who is supposed to know', the subject whom the student wants to know, the object of desire. My key questions are: what would such a strategy look like in practice; how would it differ from the position of distant superiority which feminism has necessarily rejected; is it possible for the feminist teacher to be 'passionate' without being irresponsible? (Eagleton 1998).

Eagleton's position of disinterest is strikingly like the position that Wallace takes up of the listening analyst/teacher, who renounces her subjecthood except as it is called into being by the transferential relation with the analysand/student. Despite all the efforts of feminist theory to produce embodiment, to underscore experience and recognize its contribution to knowledge, there is no place for it, for her, in the seminar room. The outspoken becomes, if not equated with, then certainly is construed as flirting with irresponsibility.

It is striking to me that the feminist engagement with tutorial authority and seminar subjectivity that I have been surveying here, including my own, took place in the decade between the late 1980s and late 1990s. The concerns that are with me still were articulated clearly even then. Consider Robyn Wiegman's summation of the situation for feminism in the late 1990s:

> This issue of reproduction is absolutely central to the tensions and anxieties that now accompany academic feminism, provoking further questions that carry deep generational weight: which feminism will be reproduced? by whom? and with what (indeed, whose) historical memory? (Wiegman 1999: 365).

Wiegman's concerns emerged out of the fractures seen within the movement in terms of the way academic feminism came to be viewed as indifferent to differences of class, sexual orientation, and race: whose version of feminism would prevail? For me, the concern is still with the central issue of reproduction, the carrying of the weight across the generations, but the anxiety is that feminism has reached a point of barrenness. It is not the case that feminism has not moved on in the last decade, but it does seem to have been moved aside.

I raised the problem of the lack of undergraduate interest in feminism with a colleague, poet and academic Harriet Tarlo, who teaches a module on American women's poetry of the 1960s and 1970s. Her specialist optional module does recruit a self-selecting group of students who already have some investment in a number of feminist ideas. Harriet suggested, off the cuff, but importantly, that there are two ways of teaching feminism. The first is to bombard the students with brutal facts, and the second way is to work the emotional response to the political situation from the inside. In her group, she chooses the latter strategy, but it does take time to build the necessary relationships with the students. Harriet says that in her group there has been no anger, particularly, but there has been emotion. Working the subject through from the inside might be possible if one has a whole semester in which to deliver a module, but in my mandatory theory class, I have no time for that. So, I suppose, I take the brutalizing option. I try to provoke emotion, anger in fact, with statistics about pay differentials, about numbers of women murdered by their male partners and ex-partners each week, about the constraints on women's reproductive rights, the scandal of genital mutilation, both at home and abroad. Perhaps it is no wonder that they feel feminism is repugnant.

Is this passion more than impersonality? Is it the irresponsible side of teaching feminism to which Eagleton refers? Beyond just provoking an emotional response, an angry response, I want to ignite in students an attraction, for theory in general and feminist theory in particular. But how can feminism be rendered attractive? I am reminded of Wolf's angry work, *The Beauty Myth*: if women do to feminism what we do to ourselves, if we primp it and preen it, depilate it, deodorize it, submit it for liposuction and surgical enhancement, will it be deemed acceptable, given equal status and seriousness to Lacanian psychoanalysis and Derridean deconstruction? And surely, in undergoing these superficial procedures, it loses its vitality, its life?

As part of a feminist roundtable discussion on what poststructuralism might have done to feminism, Ann Cvetkovich argues for an engagement which is not impersonal but, rather haunting:

> It is stories and analyses such as these that for me best exemplify the lessons of poststructuralism. Studying them has made me less obsessed by fears that poststructuralist critique mutes the urgency of lived experience or that identity politics is essentialist and that essentialism is a problem. Instead, I'm interested in looking for moments of what Avery Gordon in *Ghostly Matters: Haunting and the Sociological Imagination* calls "haunting," moments that "draw us affectively, sometimes against our will and always a bit magically, into the structure of feeling of a reality that we come to experience, not as cold knowledge, but as transformative recognition." In such moments, the best insights of both feminism and poststructuralism can be found. (Cvetkovich in Lurie *et al.* 2001: 685).

I am attracted to this formulation more than to the model of the nurturing mother, or passionate but disinterested professor, or phallic woman, that have been held up for consideration in the preceding discussion. What would be such haunting moments of transformative recognition? There is no need, of course, in Cvetkovich's and Gordon's expression, for the transformative moment to be feminist, and I suppose the hope I carry is that some of those moments will be, that if feminism is to be relevant to future generations then it is necessary that it does have that sort of affective, magical capacity.

A woman student, 18, taking a foundation year in art, tells this story. She has been printing her project work on a communal printer in the resources room at college. There has been a queue, and a number of male students are waiting for their work to appear. The woman's piece is an extraordinary work of digital photography, a complex mixture of the observed and the fantastic. The image features a woman's naked torso, partially and discreetly covered in undulating sheets (consciously like the folds of fabric from Millais' representation of Ophelia, rather than like anything from an Emin installation). The sheets are patterned with agitated sea foam, superimposed from another photograph. From the navel of the woman unravels an umbilicus made of reddish seaweed, casting its shadow (painstakingly created) on the pale flesh of the figure's belly. A boy retrieves the image from the printer and holds it out with disgust. 'Whose is *this*?', he asks, trying to touch as little as possible, keeping the image at arm's length. The woman artist claims her picture as the lad turns his face away from the other pieces of work emerging from the printer: 'I'm not looking at any more of those. I might be damaged.' Despite the beauty of the image, and the piece is quite arrestingly beautiful, the young man rejects it still. When questioned, by another male student, about her work, this heroine of my story acknowledges herself to be a 'dutty feminist'.

This young woman's haunting work represents, for me, a moment of transformative recognition. It draws on traditional artistic images of women: what can be more over-determined for the feminist fine artist, or literature student, than Ophelia? The photograph suggests a full understanding of this 'images of women' tradition, but from a completely contemporary perspective, using skill and technological mastery to produce a fusion of the natural and the artificial, and to produce a startling contemplation on the woman's reproductive body, the ties that bind it, or the ropes that can be used to pull it (to safety away from the churning sea foam?). The umbilicus is being unravelled, but it is not clear whether the woman in the image has control or whether it is being pulled from elsewhere.

The issue of the reproduction of feminism is a central concern of this essay, and the image I have been discussing seems both as anxious about this as I am, but offers also a creative confidence in changing feminism's legacy in the future. The woman artist concerned is not my student, and I cannot claim a genetic contribution for her creativity, for she is my step-daughter. And I certainly would not claim to have made any contributions to her razor-sharp intelligence, although I have loaned her a few books over the years. But what her work does represent for me is a hope that feminism can be made beautiful, vital, attractive, for a new generation. But it takes time, it takes work, and it takes commitment; and the current trend for offering feminist theory only as a small part of a mainstream, general theoretical curriculum will always diminish its attractions.

References

Berlant, Lauren (1998) 'The Subject of True Feeling: Pain, Privacy, and Politics', in *Cultural Pluralism, Identity Politics, and the Law, ed.* Austin Sarat, Ann Arbor: University of Michigan Press.

Culley, Margo and Portuges, Catherine (1985) *Gendered Subjects: The Dynamics of Feminist Teaching,* London and Boston: Routledge Kegan Paul.

Dworkin, Andrea (1988) *Intercourse.* London; The Free Press.

Eagleton, Mary (1998) 'Reading Between Bodies and Institutions', *Gender and Education* 10: 3.

Evans, Colin (1993) *English People: The Experience of Teaching and Learning in British Universities.* Milton Keynes: Open University Press.

Felman, Shoshana (1987) *Jacques Lacan and the Adventure of Insight: Psychoanalysis in Contemporary Culture.* Cambridge: Harvard UP.

Fuss, Diana (1990) *Essentially Speaking: Feminism, Nature and Difference.* London: Routledge.

Greer, Germaine (1972) *The Female Eunuch.* London: Bantam Books.

Greer, Germaine (1999) *The Whole Woman.* London: Transworld Publishers.

Gallop, Jane (2002) *Anecdotal Theory.* Durham, US: Duke University Press.

Lauren Berlant, 'The Subject of True Feeling: Pain, Privacy, and Politics', in *Cultural Pluralism, Identity Politics, and the Law,* ed. Austin Sarat (Ann Arbor, Mich., 1998).

Lewis, Magda and Simon, Roger (1986) 'A Discourse Not Intended For Her: Learning and Teaching Within Patriarchy', *Harvard Educational Review,* 56, 4, 457–72.

Lurie, Susan et al (2001) 'Roundtable: Restoring Feminist Politics to Poststructuralist Critique', *Feminist Studies,* Vol. 27, No. 3, Autumn, 679–707.

Roiphe, Katie (1994) *The Morning After: Sex, Fear and Feminism.* London: Hamish Hamiliton.

Scheman, Naomi (1993) 'Anger and the Politics of Naming' in *Engenderings: Constructions of Knowledge, Authority, and Privilege.* New York and London: Routledge.

Tompkins, Jane (1987) 'Me and My Shadow', *New Literary History,* 19. 1, 169–78.

Tompkins, Jane (1990) 'Pedagogy of the Distressed', *College English,* 52.61: 653–60.

Wallace, Miriam L. (1999) 'Beyond love and battle: Practicing feminist pedagogy', *Feminist Teacher.* 12: 3; 184ff.

Wiegman, Robyn (1999) 'What Ails Feminist Criticism? A Second Opinion', *Critical Inquiry,* Vol. 25, No. 2, "Angelus Novus": Perspectives on Walter Benjamin, 362–79.

Wolf, Naomi (1990) *The Beauty Myth.* London: Chatto.

Wolf, Naomi (1993) *Fire with Fire: New Female Power and How It Will Change the 21st Century.* London: Chatto and Windus.

4
Syntactics – Semantics – Pragmatics (Still Having One's Cake?)

Leona Toker

From time to time one has to rethink the relationship between one's teaching and one's theoretical platform – not in order to put oneself in line with current fashion but because the quality of one's work can improve if what one does instinctively is consciously conceptualized.

The theoretical basis on which I have been leaning has, of course, undergone a development over my three decades of teaching. This essay will focus on its current state, which is, I hope, still partly in transition. The development began when I was a literature student and an attentive observer of the work of other teachers, prominently including two great masters of text analysis – Irina Karsavina, my beloved French teacher, and my mother Nedda Kamenetskaitė-Strazhas, who taught our final-year English philology group at Vilnius University. Later, in 1974, I likewise attentively observed the ethically oriented methodology of my doctoral advisor at the Hebrew University, H. M. Daleski, whose intellectual influence on my work has been particularly strong: his probing discussions of the style, structure, and theme of long and complex novels combined close text analysis with holistic integration.

But this is a case of 'prolepsis' (Rimmon-Kenan 46) in my brief introductory narrative. In 1972, in the Central library of Vilnius University, prompted by our literature teacher Elena Kousaitė, I first read Wayne Booth's *The Rhetoric of Fiction* (1961), received via Interlibrary loan. This book, along with the copies of Edwin Muir and Percy Lubbock in the Vilnius Public library, turned me from linguistics to literary studies. I was undeterred even when my graduation paper on dialogue in Defoe, Richardson and Fielding was criticized by Karsavina: 'How can you write about these writers without a detailed study of their precursors and their contemporaries, just under the influence of some new-fangled

American critic?' At the time my answer was '*Ars longa, vita brevis,*' but her words have remained with me ever since.

I still believe that the principles of early Anglo-American narratology and New Criticism are an optimal theoretical base for teaching literature to first-year students. These principles become insufficient at later stages: eventually, one has to look for a different framework for combining close text analysis with other concerns – such as the civilization that produced the national literature studied and that was, in its turn, perpetuated by it. If strictly intra-disciplinary literary criticism was the one thing needful, social and political history, intellectual history, and – yes, literary and cultural theory emerged as the other, equally magnetic. What turned out to work for me was a synthesis of semiotic principles with structuralist poetics as developed by the second or third generation of scholars after Russian Formalism.

One of the first things that literature freshmen must unlearn is 'message-hunting' (Brooks and Warren xlii–xlvii) – questions such as 'what does this story teach us?' or, at best, 'what is this poem about?' Even such questions were a relief from the erstwhile Soviet obligation to discuss and evaluate the class consciousness of the writer and his characters – and I still find it disconcerting, that, as this essay will also show, my teaching of nineteenth-century novels keeps coming back to issues of class, though not along Marxist lines. Yet in the BA literature program I still emphasise close text analysis, on the theoretical basis constructed from the Russian formalist school (Shklovsky, Tomashevsky, Propp), some of the work of the Prague Linguistic Circle (in particular, that of Jan Mukařovský), structuralist and descriptive poetics (Booth 1961, Barthes 1968, 1974, Genette 1980, Harshaw 1984, Sternberg 1978, 1987, Rimmon-Kenan 1983, Bal 1997, Phelan 1987 and 2005) and reader-response theory, in particular, Wolfgang Iser (1974, 1978) and Stanley Fish (1970); see also Toker 1994/95 and 2010. The aim of the analysis at this stage is to concentrate on the *text*, the somewhat artificially abstracted middle term of the communicative model (Author–Text–Reader). Focus on the text for its own sake is as important as a daily fitness drill for an athlete. It is also an excellent antidote to the *use* of literary works exclusively as documents for the study of an epoch, a culture, or a biography, as well as to bending them for purposes of political ideology.

Yet as Vladimir Nabokov reminds us, we should 'place the "how" above the "what," ' but avoid confusing it with 'the "so what"' (66). Narratological text analysis often abuts upon the question of wages: though identification of techniques in the framework of an adopted nomenclature actually yields insights into the work's aesthetic effect, the relationship between technique and the effects that it promotes or impedes is, in practice, influenced by a variety of non-self-evident factors.

The most immediate step away from the methodological purity of descriptive poetics can be directed towards reader-response analysis, but the latter is complicated by the cognitive and sociological aspects of reception. The function of a narrative detail or technique is associated with its effect – on whom? It is useful to ask the students to discount the effect on actual individual readers, with their idiosyncrasies, and to think in terms of the 'postulated reader' (Booth 1961 156), the 'implied' reader (Iser 1974), an 'informed reader' (Fish 1970 145), a 'model reader' (Eco 8), or, at least, in terms of an 'interpretive community' (Fish 1980). And the question of effect, or the way the text shapes its reading and re-reading, compliant or resistant (Fetterley), is ultimately an issue of the ethical dimension of the Author–Text–Reader (A–T–R) model, or of its reversed R–T–A version (with the reader 'constructing' rather than 're-constructing' the world of the text). Reader-response analysis is one of the avenues of approach to the vexed question of the ethics of literary form, whose conceptualization is one of the urgent yet constantly deferred tasks of literary scholarship.

In the University teaching of literature this research horizon often takes second place to cultural and historical contextualization. In studying 'English' as an academic subject, students need exposure to the 'civilization' that has produced the literary corpus and that has, in a feedback loop, been perpetuated or modified with its help. The challenge is to combine a 'historical approach' with textual analysis without slipping back into instrumental uses of the text.

In my case, ways of meeting this challenge were suggested by a convergence of Mukařovský's theory of the multifunctionality of a work of art (1970, 1978 3–88) and Benjamin Harshaw's (Harshovski's) theory of the External and Internal Fields of Reference (1984).

Some of Mukařovský's thought-patterns (in particular, his repeated reference to the 'meaning' of the whole work) are no longer acceptable, but his view of a work of art as multifunctional (a building, for example, may have both an aesthetic function and a practical function, such as providing a dwelling or a venue) places matters in perspective. One of the functions of a literary work may well be didactic, or consciousness-raising, or testimonial. Each of these functions may enter a variety of relationships – ranging between mutual support and tug-of-war – with the aesthetic function; each may become dominant (or in the language of semiology, 'marked') at different stages of reception, whether individual or communal. In *Return from the Archipelago* (2000) I discussed the changing view of Gulag literature, in particular, the stories of Varlam Shalamov, initially read as first-hand testimony to Gulag realities and later appreciated as works of art whose aesthetic value survives their topical significance. Read by whom? Rethought by whom? In many ways the change of an individual reader's attitude models or recapitulates the change in communal appreciation (the two processes are not necessarily synchronic). Moreover, there is a mandatory element of osmosis between the two types of attitude: Shalamov's *Kolyma Tales*, like Solzhenitsyn's *One Day in the Life of Ivan Denisovich* and later Gulag works, cannot be read purely for their aesthetic value, especially since their merit is largely rooted in the appropriateness of the means to the ethical end. One of the consequences of the view of a work of art as multifunctional is that 'message hunting' need not be outlawed. It must, however, be deferred; it must be prevented from monopolizing the students' attention.

Another New Critical bogeyman that can be partly rehabilitated by the view of the works of art as multifunctional is the so-called "intentional fallacy" (Wimsatt 1954 3–18; cf. Herman). Analysis of the ethical orientation of a work and of the formal features that serve or impede it cannot, in spite of the purist self-discipline, be confined to the question of effect and avoid inferring intention from effect – as well as testing such inference against the authors' on-record statements, if available (in interviews, correspondence, essays, or public speeches) and reliable (a matter of interpretation). Again, to avoid reductiveness, it is expedient to defer questions of intentionality until after a close intrinsic text analysis.

It is less risky to introduce Harshaw's perspective in the early stages of academic literary study. With the help of the platform offered by Harshaw's 1984 discussion of the External and Internal Fields of Reference, instead of isolating the text, especially a difficult one, from its cultural–historical contexts, or, conversely, using it as a 'document to its period', one can allow the information about the period to enrich our appreciation of the text. Witness the value, for instance, of Gifford and Seidman's 1988 *Ulysses Annotated*, which not only illuminates the items in the External Field of Reference (Dublin, 1904, historical realities, intertexts) but also helps the reader to draw thick thematic links between seemingly disconnected narrative details (Internal Field of Reference).

External Fields of Reference are, in fact, a vast hypertext – now, in 2010, it is largely from various other texts that we can learn about the cultural, political, and ethnic realities of 1904. The 'cultural code'

(Barthes 1974 18–19) that the twenty-first century audience outside of Ireland might share with the author is meager in comparison with the semantic platform that Joyce shared with his immediate audience: even in the classroom analysis of 'The Sisters' one needs to gloss not only 'gnomon', 'simony', and, on a more strictly figurative plane, 'paralysis', but also the meaning of the priest's family's early home in Irishtown (a working-class neighborhood) and the concomitant understanding that the resources of the poor family must have gone into the clerical education of a gifted son who, as a celibate priest, would eventually be expected to shelter his unmarried sisters. Annotation has become an important element of literary studies whenever a regional element (definable in terms of the density of the cultural code) is prominent in the text, even if the 'region' is Joyce's Dublin or Dickens's London – or, for that matter, Barbara Pym's London of the 1950s (see Raz).

Each 'regional' work can, of course, be read predominantly in terms of the Internal Field of Reference: the motif of the sisters' disappointment in Joyce's story enters into a pattern of internal links with the priest's being 'a disappointed man' as well as with the element of malaise in the boy-protagonist's relationship with the priest and with Old Cotter from the distillery, another purveyor of spurious *spirits*. Clearly, however, awareness of the dynamics among the siblings in impoverished Irish Catholic families (External Field of Reference) enriches our understanding of the story, our sense of the saturation of its Internal Field of Reference. Formalization of the textual study in terms of EFR and IFR allows one to engage in the structural analysis of the text, including an analysis of its patterns of motifs (in Hjelmslev's terms – the form of its content; see Barthes 1968 39–40), while also providing information about the socio-cultural contexts of the story's setting, and thus bringing the text alive not only as a structure of nerves and sinews but also in its fuller human otherness. The next step – treading carefully – would be to move from showing how the EFR enriches the IFR towards suggesting ways in which the latter may enrich, or comment on, the former.

In teaching Dickens's *Our Mutual Friend*, for instance, one may relate the return-from-death formula of the plot (both the male protagonists narrowly escape death; one of them, John Harmon, is believed to be dead until he resumes his identity) to the motif of recycling, a return of the discarded back into the economy of human life. This motif is, in its turn, closely related to the motif of dust and to that of money as dust (Daleski 1970 270–336; Toker 2006–2007), to money as reducing human hearts to dust unless it is itself meaningfully reclaimed. Such a knot of motifs yields further links that organize the different episodes, images, and vocabulary of the novel into intersecting semantic vectors in the Internal Field of Reference. This field may be shown to be anchored in mid-nineteenth century realities: as Dickens's contemporary Henry Mayhew observed, 'In London, where many, in order to live, struggle to extract a meal from the possession of an article which seems utterly worthless, nothing must be wasted. Many a thing which in a country town is kicked by the penniless out of their path even, if examined and left as meet only for the scavenger's cart, will in London be snatched up as a prize; it is money's worth' (II: 6). A fortune could, indeed, be made out of what was euphemistically called dust-mounds not only through contracting for the removal of garbage but also from having it recycled. Mayhew's data form a part of the External Field of Reference for *Our Mutual Friend*. The dynamics of the relationship between the IFR and the EFR is further clarified if one accepts the suggestion made by Harland Nelson in 1965, that the prototype for Betty Higden of *Our Mutual Friend*, the 'deserving poor' old woman who has lost all her family but who is insistently avoiding the workhouse (another major channel to the EFR), is to be found, on Mayhew's pages, in the shape of a similar old woman, who is, however, a 'pure finder,' that is, a person who collects dog-dung from the street to sell it, at a few pennies a bucketful, to tanners who use it (owing to its alkaline content) to purify the skins. Dickens could obviously not integrate the latter occupation into the novel without, in the language of Mr. Podsnap, 'bringing a blush into the cheek of the young person' (129); and so he presented Betty as an artisan, a laundress (or, as a mangle operator, a laundry adjunct), and a child-minder – replacing tannery 'purification' by soapy suds and positioning Sloppy (whose name bears the echoes of the occupation of Mayhew's informant) at the mangle, a sanitized visual reflection of the workhouse treadmill (see Stokes 2001 723–24). Sloppy, incidentally, is endowed with a talent for making children's toys 'out of nothing,' which links him, before he ever meets her, to Jenny Wren, who makes dolls' dresses out of waste cloth. Thus the realia of EFR are metamorphosed into motifs, the building blocks of IFR, where they acquire new connotations, or shed customary ones, through collocation with each other.

What Harshaw formalized as IFR and EFR has also been commented on by other theorists, ranging from Northrop Frye, who spoke about the centripetal and the centrifugal movement of textual detail (73–5), to Victor Turner who adopted (20–1) the semiological distinction between syntactics (roughly equivalent to IFR), semantics (roughly equivalent to EFR), and pragmatics, that is, the interface of the sign with its senders and recipients (Morris 217–20). The pragmatics of addressing a specific target audience (see Toker 2005) can be seen as possibly responsible for the transformation of Mayhew's pure finder into Dickens's laundress. The method used thus finds further support from adjacent disciplines.

Each theory, however, becomes particularly interesting when it breaks down. The distinction between EFR and IFR is not only complicated by pragmatics (as in the Betty Higden case) but also problematized when the reference is less local than systemic. For example, what Tony Tanner terms the 'metatheatre of manners' (27) in Jane Austen's novels, or the patterns of upper-middle class female domesticity that Nancy Armstrong describes in *Desire and Domestic Fiction*, are not a matter of separate narrative details but features of a semiotic system which may be seen as reflected in Austen's novels or as perpetuated by them, along with oppositional loopholes that make the system 'livable' (Chambers 7).

Austen's novels, indeed, do not escape the feedback loop: they uphold the values of the gentry culture not only by evoking its best expressions and satirizing their corruption but also by creating that space of ludic oppositionality in which her target audience can be liberated from the socio-cultural compartmentalization prior to re-endorsing its de-automatized version. It is not easy to distinguish between the mimetic replication of EFR in IFR and the innovative processing of the former by the latter. The types of EFR information that cannot be conflated with IFR patterning are sociological, statistical, and historical data – including, for instance, the meaning of the 'Mansfield judgment' as lurking behind the central toponym of *Mansfield Park* (as soon as this detail enters IFR it develops additional meanings, such as the suggestion of the patriarchal order). An intermediate case is a theory taken from a different discipline, for example from a sociological essay such as Thorstein Veblen's *The Theory of the Leisure Class* (1899). The value of Veblen's discussion of 'invidious emulation' ('conspicuous leisure' and 'conspicuous consumption') for literary studies has been underappreciated (with the exception of critical discussions of such novels as Edith Wharton's *House of Mirth*), whether because his poetic anthropology is non-Marxist or because his book used to be so much a part of American academic education that its relevance to the nineteenth-century novel (e.g. the art of living well on nothing a year in Thackeray's *Vanity Fair*) could seem self-evident, a part of the cultural code that one still shared with Regency and Victorian novelists. Now, in the twenty-first century that platform is no longer widely shared (though Veblen's book still strikes students as quite accurately descriptive of everything they dis-like in themselves and in 'materialist' society). Pitted against a Jane Austen text, Veblen (EFR) may turn out to be both supplementable (e.g. by adding 'invidious sexuality' to 'invidious emulation' – see Toker 2001/2002) and enriching.

I shall illustrate the latter possibility by reinterpreting the Portsmouth episode in *Mansfield Park* in terms of Veblen's perspective on manners. When Fanny Price (whose last name is also an opening for EFR annotation) rejects the affluent Henry Crawford, Sir Thomas Bertram sends her back to her parents in Portsmouth, under the pretext of family pieties but actually as a punishment and a warning. This almost works. Fanny is made unhappy by the lack of emotional intensity in her reunion with her family and distressed by their disorganized, stuffy, unhygienic, noisy, ill-mannered way of life in their lower-middle class inner-city dwelling. What Fanny does not understand is that manners, apart from considerateness which comes naturally to some but must be taught to others, are not an unquestionable absolute value. Polished manners, Veblen tells us, are a conspicuous sign of leisure because a great deal of time has been spent, unproductively, in acquiring them (45–51). The privilege of the landed gentry can be peaceably main-tained only by constant reaffirmation of their superiority – manners are an integral part of this implicit contractuality. By contrast, the status of the Portsmouth family, in which all the sons are brought up to be professionals, seafaring or other, is far less dependent on manners in everyday life.

The main trouble with the Portsmouth household (not without exceptions) is lack of consideration for each other's needs in minor matters. This is presented as the result of constant hardship, of Mr. Price's egoism, and of Mrs. Price's well-meaning inefficiency. Ironically, perpetual minor discomforts may be a good training for the Price chil-dren whose prospects in life involve hard work and a struggle to keep afloat. Indeed, these children, especially the boys, seem to be doing remarkably well, which suggests that the parents have done something right after all. William, the firstborn, is the most advanced and culti-vated, but there are two more grown brothers, one 'a clerk in a public office in London' and the other a midshipman (259). There is also Sam who, like his sister Susan, seems to be ready to take responsibility for whatever needs to be done. The two younger schoolboys are full of healthy animal spirits.

Mr. Price, Fanny's father, is guilty of a less than moderate fondness for alcohol and peer company – compensations of many an impecunious retired officer. However, in the context of Austen's general sensitivity to family dynamics, the health, vigor, and success of his children suggest that he is not entirely ineffective as a father. There is something genuine in Mr. Price's rough ways. His interest in his profession is still so keen and aesthetically tinged that it infects almost all his sons. His threat to 'be after' the young ones if they continue making a noise is disregarded (260) – his presence certainly does not create restraint or cast a gloom on his family's spirits, as does the presence of the tyrannical General Tilney of *Northanger Abbey* or even of the courteous Sir Thomas in *Mansfield Park*.

For all the gracelessness and mutual elbowing in everyday affairs, the family is knit together by common concerns. When Fanny first arrives at their house, the house-maid meets the carriage at the door – not so much to help the travelers as to report the news that 'the Thrush is gone out of harbour' (254), and that an officer has been in, looking for William. The servant, however unschooled, is a faithful delegate of the family's anxieties: she has been on the lookout for William, who is almost late. The same piece of news is then repeated, in greater detail, by Fanny's eleven-year-old brother Sam (255). Soon afterwards it is also repeated by Mrs. Price. At this point the device of gradation begins to emerge: if the servant announces the main news in 18 words before she is interrupted by Sam, who has over 80 words on the subject, Mrs. Price is given 111 words, and when her husband steps into the picture, he is given 281 words to dwell lovingly on the Thrush leaving the harbor. However neglectful the Prices may be in everyday matters, they are all deeply invested in the career goals of the children. William and Sam ought to be in a real hurry to prepare for the boat that is to take them to the departing ship on which William is to start his career as an officer and Sam as a cabin-boy.

Through the shared interests of the Price family Jane Austen hints at a ranking of values that is different from that of Sir Thomas Bertram's circle yet still valid. Most of the novel's critics see the ways of the Portsmouth household as a purely negative alternative rather than as a viable one; this attitude is also shared by most students on the first reading of the novel. Does this mean that readers accept the values of the Bertram circle? Not necessarily. In the classroom, descriptive poetics comes to our help in explaining a reader-response issue: the Portsmouth episode is consistently filtered through the mind of Fanny, who is its focalizer, its third-person center of consciousness (see Genette 186–9, Rimmon-Kenan 71–105). Up to this point in the narrative, Fanny has been disadvantaged in terms of family dynamics, especially at Mansfield

Park, and readers have been encouraged to sympathize with her plight, fully expecting her principled conduct to be vindicated in the end. Hence, her disapproval of the way things are done in her parents' house is likely to shape the attitude of the audience.

Yet it may not work in exactly this way with every interpretive community. When I reread the novel after having lived through the gamut of Israeli experience, and then discussed the Portsmouth episode with a graduate class in which there were several middle-aged high-school teachers, some of the text's signals acquired a new ring (cf. Booth 1988 70–5 on 'coduction'). In particular, this was the case with Mrs. Price's remark 'here every thing comes upon me at once' (256). If on the first reading (long ago), I heard this as a banal complaint of an inefficient housewife, now, along with the students of that group, I responded to it as a quite accurate reference to the nervous strain caused by having to combine the ritual and emotion of reunion with one grown child and hasty preparations for a parting from two other children.

It is largely the mother's duty to help equip the sons who are going off to military service. Many of us in that classroom remembered parallel situations: the soldier-son or daughter comes home from the army for the weekend, dusty, tired, and eager to catch up with life, friends, movies. There must be hot water for a shower, and home-made food, and while the soldier sleeps or goes out to meet friends, the mother is laundering everything in the kitbag, drying and ironing the uniforms, sowing buttons back on, dusting the bag, darning the socks – perhaps this, and a prayer, will shield him, or her. Sometimes there is more than one soldier back for the weekend, and if the family observes the Sabbath, most of the work – a labor of love – has to be completed on Friday by dusk. Imagine long-lost relatives or friends descending on the family at exactly that moment: 'here every thing comes upon me at once'! All this joy all at once with so many strings attached! And perhaps there is not a little self-importance for the effort-coordinating matron – this might have been to Mrs. Norris's liking but is no compensation for a Mrs. Price.

Is this reading of the Portsmouth episode idiosyncratic or culture-bound (it is said that 'Israeli manners' is an oxymoron)? I believe that it can gain support from the paradoxes of Fanny's attitudes and behavior in Portsmouth – if one recollects that at the end of this episode she is beginning to slide towards accepting Henry Crawford's proposal, choosing to neglect the threat of his possible interest in her sister Susan in the future (he always enjoys being between two women). From the first moment Fanny's attitude is egocentric: she is struck by the insufficiency of the family's attention to herself rather than by the importance of her brothers' not being late to board that ship. One may mention, in her defense, that not having been privy to her family's worries and struggles, she has not developed an interest in the Thrush equal to theirs; she is pained by the noise and inelegance and oblivious of the ill timing of her visit amid the urgencies of the day. The implied author withholds comment on the dramatic irony of this situation. The only hint at the problematic character of Fanny's state of mind is given in the ironic inversion in her response to her mother, who meets her 'with looks of true kindness, and with features which Fanny loved the more, because they brought her aunt Bertram's before her' (256). Tired (one should concede) after the long ride, Fanny is then concerned not about her brothers' gear being packed but (drawing ironic chuckles in the Israeli classroom) about her not getting her tea on time.

One of the most insistently recurrent motifs in this episode is haste: everybody knows that not a minute should be lost before appraising William of the fact that a Mr. Campbell, the ship's surgeon, will come for him before six o'clock; William has no time for Fanny because he has to dress and pack; the confusion among his things (their privacy has obviously not been respected in his absence) must be put right in a hurry and with little help. Indeed, William seems to get ready just minutes before Dr. Campbell arrives.

The density of the motifs of haste emphasizes that this family has no leisure to flaunt. Though they may have a residual hankering after outer signs of leisure, the Prices do not really *need* a metatheater of manners in their own house: their sense of self-worth does not depend on conspicuous leisure. But when reasonably good manners are needed, they can display them. Indeed, on meeting Henry Crawford, Mr. Price surprises Fanny by behaving without the crudeness which he shows in the family circle: 'His manners now, though not polished, were more than passable; they were graceful, animated, manly; his expressions were those of an attached father, and a sensible man; – his loud tones did very well in the open air, and there was not a single oath to be heard '(274). Fanny, pleased enough with this performance, accounts for it by her father's 'instinctive compliment to the good manners of Mr. Crawford' (273–4), forgetting that Crawford is not only her suitor but, more importantly, the nephew of the Admiral who has secured William's promotion and can perhaps one day do the same for the other brothers. Occasional good manners are here not a matter of conspicuous leisure but a professional qualification that an officer father of young seamen cannot forgo. Mr. Price is an old professional, although Fanny cannot sympathize with his shop talk and his 'never-failing interest' in the dockyard.

Thus, behind Fanny's back 'Jane Austen' seems to be suggesting that life away from gentry estates may be meaningful, not unhappy, and not without opportunities for individual growth: it is in Portsmouth that Fanny begins to exert a positive influence on the upbringing of her younger sisters; it is there that she subscribes to the circulating library in her own name – doing something official on her own initiative for the first time in her life. Yet the suggestion is hesitant: after all, it is the surplus of the Mansfield Park education that she dispenses to her sisters, and it is the pocket money given her by the Bertrams that pays for the subscription. Moreover, the happy ending may be seen as withdrawing the alternative altogether: Fanny is vindicated, recognized by the man she loves as his true mate, and returned to the Mansfield Park family whose forgotten values she helps to restore, eventually bringing Susan along for a schooling partly similar to her own.

From the narratological standpoint, in making this claim I have moved from talking about the third-person narrator of *Mansfield Park* to talking about 'Jane Austen,' the implied author – in a moment I shall have to make a move that would be banned by New Criticism and talk about Jane Austen without inverted commas. The lassitude of the novel's ending, with its epilogue-type mopping up, may be ascribed to both the 'implied author' (a personification of a system of values) and the historical novelist. But what is the agency behind the ambiguous politics of the novel's ending? Here the syntactics–semantics–pragmatics schema comes to our help. *Syntactics*: it may be shown that the novel's final chapters are woven out of the same motifs that keep recurring throughout the novel (invidious sexuality, correctness of sentiment, sibling loves and jealousies, filial duties, parents' comfort or discomfort, education, satisfaction, etc.) so that the ending may be seen as a tucking in of the different thematic strands. *Semantics*: Fanny's outwardly uncomplaining and eventually even constructive adaptation to her life in Portsmouth may be seen as that period of resignation and retreat which sets the stage for the heroine's social self-definition and acceptance of her assigned role which usually precedes the happy ending in the anti-Jacobin novels (see Butler 1990 166); the implied author's system of values might thus emerge as that of a broadly conservative 'connected critic' (Walzer 1987 38–40 ff). *Pragmatics*: could Jane Austen (not the 'implied author' but the younger one of the spinster ladies in the Chawton cottage) be using this type of happy ending as a diversionary maneuver, a bribe to the hurdle audience, the heads of gentry families who stand between her and her target readership and whose delegates can cast aspersions on herself? Perhaps some real-life counterparts of a Sir Thomas or a

General Tilney would be likely to ban the novel from their houses if it ended in the following script: Fanny remains stuck in Portsmouth and, ceasing to rue her lot, helps her family to clean up its act and eventually marries someone like Dr. Campbell (in subversive anticipation of Esther Summerson). Or would such a plot outcome be unthinkable for Jane Austen (or for 'Jane Austen') herself, her liberalism going only part-way – in *Persuasion*, for instance, towards a Captain Wentworth, who is affiliated with the gentry rather than with the urban middle class, or a Captain Harville who emulates the graces of the gentry. The theoretical formula employed does not provide answers to such questions, but it helps to raise them, offers them for discussion and, more importantly, helps teachers of literature to eat their cake and have it too, that is, combine a close intra-textual analysis of a narrative with different kinds of contextualization. It also helps to avoid the purely instrumental use of the text. To use theory purely instrumentally is a lesser sin.

References

Armstrong, Nancy. 1987. *Desire and Domestic Fiction: A Political History of the Novel*. New York: Oxford University Press.

Austen, Jane. 1998 [1814]. *Mansfield Park*. Ed. Claudia L. Johnson. New York: Norton Critical Editions.

Bal, Mieke. 1997. *Narratology: Introduction to the Theory of Narrative*. Second edition. Toronto: University of Toronto Press.

Barthes, Roland. 1968 [1964]. *Elements of Semiology*. Trans. Annette Lavers and Colin Smith. New York: Hill and Wang.

———. 1974 [1970]. *S/Z: An Essay*. Trans. Richard Miller. New York: Hill and Wang.

Booth, Wayne. 1961. *The Rhetoric of Fiction*. Chicago: University of Chicago Press.

———. 1988. *The Company We Keep: An Ethics of Fiction*. Berkeley: University of California Press.

Brooks, Cleanth, and Robert Penn Warren. 1950. *Understanding Poetry: An Anthology for College Students*. Revised edition. New York: Henry Holt.

Butler, Marilyn. 1990 [1975]. *Jane Austen and the War of Ideas*. Second edition. Oxford: Clarendon.

Chambers, Ross. 1991. *Room for Maneuver: Reading (the) Oppositional (in) Narrative*. Chicago: University of Chicago Press.

Daleski, H. M. 1970. *Dickens and the Art of Analogy*. London: Faber and Faber.

Dickens, Charles. 1989 [1865]. *Our Mutual Friend*. Ed. Michael Cotsell. Oxford: Oxford University Press.

Eco, Umberto. 1979. *The Role of the Reader: Explorations in the Semiotics of Texts*. Bloomington: Indiana University Press.

Fetterley, Judith. 1978. *The Resisting Reader: A Feminist Approach to American Fiction*. Bloomington: Indiana University Press.

Fish, Stanley. 1970. 'Literature in the Reader: Affective Stylistics.' *New Literary History* 2: 123–62. Reprinted, with comments, in Fish 1980.
———. 1980. *Is There a Text in This Class? The Authority of Interpretive Communities.* Cambridge: Harvard University Press.
Frye, Northrop. 1957. *The Anatomy of Criticism: Four Essays.* Princeton: Princeton University Press.
Genette, Gérard. 1980. *Narrative Discourse: An Essay in Method.* Trans. Jane E. Lewin. Ithaca: Cornell University Press.
Gifford, Don, and Robert J. Seidman. 1988. *Ulysses Annotated: Notes for James Joyce's Ulysses.* Berkeley: University of California Press.
Harshaw, Benjamin. 1984. 'Fictionality and Fields of Reference: Remarks on the Theoretical Framework.' *Poetics Today* 5: 227–51.
Herman, David. 2008. 'Narrative Theory and the Intentional Stance.' *Partial Answers* 6/2: 233–60.
Hjelmslev, Lewis. 1969. *Prolegomena to a Theory of Language.* Madison: University of Wisconsin Press.
Iser, Wolfgang. 1974 [1972]. *The Implied Reader: Patterns of Communication in Prose Fiction from Bunyan to Beckett.* Baltimore: Johns Hopkins University Press.
———. 1978 [1976]. *The Act of Reading: A Theory of Aesthetic Response.* Baltimore: The Johns Hopkins University Press.
Mayhew, Henry, 1968 [1861–1862]. *London Labour and the London Poor.* New York: Dover.
Morris, Charles. 1946. *Signs, Language, and Behavior.* New York: Prentice-Hall.
Mukařovský, Jan. 1970. *Aesthetic Function, Norm and Value as Social Facts.* Trans. Mark E. Suino. Ann Arbor: University of Michigan (Michigan Slavic Contributions).
———. 1978. *Structure, Sign, and Function: Selected Essays by Jan Mukařovský.* Trans. and ed. John Burbank and Peter Steiner. New Haven: Yale University Press.
Nabokov, Vladimir. 1981 [1973]. *Strong Opinions.* New York: McGraw-Hill.
Nelson, Harland S. 1965. 'Dickens's *Our Mutual Friend* and Henry Mayhew's *London Labor and the London Poor.*' *Nineteenth-Century Fiction* 20.3: 207–22.
Phelan, James. 1987. 'Character, Progression, and the Mimetic-Didactic Distinction.' *Modern Philology* 84: 282–99.
———. 2005. *Living to Tell about It: A Rhetoric and Ethics of Character Narration.* Ithaca: Cornell University Press.
Propp, Vladimir. 1968 [1928]. *Morphology of the Folktale.* Trans. Laurence Scott. Second edition. Austin: University of Texas Press.
Raz, Orna. 2007. *Social Dimensions in the Novels of Barbara Pym, 1949–1963: The Writer as Hidden Observer.* Lewiston, NY: The Edwin Mellen Press.
Rimmon-Kenan, Shlomith. 1983. *Narrative Fiction: Contemporary Poetics.* London: Methuen.
Shklovsky, Victor. 1965 [1917]. 'Art as Technique.' In *Russian Formalist Criticism: Four Essays*, ed. L. Lemon and M. Reis. Lincoln: University of Nebraska Press, pp. 3–24.
Sternberg, Meir. 1978. *Expositional Modes and Temporal Ordering in Fiction.* Baltimore: The Johns Hopkins University Press.
———. 1987 *The Poetics of Biblical Narrative: Ideological Literature and the Drama of Reading.* Bloomington: Indiana University Press.

Stokes, Peter M. 2001.'Bentham, Dickens, and the Uses of the Workhouse.' *Studies in English Literature 1500–1900* 43/4: 711–27.

Tanner, Tony. 1986. *Jane Austen*. London: Macmillan.

Toker, Leona. 1994/95'If Everything Else Fails, Read the Instructions: Further Echoes of The Reception-Theory Debate' *Connotations* 4: 151–64.

———. 2000. *Return from the Archipelago: Narratives of Gulag Survivors*. Bloomington: Indiana University Press.

———. 2001/2002. 'Conspicuous Leisure and Invidious Sexuality in Jane Austen's *Mansfield Park*.' *Connotations* 11.2/3: 222–40.

———. 2005. 'Target Audience, Hurdle Audience, and the General Reader: Varlam Shalamov's Art of Testimony.' *Poetics Today* 26: 281–303.

———. 2006–2007. 'Decadence and Regeneration in Dickens's *Our Mutual Friend*.' *Connotations* 16.1–3: 47–59.

———. 2010. *Towards the Ethics of Form in Fiction: Narratives of Cultural Remission.* Columbus: Ohio State University Press.

Tomashevsky, Boris. 1965 [1925]. 'Thematics.' In *Russian Formalist Criticism: Four Essays*, eds L. Lemon and M. Reis. Lincoln: Univ. of Nebraska Press, 1965, pp. 61–95.

Turner, Victor. 1982. *From Ritual to Theatre: The Human Seriousness of Play.* New York: Performing Arts Journal Publications.

Veblen, Thorstein. 1899. *The Theory of the Leisure Class.* Rpt as Penguin 20th Century Classic, New York: Penguin, 1994.

Walzer, Michael. 1987. *Interpretation and Social Criticism.* Cambridge, MA: Harvard University Press.

Wimsatt, W. K. 1954. *The Verbal Icon: Studies in the Meaning of Poetry.* Lexington: The University Press of Kentucky.

5
The Motivation of Literary Theory: From National Culture to World Literature

Stephen Shapiro

With the rising backlash against the false assumption of value that neoliberalism's fictions of the marketplace deliriously promoted, it is not surprising that the Humanities, in general, and literary theory, particularly, has been called on, once more, to demonstrate tangible worth. After the hangover created by more than a decade of make-believe policies, an overwhelmed public deservedly wants reassurance that university education, as a core component to social aspirations, is still worth bearing its debt-creating burden, even when the common sense about the safety of student loans has been thoroughly shaken up. We can take up this challenge, even in theory classes, without succumbing to functionalist cost–benefit logic, by revising them as spheres of learning how to engage and interpret the newly unknown and uncharted world in which our students will be propelled, like those early astronauts facing the astral darkness.

Introductory literary and cultural theory classes are frequently uneasy ones. 'Theoretical' writing's unusual terminology and method of argument not only makes it feel like a foreign language, but also one like an ancient tongue that seems to have no practical purpose for living communication. Many students feel anxious at their incomplete understanding of the assigned readings and often experience this uncertainty as undermining the readerly pleasure that drew them to literary studies as a sanctuary from the dissatisfactions inherent in everyday modern life. One pedagogical response to student queasiness has been to lower the contact-shock by anthologizing literary criticism through abbreviated excerpts that seek to make criticism digestible by highlighting key passages or phrases. Another attempt instrumentalizes different approaches by illustrating the application of a variety of critical modes on a set text (a 'psychoanalytic' reading of *Jane Eyre*, a 'marxist' one, a 'new historicist' one, etc.). While both are well-meaning attempts to acclimatize students to literary theory, they result in further disempowering them. Literary criticism anthologies inevitably create a canon of writing that does little to demystify why these texts and terms have become significant, other than as a means of celebrity politics, where writing is famous for being famous. Because the format's compression does not show student readers the contours of an argument's unfolding, we ask our students to accept fragmentary statements without allowing them the opportunity to see criticism's reasoned elaboration. No wonder that critical writing often appears as a clutch of a spasmodic, Delphic utterances, where anything goes. Something similar occurs on courses that amble through various ways of interpreting a text. While some students may consequently internalize the basic predicates of different theoretical approaches, they are often left perplexed as to why one would choose one approach, rather than another. Under these conditions, it is not surprising that students new to critical theory see it as an elaborate imposture, an artificial set of poses lacking in emotional authenticity, and ultimately any worth at all.

On the other hand, theory classes can also be heady places of great excitement. Some students intuitively feel the critical theory classroom as an emancipatory space, a realm of resistance to the mundane, deadening instruction in the (pre-)university teaching mandated by the state-sponsored regime of regulatory testing. This cohort brings the elixir of enthusiasm to the seminar room, but this golden energy also has its own pitfalls. If a fraction of students dexterously adapts to the language of criticism, their facility can often amplify classroom divisions and deepen a sense of alienation within those students who do not adapt as quickly to the new intellectual horizon. This unevenness of reception can make discussions of theory seem like the clattering of exclusive cliques. The gap widens as many students who embrace theory do so from identitarian concerns, which can take the seminar as a ready *Battle Royal* for the often-punitive turning of tables on the perceived domination by less articulate or vocal students, who are positioned as representing the oppressive mainstream.

Gerald Graff influentially argued that theory classes should 'teach the conflicts' and show how different approaches, tendencies, and even individual critics encounter each other (1992). Every historical moment has its own responses to its current needs though. When Graff made these claims, it was both a necessary corrective to the enforced commonsense of a-theorized teaching in literature classes and as a means of bringing some cognitive order to the unruly proliferation of theoretical writing that burgeoned throughout the 1970s and 1980s. Over the last twenty years, and especially in the United States, civil discourse has become so antagonistic that 'conflicts' seem to proliferate spontaneously without any resolving reflection. A pedagogy that encourages confrontation may now mainly unleash a host of culture wars that are hard to redirect toward either a productive intellectual end or even a guarded armistice.

The deadlock between estrangement and excitement might be overcome by placing the emphasis on criticism as an endeavor that is not only a means of learning how to think, learning how to learn, but also one that develops the core skills of academic argument. It may sound paradoxical to claim that theoretical writing stands as a lesson in good exposition, but this seems perverse only because of the way in which essay-writing is often taught to students today. At the pre-university developmental level, students are encouraged to have a strong thesis statement in their essays, since we are often desperate to get some clarity in our students' writing. Yet this exaggerated focus on a thesis prevents them from learning the skill of internal reflection and the need for counter-argument. The move to a more sophisticated writing must lead to teaching the motivation behind this or that particular thesis, the energy that drives writers to say things in certain ways, using particular devices, genres, or other semantic touchstones.

For theory classes, we amplify this difficulty when we only emphasize the surface claims, techniques, and tell-tale signs of critical schools in ways that hinder students from making the leap beyond working at the level of thesis. For students, when learning theory, not only need clarity of explanation of a text's terms and statements, but also a sense of its less discernible motivation, and how motive leads to the reinterpretation of textual evidence to produce new statements. Although a media-saturated world proliferates thesis claims, we spend too little time explaining why certain theoretical questions become more interesting than others, what is at stake in theory, and the ways in which arguments take their form in tension against prior critical writing, using a motivated response and then justifying it on the grounds that it provides a more comprehensive and capable means of interpreting evidentiary matter. An anthology approach often dispenses with this diacritical encounter, since the limits of its format require stark contrast and bold statement, rather than meditated critique.

Clarifying a text's thesis as a means of then illustrating its motive goes some way to overcoming the potential mismatches in the classroom's dynamic. A discussion of motive allows students the freedom of (momentary) distance from the argument at hand, since students are not asked to identify with a text, but to consider why a critic might find it necessary to intervene within the pre-existing literary field and then evaluate the writer's relative success in the means chosen. In this way, students can consider entering within a highly politicized discussion without fear that they are either being proselytized into a new form of orthodoxy or left on the stocks for public shaming. This tutelage in the handling of contentious issues transmits, of course, the greater lesson in a basic plank of citizen democracy, the frank exchange of ideas in order to come to a decision about the allocation of social resources.

Rather than constructing a theory class's syllabus as a roughly chronological sequence of schools or representative writers, theory needs to be taught in clusters of replies where one theoretical text emerges from the reading of a prior one, not in the sense of tradition lineages or even presented within a thematic umbrella, but as an horizon that makes disagreement possible, one where the motivations that drive the need to critique the weakness of a prior one seeks to provide a more satisfying replacement. Since each motivated reply also produces a new technique or theoretically guided way of reading, students can see the stakes involved in their choice of method.

If these theory dialogues are chosen carefully so that their motivations might be explained, the surface strangeness of theory's neologisms dissolves as students may more easily see why new terms or emphases have arisen. I want to illustrate how such a dialogue cluster might occur and how these can be used in the classroom by look at a few texts that stage and interrogate the implications of using a language (English) to stand in for a coherent, uniform national identity (the English) where the call for an appreciation of the natural landscape that justifies governmental authority over its own territory (England) and beyond ("Britain" and the overseas Empire). The conflation of language, land, and literature speaks directly to the question of what has historically constituted English literary studies and what role it might have in the increasingly globalized future in which South and Central Asia are seen as centers of cultural, as well as economic and political, power.

As a teaching technique, this approach is best served when the critical writings can constantly refer back to a few chosen examples of primary materials, so that students can see how each different approach reveals how the limits of prior ones. This mode differs from one that illustrates *different* ways of reading, since it seeks to show that each theoretical approach comes about in tension with, not separation from, an earlier one, and that the difference in methodology and terms comes about as a result of hinterground concerns about the exclusions of the prior one.

The sequence chosen as an illustration here involves F.R. Leavis's 'A Sketch for an "English" School' (1943), along with aspects of his earlier co-authored *Culture and Environment* (1933). Leavis is followed by giving students the final part of Marx's *Capital Volume I* (1977) on 'the So-called Primitive Accumulation,' parts of Raymond Williams's *The Country and the City* (1973) and Edward Said's opening comments in *Empire and Culture* (1993). The section concludes with Franco Moretti's 'Conjectures on World Literature' (2000) as a way of reframing the place and traditional priority of Anglophone literary studies. Academic readers will recognize these titles as each typifying a particular critical approach – formalism (practical criticism), cultural materialism/Marxism, postcolonialism, and the new debate on comparative literature. Yet while there is no need to silence these names, students should not necessarily be directed to read these titles as exemplars of these approaches. Instead, students are asked to consider the claims of each piece as motivated replies to each other's positions.

Leavis and the reformation of English studies

Why study English literature? Surely most students who focus on literary studies have faced the need to answer this question, no matter how implicitly. A useful place to begin teaching literary and cultural theory might be to ask students to try and articulate their own reasons before having them examine one of the first, influential justifications for literary studies, F. R. Leavis's 'Sketch'. Such an introductory exercise would emphasize the roots of any theoretical question in the experience of its readers and form a personal baseline of expectations or uncertainties against which the ensuing theory texts can be compared.

Writing in 1943, Leavis lays out a conceptual groundwork for modern English studies, one crafted in opposition to the magnetic pull of normative Oxbridge (Oxford and Cambridge) literary studies. The Oxbridge curriculum was, and continues to be, organized around non-compulsory university-wide lectures that have no organic relation to a student's college tutorials, the one-on-one or very small group discussion with an academic tutor. Since a student's final degree classification is determined by her or his performance in a set of examinations taken in the last year of their study, this structure fuses a fixed notion of retrospective canonicity with a pedagogy that idealizes individual response, rather than public conversation. Writing against the assumptions embedded within Oxbridge's protocols, even as he taught within its halls, Leavis argues for English studies based on a 'liberal arts' approach that would contextualize literature within other disciplines, require familiarity with writing in foreign languages, commit itself to reviewing contemporary fiction, and teach literature mainly through seminar group discussions based on a published weekly syllabus. So many of Leavis's arguments have become commonsensical, beyond Oxford and Cambridge, that it remains astonishing to read Leavis and be reminded that these predicates ever had to be argued in favor of being established.

More interesting, though, is Leavis's definition of English Studies as the cultural response to an experience of constant social transformation. Yet despite his commitment to recording the cultural effects of change, Leavis also, paradoxically, confirms a sense that English literary studies are the self-evident product of commentary on England, a term he never puts under analysis. As we will see, both gestures can be read as the effect of his critical motivation, and this motivation can be highlighted as a teachable moment for helping to answer 'why' do theory in the first place.

Leavis begins by arguing that if English literary studies holds the 'key responsibility for education' (33), as a vocational platform for pre-university teachers, it can only justify this newly established 'high prestige' by presenting itself as a self-legitimizing field of study, a 'discipline.' Consequently, he seeks to divorce English Studies from classics, semiotics, and linguistics by insisting that 'the essential discipline of an English School is the literary critical' (34). In almost no instance will Leavis ever use the word 'literary' without attaching it to the word 'critical,' and he continually deploys a set of quasi-vocational terms – discipline, work, training, practice – that seek to distinguish literary studies from the amateurism of ersatz aristocratic connoisseurship or the nostalgic addiction to crumbling pages of forgotten lore. He sees tutorials in Classics as fundamentally different from literary studies because the former's purpose seems mainly to create a 'confident "finish"' that equips its students with a 'decorum' that is, in fact, incapable of making forward-looking distinctions between cultural performances or adjudicating actions in the post-classical world.

The discipline in English instead depends on a pedagogy that looks to transmit to its students 'the ability to profit by experience, and with it the achievement of maturity ... the judgment that is concerned inseparable from that profoundest sense of relative value which determines, or should determine, the important choices of actual life' (35). 'In a way no other discipline can,' English literary studies trains its students in 'intelligence and sensibility together' to gain the tools for evaluating contemporary changes by learning how to analyze the responses of the past's writers to their own period's social transformations.

In this light, Leavis insists that literary studies must be interdisciplinary and lead outward to involve familiarity with the arguments of other contextual fields, like history and sociology, and, consequently, the political, social, and historical influences on literature. His chief example of this kind of study involves the poetry and prose of the seventeenth century. This time is chosen as a hinge period connected to and breaking from the medieval period and 'leading directly and rapidly to what we live in now' (48), as it stages the rise of capitalism, parliamentary rule, desacralization, the rise of empiricist science, and 'the notion of society as an organism' giving way 'to that of society as joint-stock company' (49). With his emphasis on the dynamic seventeenth-century, Leavis imagines literary studies as the study of cultural modernity, and the concomitant pedagogical imperative being the need to enable students to negotiate the uncertainties produced as their own society undergoes substantive change by a comparative analysis of a similar period in the past.

The goal, therefore, of collegiate English is to produce 'neither the scholar nor the academic "star", the mind that shines at academic tests and examination gymnastic; but a mind equipped to carry on for itself; trained to work in the condition in which it will have to work if it is to carry on at all' (60). The purpose herein is to forge a new 'man' through a 'training in carrying on and going forward in spite of, and in recognition, of, incompleteness and imperfections' (61).

With these emphasizes, we can uncover Leavis's motivation for practical criticism as belonging to the larger social movement by the English middle-class in the twentieth-century to liberate themselves from domination by the old regime of landed elites and the political class responsible for leading the nation into the disaster of the Great War. While the ascent of these groups had been blunted through the 1930s depression and later war years, Leavis's sketch ought to be explained to students as existing alongside complementary activities, like Beveridge's plans for a post-war Welfare State, as a new coalition of (petit) bourgeois interests realized that the culmination of the Second World War would allow them to free England from the retarding encumbrances of its ornamental past (including the colonies) and then reconstruct the nation along more functionally efficient and egalitarian lines.

In this light, English Studies needs a new interpretive technique, a practical reading of a text's chosen words and close attention to the myriad textual details leading to the overall composition of literary work. The purpose of this discipline is two-fold. First, it provides a training ground for the future participant in the rehabilitation of England to hone their eye for details as a skill necessary for a root and branch reconstruction of society: a 'co-ordinating consciousness, capable of performing the function assigned to the class of the educated' (55). Secondly, the particular burden of literary studies is to produce the new managers of sensibility who can evaluate the cultural effects of changes to prevent a 'new' England from being destroyed by the graceless stupidity of the bureaucrats, technicians, and urban designers necessary for engineering the material environment for this new world.

Because Leavis insists on the important role of literary studies as a practical exercise that will calibrate an emerging post-war world, he feels that the study of old and middle English, as the products of a time dedicated to feudal stasis rather than progressive change, has little purpose. His desire to disencumber students from the irrelevant is why Leavis insists that literary studies begin with and anchor itself on the poetry and prose of the seventeenth century, since its leap toward modernity as a time of great transformation acts as a reference or case study for the range of options for a society in motion. We study the seventeenth century as 'a summing-up, an evaluating survey, of the changes taking place in the period – the changes as they affect one's sense of England as a civilization, a civilized community, a better or worse place to have been born into, to have belonged to, to have lived in' (54).

It is his definition of the terms of 'English' civilization, however, for which Leavis is most often known. In the earlier *Culture and Environment: The Training of Critical Awareness* (1933), co-authored with Denys Thompson, he already championed literary studies as the 'critical awareness in the cultural environment' (5). But because he has not conceptualized a role for literary studies as part of the change, his attack here is on the increasing machinery of modern living with the production of a mass culture designed for the new consumer-oriented suburbs. Insisting that 'the English people did once have a culture' (3), rather than the 'depressed and cynical aimlessness' (4) of the present, Leavis laments a lost 'organic community with the living culture it embodied. Folk-songs, folk-dance, Cotswold cottages, and handicraft products' as an 'art of life...growing out of immemorial experience to the natural environment and the rhythm of the year' (1–2). Facing the 'standardization of commodities and standardization of persons' (32) amidst a time of class conflict, Leavis looks back what he feels were the recently lost artisanal conditions of labour, where the subordinated 'were able to feel themselves fulfilled in it as self-respecting individuals...and not merely for a part of a man, a "hand", a machine-tender or a cog. The workmen were men and not "labour," not merely a factor necessary to production as "power" and "capital" are, and on the same level' (75). Decrying the 'abnormality' of the modern world that has damaged this 'national culture' (81), Leavis nominates practical criticism as a salvage operation.

Here Leavis provides his own method for teaching, one that remains a useful starting point and recurring touchstone. Looking at popular advertisements, he describes how the commercials deploy a narrative voice, often omniscient, which seeks to insinuate an emotional response within its viewers that they will be excluded from the security of communal norms if they do not become one of the new consumers of leisure-time goods. In ways that foreshadow Roland Barthes's *Mythologies* or the excellent case study-led *Representations Cultural Representations and Signifying Practices*, edited by Stuart Hall, Leavis asks that students turn to what is literally before their eyes, the paraliterature of popular culture, as the platform for their critical practice.

After encouraging our students to do likewise, by bringing in examples, the next step would be to take Leavis at his word and select some seventeenth-century lyrics and have the students repeat the exercise on the poetry. Encourage them to see the transitive relationship between their commentary on the contemporary and one on the past. In what ways does the poetry also seek to create a new identity in its readers, and how does the poet's voice manage this activity? Can all literary endeavors be seen as participating within the construction of a cultural outlook that responds to the exigencies of their own time? Lastly, students can be asked to consider the ways in which their examples hearken back to an imagined national community lacking in social tensions.

The latter may be difficult for the new readers of literary theory to see and comment on, but this tension between Leavis's two arguments, a forward-thinking one and a pained retrospection, can be used to set the stage for Raymond Williams's theoretical confrontation with Leavis on the question of the landscape-land-language nexus and Williams's creation of a replacement reading technique that questions Leavis's class-oriented motivations.

Primitive accumulation and the structure of feeling

Leavis's claim for literary studies as a training for the proper management of a dynamic England looks back to the seventeenth century as a comparative baseline when a unchanged English culture was rooted in agricultural labour. This social composition would be destroyed in turn by increasing labour unrest catalyzed by the onset of industrialization that alters the relationship of people to the social and natural environment, changing the very nature of English writing and collective identity. Yet if Leavis's motive was to intervene within his own current moment by hearkening back to an idyllic time when English language and literature had a more organic relation, the theoretical response to his thesis is two-fold.

Because Leavis himself insists that a period's writing has to be understood in relation to historical and social commentary of the time, it is worthwhile reading a competing historical account of the English countryside in the late 1500s and early 1600s: Marx's description of agrarian capitalism in *Capital Volume I*. Seeking to explain the roots of capital accumulation and the rise of modern-day class struggle, Marx argues that these emerge with the violent expropriation of small farmers, the yeomanry, through the onset of enclosures that forcibly acquire the village common land and small freehold farms for grazing sheep, which provide wool that could be sold to service the rising Continental textile manufactories. In contrast to Leavis, Marx sees the changes in agricultural relations as occurring a full century prior to the seventeenth as 'the English working class was precipitated without any transitional stages from its golden age to its iron age' (879) with the rise of a new market-oriented aristocracy in the wake of feudalism's collapse after the depopulating effects of the Black Death and the long internecine conflicts between noble lineages, such as the War of the Roses. Henry VIII's Dissolution of the English Catholic Church then accelerated rural changes, as ecclesiastic-controlled land was sold off to those market-oriented interests willing to help finance the Tudor State. Previously public or, at least, non-commercialized farming land, which had been backed by long customary social understandings, was turned into a profit-bearing instrument through a 'whole series of thefts, outrages, and popular misery' (859). Already, beginning in the last third of the fifteenth century, the 'memory of the connection between the agricultural labourer and communal property' (899) was severed, even before the middle of the seventeenth century, when 'the agricultural folk' were 'forcibly expropriated from the soil, driven from their homes, turned into vagabonds, and then whipped, branded and tortured by grotesquely terroristic laws into accepting the discipline necessary for the system of wage-labor' (989). In this light, the seventeenth century is not the period when idyllic relations were still present, but already one soured by social tensions.

It is useful for students to read Marx's account about the separation and linkage of the country and the city as it reminds them that historical evidence can be marshalled in different ways. Students might be asked what difference it makes to Leavis's claims about literary studies if his own historical account is shown to be overly nostalgic and based on cultural amnesia, which forgets that the relation of men to the countryside was far more fragile and chaotic than in his ideal of an 'organic community.' Yet even if Leavis's history is wrong, does this impact his mode of close reading? Here the classroom might be given excerpts from Raymond Williams's *The Country and the City*, as a conscious reply to Leavis, to illustrate how new critical idioms emerge from a conflict of motivations.

In *The Country and the City*, Raymond Williams rebuts the claims of his Cambridge colleague Leavis for the existence of a lost organic community that had fused English landscape, language, and literature into a national imaginary, to use Benedict Anderson's terms. Not only does Williams question the intellectual acuity and political thesis of Leavis, but he also presents, in turn, a new method for reading literary texts. While Leavis championed a practical criticism that focused on word choice and the aptness of metaphor and descriptive language to convey meaning, Williams looks to analyze a text not for what is said, but for how it presents tensions or paradoxes within, primarily, its narrative voice as an index to a *structure of feeling*. Because subordinate social groups bearing the burden of historical transformation lack the institutional mechanisms for their self-representation, they must use pre-existing forms, genres, and devices to enunciate feelings. The tension between feeling and prior formal structures produces tensions in a text's narrative that indicate the period's pressures.

Williams's theory of reading consequently moves beyond a close reading, which assumes that a text's representations articulate the vision of an assured creator representing a homogeneous society, to an examination of *perspective*, meaning both the literary technique involving the devices of narrative voice and the optics of social recognition – in what way does the literature of landscape distort or obscures the experiences of those who work the land to produce an aesthetically pleasing environment or stately manors.

As opposed to Leavis's elegiac lyric of a national organic community, Williams draws on Marx's history of agrarian capitalism and the alienation of small farmers from the land through a long history of enclosures and the State's ensuing criminalization of rural poverty to distinguish Leavis's version of community from another version, 'which is sometimes the mutuality of the oppressed, at other times, the mutuality of people living at the edges or in the margins of a generally oppressive system' (104). In his study that seeks to cast light on multiple experiences within dominant literary historiography, Williams explodes the neat binary of country and city by showing these poles exist in a spectrum of intermediary developments, like the new postwar dormitory suburbs, and chips away at the pastoral fallacy. He shows that each age, going back to the ancient Greeks and Romans, fantastically believes its immediately prior one was a time of lost harmony. For Williams, the celebration of an organic rural community that uses the myth of a happier past both papers over the history of long and systemic exploitation of rural labourers and seizure of lands and, especially in the twentieth century, enlists the reader's imagination of a rural territory into racialist fantasies of a pure homeland that must be protected against its 'contamination' by foreign groups. 'Against sentimental and intellectualized accounts of an unlocalised "old England"', we need, evidently, the sharpest skepticism' (10): Williams' rejoinder is that the reader's emotional dedication to the spheres of her or his birth and youth may easily convert into an ethnically exclusionary rhetoric.

As a child to a Welsh borderlands family that actually experienced the changes that Leavis speaks of with assumed authority, Williams personally knows the presence of rural experiences of hardship and struggle that practical criticism finds uninteresting to pursue. What may, though, simply seem to be a defence of one version of locality against another assumes a larger motivation when we examine Williams's generational motivation for producing a new kind of literary criticism. For Williams is best classified as one of the 'Angry Young Men' of post-war Britain, who emerged in the delayed boom of the 1950s. Despite the increased availability of mass-produced consumer goods, they found that their lives had been stultified, not by the cheapening of language in advertisements as Leavis argues (though this complaint also appears in Williams), but with the failure of England to follow through on the promise of lower middle- and working-class enfranchisement. Despite the long sacrifices of the war years and some small openings and institutional rearrangements, England remained, as Orwell saw it, a tea party run by self-serving elites for their own benefit. Williams's revaluation of literary criticism comes from a response of incomplete democratization, the partial opening of doors for some veterans and members of the working-class, but without the fundamental reconstruction that had been promised. As the promise of enfranchisement was contained by the shift towards a consumer democracy, where increased purchasing power was meant to substitute for actual inclusion within social and political privileges, the bitter sense of betrayal needed to express itself. Williams's theory of the structure of feeling, the half-muted expression of social otherness within swiftly obsolete institutions that were not, as Leavis thought, adjusting proactively to the social change, motivates Williams's re-reading of canonical and para-canonical writing. Williams provides different theses of reading and method to Leavis, but these can best, and perhaps only, be explained by reference when positioned against one another as consecutive responses to a social history of contestation over English identity mediated by arguments over the teaching of English literature.

For the classroom, students can then be asked to revisit their initial examples and see how Williams' comments about reading the text for its inherent tensions and the ways in which assertions of homogeneity mask assertions to power. They should be encouraged to see how the different methods of reading each lend themselves to different extratextual motivations. These 'domestic' disputes between Leavis and Williams, set the stage, in turn, for the Palestinian-American Edward Said's response to Williams, one that grounds itself on Williams' initial argument, but only to revise it by questioning why the role of the English outside of Britain and in its colonies has been excluded from the picture.

Edward Said and the imperial vision

For Edward Said, a major flaw in Williams's model of structure of feeling is the 'limitation in his feeling that English literature is mainly about England' (14). Williams's own internalized sense of national boundaries fails to uncover how even working-class structures of feeling tacitly 'support, elaborate, and consolidate the practice of empire,' the primitive accumulation of colonial lands (and the labour of the peoples on them) for the gain of the metropolitan lands. Although Said is neither a self-described marxist, nor even one who sees himself as a cultural materialist, he accepts Williams' use of Marx's argument about the exploitation locked within modern capitalism economies, just as he finds Williams linkage of the country and city a useful model for launching his own discussion of the global city (the imperial nations) and country (the colonies).

Yet even as he builds on Williams's critical moves, Said questions how Williams failed to recognize that even a study of the period's 'structures of feeling' does not uncover the institutional rise and consolidation of an assent for imperial invasion and racializing hierarchies within English society. Instead Said proposes a search for 'structures of attitude and reference,' rather than Williams's 'structures of feeling,' where the

former involves 'the way in which structures of location and geographical reference appear in the cultural languages of literature, history, or
ethnography, sometimes allusively and sometimes carefully plotted,
across several individual works that are not otherwise connected to one
another or to an official ideology or "empire" '(61).

Rather than examining tensions within the narrative voice, which
Williams felt would locate the presence of a marginalized experience
that did not have its own idiom in which to speak, Said urges us to look
from the exterior of language for marginal asides and recurring patterns
in the narrative that involve 'geographical articulations' that suggest
the presence of the colonies, always far and away, yet providing the
material foundation for the home nation's subjects and their assumptions of racial superiority. Like Leavis's examination of how popular
advertisements construct a suburbanized individual, Said looks to how
'high cultural' effects of the novel similarly construct a sense of personal
identity that relies on a common notion of a collective (national, racial)
identity. Yet while Leavis sought to examine the posters as a negative
example of what English civilization had lost, Said inverts this question to see how fictional narratives create a new set of English mental
assumptions, the ways in which the novel acts as a calibrating institution that allows for the preliminary imagination of the benefits and
justification for imperial privilege, even before any military conquest.
How was it that fictional narratives promulgated the idea of 'the right
to colonial possessions helps directly to establish social order and moral
priorities at home' (973)?

Believing that the novel and imperialism are unthinkable without each
other, Said argues that this was not because the (nineteenth-century)
novel was automatically imperialist, but that most discussions of non-
European lands often accepted a notion of power to the West's advantage, so that novels 'animate, articulate, embody the relation between,
for instance, England and Africa' (91); they do so by 'consolidating but
also refining and articulating the authority of the status quo' (91) that
has been built on the primitive accumulation of these lands by imperial
ones. These assumptions can only be recognized by our careful examining of a narrative's framing devices and attempted resolutions of seemingly insular tensions located within them.

Said consequently mandates a kind of reading different from either
of his two critical predecessors, Leavis and Williams. Said inverts the
formalism of Leavis's practical criticism by treating the externalities of
prose sentences as a gesture encouraging us to look at the outside skin
of imperialism. Likewise, he challenges us to extend the question of

perspective much further than Williams himself did. Said's motivation here, comes, of course, from the same sense of betrayal that Williams felt, but for Said this involves the broken promises of decolonization and national autonomy for the non-Western world, and raises the questions of literary criticism's role in the social adjustment of global inequalities.

Writing within the US academy, Said asks why literary studies, in the wake of practical criticism and cultural materialism, still has not risen to the challenge of thinking about how Western and non-European peoples and their literary productions need to be brought into conversation with one another. Said's motivation here belongs to a certain time period, one that felt the need to bring the pressure of the presence of the international to the classroom. Yet in the wake of Said's intervention, those in the field of comparative literature have asked if there are other ways that analogies can be recognized. For instance, can the early modern English period, with its forced urbanization, speak to the same patterns now accelerating in India, China, and elsewhere, where ever increasing numbers of rural laborers are pushed off their lands? In what ways can works in the English language speak the same idiom of historical transformation, the energies that Leavis foregrounded as the base element of literary criticism, for works emerging in different regions and tongues? For while although Said's motive was to uncover the social injustices inherent in the Empire and decolonization, the power asymmetries between the West and the Rest may no longer be so simply defined in a time when global commerce has become increasingly driven by forces outside of Europe. In order to adjust to these new arrangements, a new globally aware comparative literary theory has emerged, often under the name of 'world literature.'

Franco Moretti and world literature

Recently Franco Moretti has suggested a study of writing based on the world-systems analysis of historical sociology, mainly developed by Immanuel Wallerstein. Proposing a model of literary production based on unequal development between the European core and global peripheries, Moretti raises the question of commerce and cultural transmission to reconsider 'the relationship between markets and forms,' alongside the study 'of literary evolution in cultures that belong to the periphery of the literary system (which means: almost all cultures inside and outside of Europe).' Can the economic and social competition of the international marketplaces influence and shape the means of literary communication? To gauge these changes globally, Moretti calls for a study that moves away from close reading, which depends on the individual text's autonomy, towards 'distant reading,' a study at the sublevel of narrative devices, themes, and tropes and the supralevel of genres and literary systems. Rather than look at word-choice (Leavis), narrative voice (Williams), marginal pressures (Said), Moretti favors asking why certain genres appear at certain times and why certain narrative devices become popular. His answer seems to be that these features convey an experience of the author's locality as it encounters a global configuration determined by competing international forces. If this is the case, then works from different regions, experiencing similar conditions in their relationship to the world market, will tend toward certain familiar patterns, such as the taste for particular genres, like the gothic or the melodrama. The motivation for looking at international commerce and its relation to culture is one that needs perhaps the least explication at the current moment.

By asking readers to consider the cultural needs or interests that might take shape within familiar genres and their conventions regardless of their location in time or place, Moretti shifts away from an older model of comparative literature, wherein Western European and classical Greek and Roman cultural productions were taken as the developmental against which other national cultural productions were gauged. Similarly, he moves away from Said-influence postcolonialism that analyzes works for the deformations of their imagined community caused by imperialism. Alternately, Moretti implies that instead of seeing the West as intrinsically different from the East, both ought to be considered as bearing similar pressures, albeit at different times. For instance, nineteenth-century India might be reviewed not only against nineteenth-century England, as Said insists, but also alongside fifteenth-century England, for these are the periods when both regions express their subordinated entry into a more developed global capitalist world market through similar alterations in precapitalist caste, belief, and narrative systems. And twentieth-century India might be comparable to seventeenth-century England as both experience similar pressures of intestine war and civil disunion as a result of the development of class fractions. The key here is the assumption that the non-European is not following the stages of development that the West has set, for the 'West' is itself not a homogeneous entity. Rather each place has similar conditions when they have the similar events inaugurated for them.

By considering *every* work as world literature, formed by the pressures of the world market, students might be encouraged to disentangle land, language, and nationality. The motivation here would be to move beyond the charged air of guilt and shaming for historical events within the classroom, but in ways that do not seek to silence or erase their effects. Moretti's conjectures on world literature encourage literary studies to imagine itself as part of the world, but not belonging to or reading from any of its perspectives. This gesture escapes being a return to depoliticized formalism by acknowledging the relationship between the deployment of economic and social power and cultural codes, but not doing so at the level of a specific language, than of (often translated) narrative codes themselves.

A teaching method based on the trajectory from Leavis to Moretti offers one way to highlight the political and cultural relevance of Theory. It would involve a core set of primary texts, focus on how different interpretive techniques reshape our perception of their intrinsic nature and also, most importantly, disclose the social and political motivations that underpin critical and theoretical approaches to literature. In this way the new student is enabled both to involve themselves in and stand outside, and observe, the dynamic of reading and ideology. Politics and theory can never be disentangled but the encounter does not have to end in stalemate either.

Bibliography

Anderson, B. (1983). *Imagined Communities: Reflections on the Origin and Spread of Nationalism*. London: Verso.

Barthes, R. (1972). *Mythologies*. New York: Noonday Press.

Graff, G. (1992). *Beyond the Culture Wars: How Teaching the Conflicts Can Revitalize American Education*. New York: Norton.

Hall, S., ed. (1997). *Representation: Cultural Representations and Signifying Practices*. London: Sage.

Leavis, F.R. (1943). *Education and the University: A Sketch for an "English" School*. London: Catto & Windus.

Leavis, F.R. and Thompson, D. (1933). *Culture and Environment: The Training of Critical Awareness*. London: Chatto & Windus.

Marx, K. (1977). *Capital: A Critique of Political Economy*. London: Penguin.

Moretti, F. (2000). 'Conjecture on World Literature.' *New Left Review* 1, 54–68.

——— (2003). 'More Conjectures.' *New Left Review* 20, 73–81.

——— (2005). *Graphs, Maps, Trees: Abstract Models for a Literary History*. London: Verso.

Said, E. (1993). *Culture and Imperialism*. New York: Knopf.

Wallerstein, I. (2004). *World-Systems Analysis: An Introduction*. Durham: Duke University Press.

Williams, R. (1973). *The Country and the City*. London: Chatto & Windus.

6
Marketing Theory: An Overview of Theory Guides

Andrew James

Academic publishers often serve as barometric indicators to the state of the discipline: reading lists mean sales. The first sign that broad changes were occurring in English studies was the launch by Routledge of the New Accents series. The general editor, Terence Hawkes, appropriately enough authored the volume on that keystone to theory, *Structuralism and Semiotics* (Methuen, 1977). The series was begun in the 1970s and its appearance reflected theory's shift in status from a topic debated and written about by a relatively small number of academics – usually with specialized interests and enthusiasms beyond the mainstream of straightforward literary criticism – to one which was taught to undergraduates, albeit in courses which remained outside the traditional framework of curricula based on the English canon. Significantly, the title list of New Accents also indicated that theory was acquiring its own framework of sub-categories and components – structuralism, deconstruction, formalism, Marxism. Theory was becoming an academic subject in its own right with a layout that would fit comfortably into a ten to twelve week semester and satisfy the requirements of examinations and coursework. Though radical by its self-proclaimed nature, it was adapting itself into the customs of university teaching. The fact that Routledge judged that there was now a viable market for single, explanatory texts covering the various aspects of theory shows that it was gaining ground within the university curriculum. Previously the standard text was Jefferson and Robey's single volume guide, *Modern Literary Theory* (1982), offering a concise chapter on each of the topics that New Accents would deal with in 50,000–70,000 word texts. At the other end of the spectrum the arrival of New Accents coincided with the publication of Jonathan Culler's *Structuralist Poetics* (1975), nominally an explanatory textbook but demanding enough to unsettle academics themselves.

Fifteen years after New Accents was launched, Blackwell went a step further and founded Rereading English, a series of short student-targeted guides based not upon theoretical concepts but upon literary authors. This was theory in practice and was, one assumes, indicative of theory's inclusion in the English studies curriculum. Ironically, the series was shaped around that monument to traditionalism, the canon, with its general editor, Terry Eagleton, authoring the volume on one William Shakespeare. Impressions can, however, be misleading. The assumption that all courses on Shakespeare would reflect on the radical agenda of Eagleton's volume in the teaching and examination of the plays was somewhat optimistic, perhaps even delusional.

Also significant was Routledge's Critics of the Twentieth Century series, launched at the beginning of the 1990s. More detailed and intensive than New Accents, these volumes concentrated upon what were thought to be the formative presences in the history of theory, marking a further ironic twist in this genre since theory now appeared to have a grand canon of its own. (Continuum have launched a similar series.) Routledge's New Critical Idiom series from the late 1990s onwards represented another intriguing development in that it replaced the original set of volumes, called simply The Critical Idiom, offering a traditional overview of matters such as humanism, mimesis, rhetoric, and literature. Some of these titles re-emerged in the new series alongside historicism, ideology, and sexuality and throughout the impression was that theory now informed all interpretive perspectives and practises.

While the development of a vibrant theory guide market suggests that theory is now an integral part of English studies, many pedagogical concerns remain. Most degree programs in English studies are still based upon the study of literary history and the modules only allow time for a selected number of texts. Fitting theory into undergraduate literature courses often depends upon how much the texts lend themselves to theoretical interpretations. A post-colonial reading of *The Tempest* in a Shakespeare course might help to provide the perspective of historical change but, with so many theories and so little time, the consistent application of theory is for the most part simply impractical. Theory questions the intrinsic characteristics of literature, which is surely beneficial for English studies students, as it forces them to consider the essence of their discipline. But one of the premises of theory has been that literature cannot be conceived of as a self-defining aesthetic pursuit superior to popular culture and most theory guides today still reflect this belief in their dismissive treatment of the New Critics.

It is therefore difficult to understand why, if theory has so little respect for literature, the major theorists continue to define their ideas in relation to literature. And while many of the central figures in theory have insisted that the socio-political ramifications of theory exceed the limitations of the written word, its relevance outside the classroom is still unclear.

The most obvious way that theory makes its presence felt in the real world is commercially. Twenty years after the first theory guides appeared, the sheer number of introductory volumes aimed at students suggests that theory has evolved from a radical political enterprise into a business. A sampling of available theory readers includes Brooker and Widdowson's *A Practical Reader in Contemporary Literary Theory* (Prentice Hall, 1996), Tallack's *Critical Theory: A Reader* (Pearson, 1995), Easthope and McGowan's *A Critical and Cultural Theory Reader* (2nd edn,Open UP, 2004), and Lodge and Wood's enormous *Modern Criticism and Theory*, (3rd edn, Longman, 2008). While theory readers contain selections from the original writings of seminal theorists, theory guides summarize and explain the tenets of established theories. In a sense, guides help theory teachers to avoid doing their jobs for, while few literature modules would teach novels through plot summaries, guides make it possible to bypass the original texts and still teach and discuss theory with deceptive fluency.

Arguably the greatest change in theory guides over the last twenty years is in their increasing topicality and complacency. 'It is easy to see,' proclaimed Terence Hawkes in the preface to the New Accents series, 'that we are living in a time of rapid and radical social change.' These changes were most apparent in the field of literary studies and the New Accents series 'would seek to encourage rather than resist the process of change' (7). However, in the fifth edition of Selden, Brooker and Widdowson's *A Reader's Guide to Contemporary Literary Theory* (Longman, 2005), the editors seemed to announce that the process was complete in warning theory teachers that 'occupying a theory-free zone is a fundamental impossibility, and to allow our students to think that it is not would be a dereliction of intellectual duty.' This opening is reminiscent of Terry Eagleton's in *After Theory*: 'Those to whom the title of this book suggests that "theory" is now over, and that we can all relievedly return to an age of pre-theoretical innocence, are in for a disappointment. There can be no going back' (1). The message is that theory has arrived and will continue to be of significance, and the tone is decidedly aggressive. The defenders of theory are no longer defensive, as Catherine Belsey was in justifying, in *Critical Practice* (Methuen, 1983), her use of theoretical jargon through jargon:

> Of course jargon exists, but from a perspective in which ideology is held to be inscribed in language, so that no linguistic forms are ideologically innocent or neutral, it follows that terms cannot be seen as unnecessary simply on the basis that they are new. To resist all linguistic innovation is by implication to claim that we already know all we need to know. In this book I shall try to make the new theories as accessible as possible without recuperating them for common sense by transcribing them back into the discourse of every day. (6)

In part this change in tone is due to the relatively comfortable position theory now occupies in the university. Theory's place on the English studies curriculum may be secure, but an examination of the currently available guides points to a political divide between those who believe that theory ought to inform every literary interpretation – that deep knowledge is essential – and those concerned to widen theory's base of followers through demystification. In the second edition of *Beginning Theory* (2002; 1st edn, 1995), Peter Barry uses the art of soft persuasion, stating that 'At the undergraduate level the main problem is to decide how much theory can reasonably be handled by beginners' (3). 'Literary theory,' he adds,' 'is not innately difficult' (7), which is a rather dubious claim implying that troublesome figures like Derrida and Lacan came along and made it unnecessarily complex.

With so many theory guides now available it is difficult to generalize, but here are some common features. Regardless of whether they hector or woo the reader, guides typically begin with a statement of purpose and a confession of theoretical bias. The authors or editors then claim that theory is either important or accessible (though rarely both) and this claim affects the presentation of content. Guides emphasizing theory's significance are likely to focus on recent theoretical trends with an overtly political or socio-cultural outlook. Those that take the accessibility angle prefer to deal with theory in broader strokes and place it within a general historical context. Regardless of which approach a guide follows, there are, however, some universal features. All guides define theory, explain where it came from, and predict where it is headed. And no guide ever achieves complete neutrality because, in order to provide perspective, it is necessary to have one. Some theories are inevitably elevated to a favoured position while others are relegated to the periphery. It is interesting, then, to look at guides not only as packaged highlights of theory for undergraduates but as indicators of the state of theory which tell us about its past, present, and the direction the authors hope it will take in the future.

Two examples of recent efforts to make theory accessible are Peter Barry's *Beginning Theory* (1995) and Jonathan Culler's *Literary Theory: A Very Short Introduction* (Oxford University Press, 2000). It is not surprising that two theorists with ties to structuralism have written similarly structured guides. In *Structuralist Poetics* (Routledge, 1975) and *On Deconstruction* (Routledge, 1983) Culler was not particularly concerned to explain theory to laymen. In fact, the explications themselves were challenging for academics. However, the mandate of the *Very Short Introductions* series required him to make the story of theory short, entertaining, and devoid of jargon. Culler's book is indeed short, running just over 120 pages, and readable. Continuum targets a similar audience of disinterested undergraduates through its *Guides for the Perplexed* and Mary Klages's 2006 contribution to this series resembles Culler's in length but not in format. While she employed key theorists and theories as her organizational principles, Culler deliberately avoided this method, arguing that 'To introduce theory it is better to discuss shared questions and claims than to survey theoretical schools' (22). He begins with a discussion of literature and its defining characteristics and compares the reader to a gardener who, when confronted by something not to his or her taste, labels it a weed. Determining what qualifies as literature is highly subjective, since one gardener's weed may be another's flower. In contrast to the vagueness of the literary genre, the aims of theory are presented as definitive and clear. Culler argues, just as Catherine Belsey did twenty years earlier, that one of modern theory's purposes is to challenge common sense, encompassing topics such as literary excellence and the construction of personal identity. In an apparent effort to make his material entertaining, Culler at times offers aphorisms and one-liners in lieu of fully developed argument. Thus, the reader is told that the idea of the original is created by the copies (12) in a discussion of the literary, with soul singer Aretha Franklin's claim that her lover makes her feel like a natural woman cited as proof that she is not (14). 'Meaning is context-bound,' he later ephemerally adds, '"but context is boundless' (67). Overall, Culler's guide is accessible and interesting, but it leaves the impression that theory is more easily marketed than properly explained.

Peter Barry opens *Beginning Theory* by revisiting Eagleton's *Literary Theory: An Introduction* (Blackwell, 1983), which also began with a discussion of liberal humanism. He reminds us that Oxford and Cambridge were sceptical of English's suitability as a university course of study and held out against it until 1894 and 1911 respectively (14). Some of the more ardent supporters of English as an academic subject were those who linked literature with morality: Henry James, Matthew Arnold, and

F.R. Leavis. Perhaps the purpose of this discussion is to hint at the inevitability of the changing of the academic guard, with English studies supplanted by theory just as the authority of Leavis and the New Critics was long ago usurped. Barry favours intensive, rather than extensive, reading, recommends key chapters in primary texts, and provides 'stop and think' exercises to assist students in understanding theory's practical applications. He admits to having changed his mind about theory since the appearance of his guide's first edition in the early 1990's, now finding structuralism more alluring than poststructuralism. His primary concerns seem to be familiarizing students with the background and aims of each of the main theoretical schools and showing how a particular theorist views language or a text. Barry's guide is a favourite on university reading lists because it is accessible, more detailed than Culler's guide without becoming cumbersome, and it offers a glimpse of future trends. Barry claims his guide was the first to discuss ecocriticism. The most intriguing part of the book is the author's hypothesis of a super-reader capable of performing multiple interpretations of any given text. He rightly questions the desirability of the creation of super-readers on the grounds that they would only succeed in rendering superficial, generic interpretations (198–9). Unwittingly, perhaps, he has pointed out one of theory's greatest challenges. In training literature students, a general aim is to cultivate the ability to provide original textual interpretations. Though the New Critics are no longer in vogue, they at least accorded primacy to the individual's reaction to literature. Original interpretations of texts are valued more highly than regurgitations of standard views, yet theory guides often seem to lead students towards the latter option. For theory teachers who like the short approach but would prefer slightly more detail, Hans Bertens' *Literary Theory* (3rd edn, Taylor and Francis, 2007), which begins with a chapter on practical criticism, is another option.

Selden *et al.*'s, *A Reader's Guide to Contemporary Literary Theory* (Longman, 2005) is somewhat less accessible but it is has become one of the genre's standards and is now in its fifth edition. It introduces theoretical schools according to historical principles in ten detailed chapters which culminate in lengthy reading lists. The editors are less concerned with making their subject immediately comprehensible than with proving its importance and topicality through intelligent, thorough chapters on such topics as gay, lesbian and queer theories, genetic criticism, and political criticism. Theory is depicted as flourishing and politically relevant. The greatest difference between *A Reader's Guide to Contemporary Literary Theory* and Barry's and Culler's volumes is that

Widdowson and Brooker (Selden being deceased) require the reader to approach theory with a zeal that matches their own. The guide covers a vast amount of material in just over 300 pages and is a better alternative in the university class room than, for example, Groden *et al.*'s comprehensive but unwieldy *The Johns Hopkins Guide to Literary Theory and Criticism* (Johns Hopkins University Press, 2005). Another work that is excellent, though cumbersome at 600 pages, Patricia Waugh's *Literary Theory and Criticism: An Oxford Guide* (Oxford University Press, 2005), is composed of commissioned essays covering the history of theory and offering glances into the future. In spite of its attractive size and price, Selden *et al.*'s, Widdowson and Brooker's guide does have its drawbacks. Perhaps the authors have forgotten what it is like to be a student, but there is no better way to ensure that a task will be neglected than to tell undergraduates simply that it must be done without offering any justification. The editors are prone to making grand statements such as the following: 'some familiarity with theory tends to undermine reading as an innocent activity' (4). Surely, though, not every reader unacquainted with theory reads simply to pass the time just as all theorists are not revolutionaries but include some comfortably tenured academics in their midst. A challenge at the end of the guide might unintentionally invite some students to turn away from theory: 'when we go back to read the text, what theory do we take with us?' (270). The question of which theory one ought to follow points to the greatest weakness of guides with a political agenda. Such guides are at least as interested in recruiting followers as they are in educating novices.

Another common feature of guides that highlight the political side of theory is their invocation of music and film for interpretive purposes. By shifting the focus away from literature, theorists can stress theory's independence while showing that it is aware of the latest trends in popular culture. When theory removes literature from a position of privilege within culture it declares, by extension, that texts cannot be conclusively evaluated in terms of artistic excellence. Bennett and Royle's *Introduction to Literature, Criticism and Theory* (3rd edn, Longman, 2004) is a political guide that interweaves the practical application of theory with broad philosophical questions. The first chapter, 'The Beginning,' asks, 'Where – or when – does a literary text begin?' (1). To answer the question, the authors consider literary classics including *Paradise Lost, The Divine Comedy*, and *Tristram Shandy*. But many of the other chapters betray the authors' deeper interest in the political side of theory. Four new chapters were added to the second edition – 'Monuments,' 'Ghosts,' 'Queer,' and 'The Colony' – and four more have joined the third: 'Creative Writing,' 'Moving Pictures,' 'Mutant,' and 'War.' Each theory is concisely explained with appropriate (predominantly) literary references, but one weakness is the authors' tendency to be judgemental. After referring to American President George Bush's ideological abuses of the English language, they urge the reader to log onto 'bushisms.com' for further examples (171), and John Fowles's *The Magus* is dismissed as 'verbose, dull, self-regarding and [...] overrated'; (227). Such remarks suggest that writing can be ranked according to quality, which would seem to contradict the aim of a theory guide which features so much cultural critical content. The authors also risk confusing undergraduates who already struggle to offer objective evaluations of texts untainted by personal tastes and biases.

One of the safest organizing principles for a theory text that hopes to makes its way onto English studies readings lists has been the historical one, but it is an approach that seems to be losing favour. Many guide writers are now more concerned with alerting readers to current theoretical trends than in reviewing long-established theoretical branches that have fallen out of favour. Chris Baldick's *Criticism and Literary Theory 1890 to the Present* (Pearson, 2003) possesses both a familiar historical framework and a clear statement of purpose, opening with an editor's preface, an author's preface, and a lengthy introduction. Baldick focuses on the 'changing "agenda" [...] of critical discussion in the English-speaking world' (xiii) rather than introducing principal figures in criticism and theory, which is in accord with the stated aim of Longman's forty-seven volume Literature in English series: to 'show that the most valuable and stimulating approach' is the historical one. He discusses criticism and theory simultaneously, spending more time than is usual on critical pronouncements made by literary figures such as Wilde, Yeats, and Henry James. Another unique aspect of this text is that Baldick confines his argument to critical theory written in English. Russians and continental Europeans do receive occasional mention, but the author has endeavoured to 'place these influences [...] "offstage" for the purpose of this exposition' (xiv). He describes criticism as a 'hybrid or bastard discourse' (3) in which 'the "great" critics work in dialogue with a range of other voices' (10). Although it could not have been easy to remove all of the non-English theorists from his argument, Baldick has done well and he provides valuable analysis for English studies undergraduates overwhelmed by both theory and criticism. Until 1918, writes Baldick, the critic's job was to focus on the author's sensibility and to delineate a work's principal moods and character portraits, but not to 'delve into detailed questions of style, structure, or meaning' (58). Criticism was primarily written by men-of-letters, such as Wilde and Shaw. Though Baldick's own position is not overly stated, he is something of a literary purist, quoting Allen Tate's remark that the insights of critical evaluation cannot be taught to college students. Perhaps this is the reason he has largely limited himself to cataloguing names and dates. He is most convincing when dealing with the Chicago critics, as he uses Crane's analysis of *Tom Jones* to indicate their critical tendencies (130). In general, he offers perceptive insights but the book serves less as an introductory guide than as enriched reading for the initiated. It fails to convince the reader of either theory's importance or its accessibility, which makes the guide seem lacking in purpose, in spite of its attempt to distinguish itself from the competition by focusing exclusively on English thinkers.

Yet the chronological method can work well in theory guides, as Richard Harland demonstrates in *Literary Theory from Plato to Barthes: An Introductory History* (Macmillan, 1999). Like Culler and Barry, he is partial to structuralism, though he suspects his ' "other' career as a writer of SF/fantasy fiction' has coloured his perspective. If anything it seems to have to given the guide admirable balance. Throughout, Harland suspends disbelief and shows how earlier theoretical perspectives 'can make perfect sense in their own terms, no matter how odd or unappealing they may appear nowadays' (xii). He focuses on links in critical positions from Plato to the present without straining to be topical or making references to popular culture. In a genre full of guides eager to predict the next theoretical trend, Harland's is conspicuous, for it takes more than half of the book for him to enter the twentieth century. When he does reach the radical Russian theorists, Harland notes that they 'are not so much critics of literature as critics of social reality, with literary texts serving as a particularly useful point of entry' (87), an observation helpful for undergraduates in clarifying the direction of modern theory and its connection to literature. One problem with the guide lies in its lack of emphasis on theory's application to literature. Though it is readable and well-organized historically, the ways in which theory informs our understanding of landmark texts could perhaps be better demonstrated. Of course, theory guide writers must make choices and in Harland's case historical balance has been given precedence over politics and practice. Another recent guide which may be compared to Baldick's and Harland's efforts is M.A.R. Habib's *Modern Literary Criticism and Theory: A History* (Blackwell, 2008), which focuses on the last century of theorists and critics, offering short biographical entries for the key figures. Habib packs a great deal of information into 250 pages and, though it is comprehensive, proves the difficulty in writing a historical theory guide that does not read like an encyclopedia full of dates and names.

The only type of theory guide which makes a consistent effort to put theory into analytic practice is arguably the most flawed and the explanation for this might be, as Allen Tate suggested, that there are some things which cannot be effectively taught. One problem with practical guides is that they simplify both theory and practice to such an extent that students generally require another, more comprehensive, supplementary theory text. It is also possible that the strict adherence to a practical guide might result in the creation of super-readers capable of analyzing texts from a variety of perspectives but without any deep insight. By extension, the practical method also might discourage students from pursuing original ideas uninformed by theory. Raman Selden's *Practising Theory and Reading Literature: An Introduction* (Harvester Wheatsheaff, 1989) contains most of the flaws inherent in the practical method. While he insisted that radical contemporary theories opposing Romanticism, humanism, and empiricism have shown that' "we can and must learn to *read differently'* (4), he neglected to explain how people were reading at the time. At least he admitted to being biased – to writing from a 'materialist' perspective (6) – and expressed concern that by attempting to put numerous theoretical positions into practice he might 'appear to convey a judicious but deceitful neutrality' (7). He need not have worried, as his dissection of F.R. Leavis on Bunyan's *Pilgrim's Progress* illustrates (20–4). Selden refuses to give serious consideration to either Leavis or Moral Criticism, saying of the former that 'It is not possible to adopt Leavis's method except at an intuitive level,' and of the latter that the weakness of the approach 'lies in its self-deceiving claim to disinterestedness and universality' (24). Selden foreshadowed the attack in the introduction, declaring: 'the long established "hegemony" of Leavis and the New Critics is over' (7). But Selden's pioneering practical guide does teach us a valuable lesson in the mutual exclusivity of theoretical schools. Thus, it is almost impossible for a Marxist critic to sympathize with Moral Criticism and Selden's self-professed 'commitment to unravelling the entire project of Western "bourgeois" humanism [...] and the universality of essential human values' (6) doomed Leavis from the start. This also means that students are lead to believe that some theories are less applicable than others. The tendency of practical guides to be over-inquisitive poses another problem. A few general questions would suffice to arouse students' interest in exploring texts theoretically, but Selden and other practical guide writers often provide pages of minute questions. These question lists may give undergraduates the discouraging feeling that there are no new questions to be raised.

Almost twenty years after the publication of Selden's guide, Michael Ryan's *Literary Theory: A Practical Introduction* (2nd edn, Blackwell, 2007) has appeared and it features all of the familiar attendant problems of the practical approach. A statement of intent is provided on the back cover: 'The edition is unique in that it expands the range of texts to include film, from *The Matrix* to *Run, Lola, Run,*' offering 'accessible accounts of the full range of theoretical approaches.' Perhaps Ryan was overly eager to launch into practical analyses, but the absence of an introduction or preface suggests that now no such justification is required because theory has become part of our lives. 'Political Criticism,' Ryan's contribution to the essay collection *Contemporary Literary Theory* (Macmillan, 1989), edited by Atkins and Morrow, could have served as the introduction to his practical theory guide. 'It is no longer possible,' he wrote, 'to speak of "Marxist criticism" as a category apart from a broader critical undertaking that includes work being done by non-Marxist radicals and that might most suitably be called either "political criticism" or "cultural criticism."' Ryan chose the label 'cultural' because the genre deals not only with literary classics but television, film, popular literature, and 'the symbolic elements of everyday life' (201). Although the title of Ryan's 2007 practical guide claims that it is literary, roughly half of the works under consideration are popular films. He is, therefore, performing cultural criticism, but the misnamed guide begins with a definition of literature: 'One of the first things one notices about literature is that it consists of language that has been formed and shaped so that it no longer looks like ordinary language. It is easy to tell a novel from a weather report' (1). If this statement is true, and literary works can be qualitatively ranked, then it becomes difficult to justify the inclusion of an analysis of a rap song ('The Nigga Ya Love To Hate') and the screen version of a novel (*Lord of the Rings*) alongside *King Lear*. It is also rather sad to note that when practical guide writers tirelessly catalogue every image, metaphor, and alternating vowel in a poem, as Ryan does in analyzing Elizabeth Bishop poem 'The Moose,' literature and theory become almost as stimulating as a discussion of the weather.

Another of the pitfalls of a practical guide is the tendency to blur subjective and objective analysis. In his reading of the Alice Munro story 'Five Points,' Ryan imagins how a formalist would view the character Maria's behaviour. But the following remark is more opinion than informed theory: 'Maria's "gross" appearance makes her convert sexual love into a financial transaction devoid of affection or feeling of any kind' (23). And so one finds two unsatisfying extremes in practical guides: catalogues of detail that overwhelm the reader and fail to inspire; and political appeals that may alienate readers who do not want to be indoctrinated. For those teachers intent on using a practical guide in the classroom, another alternative is Gregory Castle's *The Blackwell Guide to Literary Theory* (Blackwell, 2007). This is an interesting recent effort to integrate the potential merits of the practical approach into a standard introductory guide containing fairly extensive background information on theories and thinkers.

Overtly political theory guides can also mislead students into believing that every serious literary interpreter subscribes to a theoretical doctrine. Students of both literature and theory would benefit from the knowledge that there are contemporary critics who follow organizing principles that ignore theory altogether. James Wood, for example, approaches literature from a theological perspective. In the preface to his collection of literary essays, *The Broken Estate* (Jonathan Cape, 1999), he writes: 'It will become clear that I believe distinctions between literary beliefs and religious beliefs are important,' and he admits to being 'attracted to writers who struggle with those distinctions' (xv). He is fascinated by Melville because he saw 'that language helps to explain God and to conceal God in equal measure' (45) and is disturbed by Sir Thomas More, who, when he 'was not lying, [...] was dissembling' (4). Wood passes moral judgments in a manner that Raman Selden thought had come to a merciful end with the death of F.R. Leavis. Martin Amis is deemed important because 'He has produced a true literary slang, fattened on contemporary swill' (186); his 'greatest weakness as a writer is not that he is not innocent enough, but that he is too knowing.' According to Wood, 'the opposite of innocence is not knowingness, it is guilt' (192–3); clearly, the word 'innocent' has different connotations for Wood than it did for Selden, Brooker and Widdowson when they referred to the reading activity they hoped theory would undermine. John Updike is also chided for being a 'complacent' theological writer (227). Throughout, Wood is unapologetically subjective: a passage in Philip Roth is described as 'very moving, because it seems true, real, lifelike' (xiii). 'Pynchon's characters,' on the other hand, 'do not move us, because [...] they are serfs to allegory' (206). Wood likes what he likes and he has his reasons and, if one substitutes politics for religion, Wood is not so different from Selden, Ryan, or Eagleton in seeing the critic in the service of a higher ideal. 'We live in a world where the political

right acts globally and the postmodern left thinks locally,' (72) wrote
Eagleton in *After Theory*, and the solution to this situation is for cultural
theory to 'start thinking ambitiously once again' (73). Political literary
theory may have high ideals, but so does Wood's version of moral criticism, which continues to exist even if theorists ignore it in their guides.
While one expects to encounter strong, provocative opinions in the
writings of both literary critics and theorists, theory guide writers need
to restrain the impulse to offer such views and allow readers to make
their own decisions about theory.

The fact that theory guides can be divided into those that aim to
please and those with a political agenda reflects a schism within the
genre. Theory's inclusion on the English studies curriculum has resulted
in the creation of a commercial niche. Even the openly political guides
show an awareness of the consumer, as staid literary texts traditionally
used to demonstrate theory have been replaced by items from popular culture. Some guides which call themselves 'literary,' like Ryan's,
would be more appropriate for cultural studies than English studies. In
truth, theory and English studies are an awkward match. While novelists and poets are occasionally rehabilitated and added to the English
literary canon or, conversely, dropped as time alters reputations, the
theory canon operates in an entirely different way. The elite theorists of
today could have their ideas proven wrong at some future date and
become objects of ridicule within theory circles. While F.R. Leavis is
now used by theorists in negative example, to show how far theory
has progressed, it would be unimaginable for Dickens or Hardy to be
declared obsolete. Simply put, there is flux in the world of theory while
literary circles continue to value tradition. Theory's persistent declara-
tions of independence from literature ring hollow when theory guides
lean on the literary classics to explain themselves and it is ironic that
the most valuable questions raised by both theory and the guides are
unanswerable. What are we expected to do with theory once we have
learned it? Is the goal of theory merely self-perpetuation or can its lessons be applied outside the text? And could theory ever conceive of a
life without literature? Suppositions of super-readers and innocent readers undermined are also helpful in understanding theory's goals and
concerns. What looks like complacency in the tone of some contemporary theory guides may actually be defensive anxiety, for those who
claim that theory is an important field probably would not protest quite
so much if there was general agreement in English studies programs on
these very points. Likewise, the insistence that theory can manage on
its own may be nothing more than an expression of discomfort over

the realization that theorists would be at an analytical loss without literature.

Slim theory primers like Culler's and Barry's, which present theory as both entertaining and immediately comprehensible, offer a microcosmic version of the challenges theory faces. In spite of Barry's reassurances, theory is innately difficult. If it was not, there would be no need for theory guides. If theory really has been misunderstood and it is so easy to grasp, one wonders what was wrong with the defenders and interpreters who offered complex analyses in the 1970s. The explanation lies in marketing. Jonathan Culler has not recently seen the error of his erudite ways, but responded to a commercial need. While theory is not simple, the market dictates that it appear so. Many current theory guides make their subject approachable by eliminating jargon and relating theory to popular culture. But these guides are poor substitutes for the original texts and when students, who have been lead to believe that Derrida and Lacan are not really so difficult, encounter the original texts they may be surprised to find few references to popular culture and plenty of jargon.

If one assumes that a guide is necessary in theory courses, perspective is certainly a key factor to consider in the selection process. Perspective should not be confused with neutrality, but should be understood as a framework to shape students' existing knowledge of criticism and theory with suggestions about how to expand that knowledge. When a guide is used to supplement, rather than replace, original texts, there is no need for it to be exhaustive. While theory guides have become more accessible of late and there are concise, comprehensible options on the market, theory guide writers still assume too much. Without sufficient justification, they routinely make claims for theory's importance and although theory itself is almost invariably introduced through literary examples, guide writers insist that they do not need literature. With so many different guides now available which blending theory, literature, criticism and popular culture, the educational options can be as overwhelming as the theories themselves. The key question is not which of the competing theories we should take with us when we return to the text, but how to make students want to return to theory. This is why so many guides argue for either necessity or accessibility. Perhaps theory will really have gained its independence when it starts encouraging students to challenge the assumptions behind all branches of theory, and not just the widely denigrated ones like New Criticism. The expectation seems to be that students use guides to understand different schools of theoretical thought, then to apply theory to literature, but there is rarely any sense conveyed that it might be acceptable to disagree with theory. This is the problem with asking which theory we should take with us when returning to the text. One of the tacit goals of theory guides is to perpetuate the discipline while strengthening theory's foothold in English studies programs. Clearly theory's fight for territory with English studies is not over and this is why theory guide writers continue to warn teachers to remember their duty and talk of occupying theoretical zones. But the battle for adherents has taken an oddly commercial turn now and the image cut by Marxist theorists catering to the needs of the student consumer is somewhat incongruous. It would not be surprising to see more theory guides appearing in the near future which recognize that, in order to survive on the open and competitive theory guide market, they must recognize the student's rights as consumer.

Bibliography

Atkins, G. Douglas and Laura Morrow, eds. *Contemporary Literary Theory*. Massachusetts: Macmillan, 1989.

Baldick, Chris. *Criticism and Literary Theory 1890 to the Present*. London: Pearson, 2003. (1996).

Barry, Peter. *Beginning Theory*. 2nd edn. Manchester: Manchester University Press, 2002.

Belsey, Catherine. Critical Practice. London: Methuen, 1980.

Bennett, Andrew and Nicholas Royle. *Introduction to Literature, Criticism and Theory*. 3rd edn. London: Longman, 2004.

Bertens, Hans. *Literary Theory*. 3rd edn. London: Taylor and Francis, 2007.

Castle, Gregory. *The Blackwell Guide to Literary Theory*. Oxford: Blackwell, 2007.

Culler, Jonathan. *On Deconstruction: Theory and Criticism after Structuralism*. London: Routledge, 1983.

Culler, Jonathan. *Structuralist Poetics. Structuralism, Linguistics and the Study of Literature*. London: Routledge, 1975.

Culler, Jonathan. *Literary Theory: A Very Short Introduction*. Oxford: Oxford University Press, 2000.

Eagleton, Terry. *Literary Theory: An Introduction*. Oxford: Blackwell, 1983.

Eagleton, Terry. *After Theory*. London: Penguin, 2003.

Easthope, Antony. *Poetry as Discourse*. London: Methuen, 1983.

Groden, Michael, Martin Kreiswirth and Imre Szeman, eds. *The Johns Hopkins Guide to Literary Theory and Criticism*. 2nd edn. Baltimore: Johns Hopkins University Press, 2005.

Habib, M.A.R. *Modern Literary Criticism and Theory: A History*. Oxford: Blackwell, 2008.

Harland, Richard. *Literary Theory from Plato to Barthes: An Introductory History*. London: Macmillan, 1999.

Jefferson, Ann and David Robey, eds. *Modern Literary Theory: A Comparative Introduction*. 2nd edn. London: B.T. Batsford, 1988.

Klages, Mary. *Literary Theory: A Guide for the Perplexed*. London: Continuum, 2006.

Ryan, Michael. *Literary Theory: A Practical Introduction*. 2nd edn. Oxford: Blackwell, 2007.

Selden, Raman. *Practising Theory and Reading Literature: An Introduction*. Herfortshire: Harvester Wheatsheaf, 1989.

Selden, Raman, Peter Brooker and Peter Widdowson. *A Reader's Guide to Contemporary Literary Theory*. 5th edn. London: Longman, 2005.

Waugh, Patricia, ed. *Literary Theory and Criticism: An Oxford Guide*. Oxford: Oxford University Press, 2005).

Wood, James. *The Broken Estate*. London: Jonathan Cape, 1999.

7
From Theory to Practice: Literary Studies in the Classroom

Katherine Byrne

It seems to me impossible that we should teach literature at university level without also teaching the theory behind the subject. It is not my purpose in this chapter to defend theory against the humanist questions which inevitably accompany any discussion of its value to teaching: it is important to bear in mind the epistemological complexities posited by theory's undermining of the foundations of traditional literary study, but to consider that any university syllabus could not engage to acquaint its students with an understanding of theory is reductive, given the events of the last fifty years of scholarship. We can and should continue to debate the value of theory to literary studies, but in the meantime students need to be made aware of the critical thinking which has informed the study of their subject in particular and our understanding of our culture in general. For the student, the gains in understanding outweigh the difficulties posed by the process of learning such a problematic topic. They may not be convinced by every aspect or conclusion of the theory they are taught but the process of learning theory is to interrogate and examine aspects of our society, understanding and perception which may otherwise be overlooked and taken for granted. From our relationship with the language we all "use", to the meaning of the signs that surround us every day, down to the question of whether our minds are as free and independent as we would like to believe: modern theory undermines and challenges established views about the world in very important ways. However, the very breadth of its approach – what David Lodge (1988) has described as "nothing less than a totalizing account of human consciousness and human culture" – renders theory an unwieldy interdisciplinary monster which demands student engagement with history, politics, linguistics, psychology and anthropology, to name only a few. Added to this are difficulties in interpretation and understanding associated with the way in which theory is written about, and perhaps most fundamentally of all, the uneasy relationship which critical thinking has with other methods of teaching literary studies. All contribute to making the teaching of theory a problematic undertaking, yet a necessary one, and so this chapter will consider some of the issues, both philosophical and practical, which surround its place in our classrooms.

The most general problem is a curricular one. Teaching critical theory presents a "chicken and egg" type dilemma for the lecturer, regarding its place in the English syllabus. It is fundamental to an understanding of the study of literature and yet because of its difficulty is not an accessible entry level topic for most first year undergraduates. Hence most of our degree programmes begin with historical or genre-based modules and theory is either introduced later, perhaps in the second semester of the first year, and/or as a separate component, rather than a direct companion to, and in dialogue with, other courses. The issue here is that we are acknowledging that theory is a vital element in literary studies and yet the practice of our teaching often shies away from it, or attempts to conceal pieces of theory beneath other approaches to render it more palatable. It is impossible to engage effectively with texts without a working knowledge of literary theory and yet, because of the structure of their degree programmes, this is essentially what many students do on a regular basis.

I teach critical theory at a very basic introductory level for first year undergraduates, and on a more detailed and developed module for second years, but only the first of these is compulsory for all students and I have come to the conclusion that, in an ideal world, both would be taken by all. That is not to say that it is impossible to achieve sophisticated readings of texts, high essay and exam marks and indeed a good degree with only the most vague and sketchy grasp of the tenets of literary theory, for this happens all the time. Students do regularly adopt an author-centred approach to their interpretations of texts and follow this throughout their academic careers, to avoid too much involvement with the frightening notion of "theory". However, only engaging with the practice, rather than the theoretical perspectives, of literary studies results in students analysing, interpreting, and deconstructing literature without knowing the reasons, the logic and the history behind what they are doing, and why they are doing it. Without an awareness of New Criticism, Formalism and Structuralism, say, undergraduates feel that they are "reading things into" texts which aren't actually there, that much that they have been taught to look for in literature is actually nonsensical and irrelevant – namely because it may not be what the author intended. The whole nature of modern literary studies and its differing reader-orientated approaches seems to have no basis in reality for students schooled, both from A-level and from the world-view of culture in general, in author-centred criticism.

Chartering this move away from the figure of the author is one of the most fundamental yet problematic issues in the teaching of theory. This is especially pertinent given that so much university teaching continues to attach primary importance to the author and suggests that the most obvious way in to the interpretation of any text is via biographical criticism. There may be a handful of theory based modules on a university syllabus which suggest that there are other ways to approach texts, but the majority are organised around a historical perspective. Hence the majority of lectures begin with an account of the life, artistic preoccupations, and political agendas of the author, even though they often broaden out into wider – though still usually author-centred – historical contexts as well. So undergraduate syllabuses are therefore inherently and perhaps inevitably, contradictory: on the one hand they make students aware, in some classes, that the author can and should be removed from the reading of texts, and yet the dominant form of critical analysis we teach re-instates the author as the owner of the work and the central source of its meaning. These methods of teaching are also reflected and reinforced by the assessment process, of course. An undergraduate essay which disregarded the author entirely and did not include any information about their life, influences or intentions would be unlikely to get a good mark, simply because of the nature of most classes and courses and their learning strategies: lack of engagement with the author is usually regarded as lack of engagement with the most important element of the text.

Most of my students are themselves uncomfortable with the notion that a text can be considered as other than a product of its author and that there is no such thing as ownership of writing. Modern critical thinking may open up possible interpretations of a text, but its simultaneous rejection of the originality of words and images, and of the concept that there is one absolute meaning behind a text is hard to accept. All of these are innate, inbuilt cultural beliefs widely held in the outside world and therefore hard to shake off in the classroom. A recent seminar I taught following lectures on New Criticism and Formalism demonstrated this. It was an attempt to put the theory into practice via close reading of an "unseen" poem, which was to be analysed via its form and language. For this class I handed out copies of a piece, "Echoes" by contemporary Welsh poet R.S Thomas, with the authors name removed, and asked for comments upon it.

Deprived of the biographical or historical information they would have been equipped with at the beginning of such an exercise in any other class, my students struggled with the process of interpretation. In most undergraduate modules, readings of poems would be inevitably accompanied by details about the author and about his historical context. Hence I had essentially denied them their usual "ways-in". Despite this, however, they continued to dwell on, and speculate about, the intentions, gender, and political and religious beliefs of the author, even though they didn't know anything about him or her. The lack of a date or place of composition proved equally frustrating, and there was much speculation about these too. The poem was approached by them like a puzzle of origins which they had to solve, using its words and images as clues; a puzzle to which I alone, as the possessor of the relevant background information, had the key. In the process of their speculation about contexts, however, very interesting readings of the poem did emerge. Opinions were divided as to whether it could be considered a religious poem or a critique of religion; one student suggested it might be an eco-critical attack on global-warming, another agreed but pointed out that it seemed to be specifically about the destructive nature of industrial capitalism. Another suggested that a reference to skin colour constructed the poem as a post-colonial comment on Western civilisation. When questioned as to why they identified these readings, it emerged that the latter student was doing a module on post-colonial fiction and so was programmed to recognise any reference to "white" as politically charged; the former was currently writing an essay on green Shakespeare and was sensitive to any possibly eco-critical connotations. This seemed to me to beautifully illustrate some of the principles of reader-response theory and the ways in which readers construct their own meanings from texts, but when I put this to my class they were more concerned with whose interpretation was the "correct" one. They were able to appreciate that readers coming from alternative perspectives might interpret the poem differently, but there was within this the inescapable sense that only one of those readings could be right, and that information about the author was the only way to find out which, to get closer to the "true meaning" of the poem. This view was undermined, however, when I finally told them who the author was and gave them some biographical information about him, at the end of the class. Up to a point this did provide the answer the students were looking for: the knowledge that R.S Thomas was interested in wildlife and conservation issues validated for them the eco-critical reading of "Echoes", which no longer seemed a random guess based on a few words. More disturbingly for them, however, being told that he was a minister actually did not end the dispute we had been having about the kind of religious attitudes expressed by the poem. The class agreed that returning to the text knowing its author was a religious man did not resolve the undeniable tensions, ambiguities and questions about faith it contained: if anything it complicated interpretation further. This was an effective demonstration of the limitations of biographical criticism, then, but that had not been the initial object of the exercise, which was to make them function as New Critics and consider only the words on the page. The way in which most of our class time had been spent instead taught a different lesson, and one as valuable for me as for my students: that the desire to reconstruct the author's meaning and intention was intrinsic, fundamental, and extremely hard to overcome. Stanley Fish's famous experiences in *Is There a Text in this Class* revealed how his students, when they began to interpret a 'poem', appeared to be "following a recipe" which created the meaning which it set out to find. My experimentation with unseen material displayed that the principle ingredients in that interpretive recipe are the author and the historical context – and when deprived of these, my students become extremely uneasy about their culinary skills.

The debate about of the author is indicative of the greater difficulties regarding the integration of literary theory into the curriculum as a whole. Theory should, logically speaking, exist as the backbone and foundation of all literary studies. In practice, university courses merely dip into some, more readily applicable and accessible, forms of theory in some modules, as and when it may be beneficial and necessary. A women's writing module, for example, would probably engage with basic feminist theory, or one on the Condition of England novel might consider Marxist approaches. This seems like the most accessible or palatable way of getting students to work with critical concepts, given that it allows them to focus on specific areas and put ideas into practice, showing how they underpin readings of relevant texts. Hence this approach is accepted as the usual means of putting theory to work, but it may also have the effect of fragmenting and isolating these concepts from wider theoretical issues. For instance, the theory aspect of the women's writing class I teach familiarises students with the ways in which a feminist critic might approach a text, but does not 'validate' that approach by locating feminist criticism in the context of structuralist and reader-response theories which pre-figure the shift to the reader. This implies a certain falsity about the process of interpretation: some approaches seem legitimate enough, but others irrelevant in their premise.

My students seem to readily comprehend the need to examine, say, the representation of women in a text, as given that feminist thought justifies the notion that female characters provide an insight into gender roles and stereotypes. Without a knowledge of other critical theory, however, students are sceptical about feminist readings of texts which seem to be accepting and reinforcing patriarchal structures. Mary Shelley's *Frankenstein* provides a case in point, being a novel which appears to be only concerned with the masculine society it represents and in which women are marginal and largely unimportant characters. So my first-year students were unhappy with feminist readings of it which seemed to be unnecessarily prioritising and centralising gender issues which they considered incidental to the real concerns of the text. The question then arose as to whether feminist criticism was appropriate for this novel at all, and it was not an easy one to answer without recourse to psychoanalytic theory which might reveal the latent content of Shelley's work. Similar difficulties arise with almost any mode of reading, of course. My first-years were particularly sceptical about an eco-critical interpretation of *The Tempest*, which they considered a completely anachronistic imposing of our contemporary concerns and preoccupations on a play which seems to be only concerned with nature on a superficial level, and was written hundreds of years prior to our concerns with climate change and the environment. It is apparent that such a reading is difficult for students to accept without a knowledge of the theoretical perspectives – both linguistic and philosophical – which enable this kind of polemical reading of a text, irrespective of the alleged or assumed views of its author.

Teaching literary theory is also problematic in terms of the political dimension of many of its critical approaches. Many students are, perhaps understandably, confused about where the political agenda ends and the aesthetic appreciation of a text begins, and uneasy about the problematic value judgements implied by modern forms of criticism. Certain modes of reading are, for some undergraduates who are beginning their relationship with theory, irrevocably contaminated by their cultural resonances. In one notable essay the student appeared unable to lay aside their preconceived notions about communism in order to engage impartially with Marxist literary criticism because, in their view, communism was fundamentally flawed in its assumptions: therefore Marxist theory must be similarly tainted. This student rejected as reductive and politicised the notion that culture may be influenced by economic forces, and considered that literary interpretations based on such views are politically manipulative.

It is also difficult to teach perspectives which seem to have relevance only for the fiction of a previous era: students can appreciate the relevance of Marxist theory for the nineteenth-century realist novel, but insist that class struggle, for example, is not a defining part of the twenty-first century, western society in which they live. This does not prevent them engaging with Marxism in their work, of course, but it does mean that much of the philosophical impact and wider cultural applicability of such ideas is lost. Similar reservations are directed at feminist theory, which seems to articulate a narrative of paranoia and marginalisation which students accept may be appropriate in relation to the texts of the past, but which they do not consider relevant today. When discussing feminism's desire to reclaim a female literary canon in class recently, I was met by blank stares from those who felt that there was no inequality in the numbers of texts by women that they studied or read. They were prepared to accept that women authors had been neglected by previous generations of critics, but the prevalence of women-centred scholarship from the seventies onward seemed, for them, to have redressed the balance successfully enough to make such concerns appear unnecessary to today's readers. This was just an instance of the overwhelming sense from my students that feminist literary theory has done its work and is now redundant, a victim of its own success – simply because that was how they viewed feminism itself. My response was to draw their attention to contemporary social issues like unequal pay and sexual discrimination, and in a literary context, to the dominance of male writers in their own canonical university syllabus, in order to convince them that there might still be a need for feminist approaches. Marxism required the production of some current statistics about the continuing relationship between social class and university attendance, and hence between background and future earning potential. The sense I got here was that it is necessary for the teacher to validate the need for theory, before it can be successfully taught. Once again, however, one of the central purposes of teaching theory is to encourage students to question the truisms they hold about life and reality – given that theory itself questions the whole nature of that reality.

The question of how to teach the practical application of theory, putting it to work on literary texts, presents its own separate set of problems. I began teaching my second year critical theory class with no literary texts on the reading list, which enabled students to give almost exclusive time and attention to the writings of theorists themselves. The idea behind this was that essays by Saussure, Barthes, Lacan and others provide more than enough reading material for students to work with, and the focus of the module remains concentrated on engagement with that material. Additional primary texts risked rendering the workload for the module too great, and distracting students from the study of the theoretical approaches. This was successful up to a point – though reading theorists of course presents its own challenges, as I will discuss below – but it did mean that the emphasis of the course was on the teaching of critical concepts, rather than the demonstration and application of these concepts, as the means of doing this was not available. The onus was then on the students to apply theory to literary texts themselves, both via seminar discussion and especially via other modules in which they can put these ideas to the test. I learned that this was, however, only really achievable for a few very strong or theoretically-minded students, and that generally undergraduates did not like being deprived of the 'literary' in order to focus solely on the 'theory'. They found it much easier to grasp new ideas when demonstrated by readings of familiar texts: practical application, probably unsurprisingly, was key to understanding. Hence I have found it ultimately impossible to separate the two, and so demonstrate each mode of reading by putting it to work on a novel, poem or film. In order to lighten the workload a little, and to maintain the focus on reading and interpretation of the theorists, these texts are usually popular films and well known books. This ensures, at least, that students are not distracted by getting to grips with unfamiliar texts, given that the concepts they are studying are unfamiliar enough, and has the added advantage of allowing them to view texts they know already in fresh ways.

My basic "introduction to theory" class works on similar principles though the emphasis of the course is reversed. Students are presented with several key, canonical literary texts and are shown the different ways in which alternative critical perspectives can enable them to differently interpret that text. This has the effect of demonstrating "theory in action" and making the students adopt a hands-on approach which makes difficult concepts more accessible and readily graspable. It does, however, also mean that students at this level don't engage with the actual writing of theorists themselves, at all. This is at once necessary to the simplification of the course, to make it palatable for first years – but it is also the equivalent of teaching Shakespeare without actually picking up a play. Furthermore, the texts which are on the module are selected because they lend themselves well to alternative modes of reading, not for readability or enjoyment. For example, the core text, *Frankenstein*, can be interpreted very easily from Marxist, feminist, psychoanalytic and eco-critical as well as biographical perspectives, and there is a vast amount of secondary criticism available on it which covers all these approaches. This does not, however, endear it to the many first years who frequently find its long and rambling structure more impenetrable that the theoretical ideas they are putting to work on it. I am hence still continuing my search for accessible yet pedagogically appropriate alternatives.

Of course even when students are expected to engage in detail with the writings of theorists, and when the module is designed to facilitate and encourage that engagement, this does not guarantee that any meaningful engagement actually occurs. This is probably the most obvious and also the most fundamental difficulty facing the teacher of literary theory. Every week in my second year module I open a discussion workshop by asking my students if they can summarise the main points of the essay they had to read for that day's class, and almost without fail I am greeted with silence. Students who can happily grasp the concepts of theory after a lecture are unable to draw the same concepts from their private reading of the primary text. As Peter Barry puts it, the difficulty is not so much with the ideas themselves but with the often tortuous prose with which they are described:

> "literary theory is not innately difficult. There are very few inherently complex ideas in existence in literary theory...what is difficult, however, is the language of theory. Many of the major writers on theory are French, so that much of what we read is in translation, sometimes of a rather clumsy kind... [Barry, 1995:7]

We might add to this that the deliberate playfulness with language which characterises the writing of many post-structuralist theorists is enough, even without considering the translation issue, to render "the language of theory" impenetrable for many undergraduates. Many of the essays involved are written to display, among other things, the slipperiness of language and the problematic pursuit of meaning – not to be easily understood by the reader. It is therefore unsurprising that the undergraduate trying to come to terms with new ideas finds their expression opaque, and that they turn instead to the study guide. Yet some students find the language of Renaissance England difficult to understand and yet that would not be cited as justification for ceasing to explore Shakespeare's rhetoric: this would, effectively, be missing the whole point. So the challenge here is to familiarise students with the primary texts and encourage close readings of them, without too much reliance on the theory textbook. This can best be achieved, it seems to me, by the devotion of considerable amounts of class time to a line-by-line analysis of the most relevant passages of each theoretical text, so that students are directed at the most important ideas rather than trying to take in the whole essay or chapter, which usually engages with ideas and issues extraneous to the necessarily narrow focus of the class. This is a far-from perfect solution, of course: it is at once an extremely time-consuming process and a selective one which, it can be argued, prioritises small aspects of critical writings rather than over-viewing the whole. However it is hoped that such a "way in" to understanding important aspects of a theorist's writing may encourage the student to go back for the necessary repeated readings, and will also, in the long term, familiarise students with the ways in which theorists write, and as a consequence renders their work more accessible. I have also begun the practice of spending five minutes at the end of each class summarising the key ideas in the essay which has to be studied for next week, so that my students know what they are looking for before they begin to read.

It should be noted here that essays and extracts form the bulk of the theoretical material I teach. This is the way most critical theory courses are constructed and it allows students to buy a reader which contains the relevant material in one volume – or a reasonable selection of it at least – and to each week pursue a piece which is rendered more accessible by its brevity if not by its language. However while this approach makes sense for the most part it does have the effect of limiting the engagement with each topic and with the writings of each theorist. The brief extracts from Saussure's *Course in General Linguistics* as reproduced in Lodge's *Modern Criticism and Theory* (1988) are fragmentary at best, for example. Similarly Derrida's "Structure, Sign and Play in the Human Sciences", even though a complete essay in itself, is not a substitute for reading the whole of *Writing and Difference*, or *Of Grammatology*. Given both the time limitations implicit in any undergraduate module, and the aforementioned student resistance to reading difficult theoretical texts, there is very little that can be done about this issue, but we should be aware that studying such a small sample of a larger work does present a problem. In some cases it is rather like being expected to offer an analysis of *Jane Eyre* but not reading beyond the first chapter: the main ideas of the text are present in the sample essays the students are given, but the development of those ideas can't be appreciated without reading the rest. We should, at least, be supplementing the essays and extracts in critical theory Readers with important pieces from other texts, which might indicate the broader context of these, and provide some guidance as to the direction students might take to broaden and strengthen their understanding of a given topic.

Which collection of essays is selected as the core text for a theory module has a considerable impact on the teaching of that class, of course. There are quite a number of readers on offer, but some are more inclusive than others, and it is difficult to find all the desirable texts collected in one volume. Of course this does depend on personal choice and of the nature and aims of the course, but in most ways, the more comprehensive the better. The aforementioned David Lodge's *Modern Criticism and Theory* remains a classic for undergraduate purposes, and is a manageable and largely unintimidating size for students. It does, however, seem to me to be a little light on psychoanalytic theory and so cannot be used as a solitary set text on a module which wishes to teach Freud. I have supplemented my teaching with essays from Neil Badminton and Julia Thomas's *The Routledge Cultural Theory Reader,*which has an interesting, slightly alternative range of texts, and stimulating "suggestions for further reading" after each. This collection, however, is not designed or intended to be for undergraduate use in the same way, given that there is no introduction to or discussion of any of its essays, and that any attempt to order and organise them according to approach or theme is deliberately resisted. Such an ordering may indeed be "restrictive", as the editors suggest, but it is also, it seems to me, essential for those relatively new to theory[1], and I feel it has become a convention of this type of volume for that reason. Structuring is also an issue in Easthope and McGowan's *A Critical and Cultural Theory Reader,* which groups together essays under sections such as "ideology"and "subjectivity", which renders them rather inaccessible to students who are as yet unclear what these terms even mean. Probably the best collection I have used is the weighty *Literary Theory: An Anthology* (2nd edn) edited by Julie Rivkin and Michael Ryan. This impressed me with its seemingly all-encompassing approach, and also by the introductions to each section – though not to each essay, annoyingly – which are detailed and informative, if pitched slightly high, as is so often the case, for the theory beginner. And also worth considering as an interesting accompaniment to any of these Readers is K.M. Newton's *Theory Into Practice* (1992), which is a collection of readings of literary texts by well-known critics, which offers an insight into different theoretical perspectives put into action. In order to work in a seminar these essays require that the students are familiar with their literary subjects, however and hence some are more workable than others.

When they are based on a text on the syllabus they can function as a revealing demonstration of theory in action. Elaine Showalter's reading of *Hamlet*, for example, displayed a feminist approach to a play which my students had studied, without engaging with theory, the previous semester.

Given the problems involved with the commonly-used primary texts I mention above, then, as well as the difficulties involved in understanding the language of theory, it is unsurprising that teaching in this area does depend to a considerable extent on the use of the study guide. Hence I intent to conclude by devoting some attention here to an examination of their respective strengths and weaknesses of those most widely used by my classes. The very obvious but important point to begin with is that even though guides are of course no substitute for reading the original texts, they are very frequently used as such by students. One of the most common pitfalls of the undergraduate essay on theory is that it often quotes heavily from the secondary sources rather than the primary material, so that the end product of an essay on structuralism, say, appears to be more of a exploration of Jonathan Culler or Peter Barry's ideas on the topic than it is about structuralism itself. This is of course not an easy problem to solve, though it can be to some degree alleviated by ensuring that students are familiar with the critical texts, as discussed above. The difficulty is compounded, however, by the fact that my students tend to become attached to and focus on just one study guide and do not even generally compare and contrast the view of different secondary critics, which would enable them to offer a wider perspective on the relevant topics. This is mainly because even though there is now a plethora of theory guidebooks most of these so-called "introductory" texts are simply not introductory enough for the average first and second-year student. Hence the most readable of those available are over-used in isolation by the majority of undergraduates. Barry has a ubiquitous presence in student essays simply because *Beginning Theory* is probably the most user-friendly guide: it is readable mainly because it is aware of the linguistic and explanatory challenges involved in writing about theory and, unlike other guides, it does not forget that it is directed at a student audience. As a result it is quite conversational in tone and gives the sense of being in dialogue with the reader, rather than being straightforwardly and drily didactic. Jonathan Culler's *Literary Theory: A Very Short Introduction* (1997), in contrast, seems less popular with my students, some of who complain that its brevity is not, in this case, a substitute for directness and simplicity, and that Culler's prose resembles too closely the language of the theorist rather than the language of the simple study guide – even though the short and snappy nature of the text makes it appealing to others.

The structure of many of the guides also makes them inaccessible in certain ways. It is desirable, for an introductory volume, for students to be able to quickly find a discussion of the mode of reading they are studying and to be able to visit that section without ploughing through the whole book. It makes life easier if they can identify at a glance the definition and practice of each critical approach, especially for assessment purposes when they are expected to differentiate between them. Barry's clear chapter headings and divisions (and his summing-up, "what critics do" sections throughout) facilitate this: so too does Ann Jefferson and David Robey's *Modern Literary Theory* (1986), which although now out of print is still very useful. Both these volumes move more or less chronologically through the history of modern theory, beginning with Formalism and New Criticism and devoting a chapter to each critical approach. Students find this helpful in that it gives a sense of the historical context and the evolving nature of theory, and indicates the ways in which one critical school of thought may give rise to, or even displace, another. This does assume, however, that the whole book is read from start to finish, which, clearly, given the "tourist" approach taken towards most textbooks, will not always be the case. Approaches like Hans Bertens in *Literary Theory: The Basics* (2001), another fairly readable guide, takes a similar historical approach but makes it harder on the reader to dip into and out of the text. His exploration of structuralism is, for example, divided into "Reading for form" sections one and two, the first dealing with pre 1960-criticism – Propp and Jakobson – and the second with 1950–75. This is not without its usefulness but does not make things easy for an impatient, time-limited student reader who is new to literary theory and hence less interested in following the history of the subject than they are in the central issues and ideas with which they have to engage. Culler's *Introduction* takes an interesting departure from the historical approach via its posing of important questions and answers about theory, but again this seems more designed toward the slightly more advanced student who is reading at a leisurely pace to test and develop their knowledge, rather than the confused beginner.

While these guides differ in terms of accessibility and style of presentation, most of them do contain an overview of literary theory which is comprehensive and useful provided it is considered with specific reference to the primary texts themselves and not as a substitute for them. However, content-wise one of the most significant difficulties common to many of the texts I've discussed above is their near-neglect of reader-response criticism and reception theory, and indeed something of a reluctance to engage directly with the role of the reader at all. Bertens discusses Barthes's "Death of the Author" in only three lines, for example, and Wolfgang Iser is not present in any of the three. The shift in allegiance and focus from author to reader that has occurred during the last half century is of course considered in reference to the critical theories it prefigures, but is somewhat taken for granted by these texts – whereas for the early stage undergraduate this is the most important, intriguing areas of modern theory, as I have indicated. This does result in a chunk of important theory being missing from these guides. James Knowles's chapter in Bradford's *Introducing Literary Studies* (1996) is one of the few useful examinations of reader-response criticism which is compact and easy to read, and which includes analysis of the writings of Iser and Stanley Fish. Raman Selden's *Practicing Theory and Reading Literature: An Introduction* (1989) has a chapter on reader-response but as with the rest of this volume this section is more focussed on illustrating theory of via examples from, and discussions of, specific literary texts than discussing the implications of the theory itself. This is an approach with which students find useful only if they have already integrated the theoretical concept they are studying and wish to see those concepts put to work – so it is not an ideal medium for introducing topics, despite its title. Mario Klarer's *An Introduction to Literary Studies*, although a general textbook to introduce first year students to the study of English with just one section on "theoretical approaches to literature", does include a useful piece on Reader-response. Klarer also has a nice clear way of organising theory, which is divided up here into reader-based approaches, author-based approaches, and so on. Undergraduates have complained to me that it is difficult to remember which mode of reading "fits in" where, and which have certain aspects in common. Klarer includes a diagram of "theoretical schools subsumed under four basic rubrics" which goes some way towards solving this problem. This is especially pertinent given that my students always fall upon any diagram or table with enthusiasm, and so I too have embraced them as a means of clarifying and ordering the material, even at the risk of making it reductive. Visual representations also play a useful part in Chris Hopkins's *Thinking About Texts*, another introductory textbook which is not designed for explicitly theory courses but which engages with the relationship between author and reader in very interesting ways. Moreover, unlike Barry, and many others, this includes a discussion and close reading of Barthes's "Death of the Author" which I have found very helpful in class.

Perhaps the most detailed and comprehensive study guide I've used, however, is Waugh's *Literary Theory and Criticism,* which is a collection of explanatory essays with something on pretty much all the important aspects of literary theory. This really does feel like it covers all the bases, and each topic is introduced at the beginning, and thoroughly discussed. Of course as the chapters are written by different authors some are more readable than others, however, and some lack the direct simplicity of Barry; indeed, this volume is generally too dense and hefty to be non-intimidating for a beginner. Furthermore, a number of the chapter headings are based around the names of critics rather than the schools of thought associated with them. This seems to assumes either that the reader has some prior knowledge of these figures and the ideas they represent, or that they are not simply looking for some quick information on a specific topic. These are both dangerous assumptions to make about undergraduates, but are ones shared by many supposedly introductory texts. Waugh's guide is, once a way in is found, better than most, but the ideal literary theory textbook for beginners, like the ideal approach for teaching theory at university, is yet to be written.

So, given the innumerable difficulties involved in teaching theory, how could it be more successfully and accessibly integrated into our university syllabuses? Most of the problems I have addressed here do not have small and simple solutions: instead they are fundamental obstacles which the individual lecturer would find next to impossible to overcome. It is only really by shifting our whole approach to literary theory that it could become an established and accepted part of English in the classroom. This necessitates, however, a move away from the traditional means of teaching literary studies, a abandonment, even, of traditional author-based, historically located criticism. It is really only a complete shift in emphasis to the reader and the work which would utilise, clarify and put into action the principles of modern thinking. This of course has implications for what is taught as well as the way it is taught: if we move away from author-centred criticism we also must to some extent move away from the traditional literary canon and its domination by the select, still predominantly male, chosen few. The lives, politics and intentions of the great literary men of history whom we spend so much of our time studying would become less relevant. Of course to some degree this has occurred already, in that most universities now have components of their teaching devoted to non-canonical texts, but this is almost always a small part of curricula full of familiar names. Those modules which challenge the established ways of teaching literature – by teaching lesser-known authors, by moving away from historical approaches – are still seen as maverick, quirky choices, at odds with the literary mainstream.

Similarly, it is because of the rarity value of theory, the way it is seen to be challenging established ways of approaching texts, that makes theory difficult to teach. It is generally viewed as a necessary evil which must be squeezed on, with time-restrictions, to a syllabus which spares ample time for traditional approaches, and so it is bound to be perceived as difficult, unpopular, and controversial. In practice students, once they get past the initial difficulties, find theory useful and worthwhile perservering with. One of my students told me recently that they had been unsure about choosing my theory module but at the end of the semester were glad they had done so, because it was different from the others they had done as part of their degree, and it had encouraged them to challenge their established ways of thinking. As a lecturer it was very gratifying to hear this, but it would be much better to have no reason to say it: not only should theory not be different, new, but also it should not be the only undergraduate module which challenges students to think in different ways.

Bibliography

Barry, Peter. *Beginning Theory*. Manchester: Manchester University Press, 1995.
Badminton, Neil and Thomas, Julia (eds). *The Routledge Critical and Cultural Theory Reader*. London: Routledge, 2008.
Bertens, Hans. *Literary Theory: The Basics*. London: Routledge, 2001.
Bradford, Richard (ed.) *Introducing Literary Studies*. Hemel Hempstead: Harvester, 1996.
Culler, Jonathan. *Literary Theory: A Very Short Introduction*. Oxford: Oxford University Press, 1997.
Easthope, Anthony, and McGowan, Kate (eds). *A Critical and Cultural Theory Reader*. Open University Press, 2004.
Fish, Stanley. *Is There A Text In This Class?*. Cambridge: Harvard University Press, 1980.
Hopkins, Chris. *Thinking about Texts*. Basingstoke: Palgrave, 2001.
Jefferson Ann, and David Robey (eds) *Modern Literary Theory: A Comparative Introduction*. London: Batsford Academic and Educational, 1986.
Klarer, Mario. *An Introduction to Literary Studies*. London: Routledge, 2004.
Lodge, David. *Modern Criticism and Theory: A Reader* . Harlow: Addison Wesley Longman, 1988.
Newton, K. M. *Theory Into Practice: a Reader in Modern Literary Criticism*. Basingstoke: Macmillan, 1992.
Rivkin, Julie and Ryan, Michael. *Literary Theory, An Anthology* (2nd edn) Oxford: Blackwell, 2004.
Selden, Ramon. *Practising Theory and Reading Literature: An Introduction*. London: Harvester Wheatsheaf, 1996.
Waugh, Patricia. *Literary Theory and Criticism*. Oxford: Oxford University Press, 2006.

8
At Home in theory? Teaching One's Way Through the Theory at Home

Madelena Gonzalez

France is generally thought of as the home of Theory with a capital T, the country that spawned such intellectual giants as Althusser, Barthes, Bourdieu, Derrida, Foucault, Lacan, with Paris the vibrant epicentre of a movement that revolutionised the teaching and study of literature in the last few decades of the twentieth century. However, it is in the home of Theory that this most contentious object is the least subject to scrutiny as such. Theory is everywhere, one might almost say, part of the very fabric of life for anyone who anxiously walks the floor of academe, but its presence is implicit rather than explicit in the classroom and it is almost never taught as a subject per se at either under- or postgraduate level.

I intend to examine here some of the historical and sociological reasons for a silence that may appear little short of deafening to those on the outside, looking in, who are unfamiliar with the constraints of a system geared to producing the well wrought urn of the institutionalised textual commentary or Cartesian 'essay' – the word is hardly appropriate in the French context[1] – in order to guarantee success in the prestigious *concours*, the highly competitive exams which are the passport to intellectual deference and a life-time job as a servant of the state, in the excellent public-sector high-school system.[2] If the French academy seems to have remained paradoxically immune from the Theory course, that staple of university education in the Arts Faculties of the English-speaking world, introduced thanks to the onslaught of what David Lodge (1986: p. vii) once termed, 'Continental structuralism', it is also because of the degree to which Theory is a way of life, as well as of literature, on its home turf, not just one element of Bourdieusian cultural capital for university teachers, but a quasi-religious belief or scientific faith in a certain method of analysis of the word as world, to the exclusion of all others, till death do us part.

127

In such an environment, choosing to teach Theory as a subject ranging from Structuralism through Marxism and Feminism to Queer Studies and Ecocriticism, as suggested by textbooks such as Peter Barry's *Beginning Theory: An Introduction to Literary and Cultural Theory*, is, on the one hand, a risky and intellectually suspect enterprise, subversive of the established academic order.[3] The charge of ideological naivety or irresponsible relativism could easily be laid at its door, thanks to the grouping of so many disparate approaches under the vast umbrella of 'Theory'. 'Doing' Structuralism in week two and moving blithely on to Poststructuralism in week three, without examining in detail several decades of philosophical background and reading all the foundational texts may be, after all, only another form of 'Theory tourism' (Cunningham 2002, p. 28). Finally, the Theory course might simply be considered misguided and irrelevant to the needs of French students, expected to perform their textual tour de force at the hurdle of the aforementioned *concours* without the unnecessary hindrance of a theoretical conscience of what they are doing. I hope to show that, despite the odds stacked against such a choice, there are, after all, some benefits to be gained from speaking up within the context I will be describing.

A love that dare not speak its name: the silent politics of science

'To understand a science it is necessary to know its history' (Auguste Comte)

My first experience of a French approach to teaching literature was in the late eighties, when, fresh from happy memories of what David Lodge (1986: p. viii) calls 'bland, old-fashioned tutorials' in a respectable red-brick university, I arrived in a third-year undergraduate class on the nineteenth-century novel in the English department of a French university. The shock was considerable. Having been taught to espouse a vaguely Leavisite attitude to literature, based on sensibility and an individual response, I was suddenly confronted with a totally alien approach to what was now being called the 'text'. At first bewildered, and frankly terrified, – the teacher seemed to be doing something very bizarre and technical, in fact, to my mind, unliterary, to a passage in Gaskell's *North and South* – I experienced a gradual epiphany as I understood that he had a system for textual analysis and that it 'worked'. His analysis was based on a series of binaries in the text, male and female, light and dark, hard and soft, etc. woven together in a subtle, but seemingly irrefutable, explanation for every single component of the passage under scrutiny, and backed up with an impressive barrage of technical terms and linguistic terminology. Both shocked and excited by such a masterly display of authoritative exhaustiveness, and thrilled to have this impressive tool at my disposal, I quickly became an avid devotee, unquestioningly following the model and earning praise for doing so. The method was applied to all the books on the syllabus and scored top marks every time.

The point of this anecdote is, that at no point did the teacher, whose absolute conviction of his rightness, let it be said in passing, was refreshingly welcome to the hazy impressionist that I then was, make clear what method he was using and why. Many years later, I understood that I had experienced Structuralism, but the word was never pronounced in that class or, indeed, in any other. One of the reasons for such silence, which I will discuss in more detail later on in this essay, is of course the following: if presuppositions and positions are not stated, they have a crushingly inevitable authority which it is difficult to attack, precisely because they *are* unstated: ours is not to reason why the text is a closed system, but to accept that it is. This brings me to the other point of the anecdote, which is to show the importance of method in a country where 'methodology' is frequently found on the syllabus, even if Theory is not. In order to give an idea of what is meant by this term, I will start by referring to one of the numerous textbooks on the subject, written by a professor of French literature at a university in northern France:

> The efforts that you make to master the mechanisms of the essay are particularly worthwhile, for you will be judged on method as much, if not more, than on your knowledge of the syllabus. ... Knowing all there is to know about Racine is of no use for an essay on Zola. Methodological proficiency, on the other hand, will always be of use to you, for it remains fundamentally unchangeable.[4] (Rohou 1993, p. 143)

Thus methodology is a passport to success, providing, of course, one chooses the right method, as Antoine Compagnon (1998: p. 10) does not fail to point out:

> It is impossible today to succeed in a competitive state exam without mastering the subtle distinctions and the jargon of narratology. A candidate who is unable to say whether the text in front of his eyes is 'homo-' or 'heterodiegetic', 'singulative' or 'iterative', 'internally focalised' or 'externally focalised', will simply not succeed, just as, in

former times, one had to be able to distinguish between analocuthon and hypallage and know Montesquieu's date of birth. In order to understand the specificity of higher education and research in France, one must always bear in mind the historical dependency of the university on the requirements of the competitive teaching exams.

Compagnon's plain speaking is rare and of course he is secure in his prestigious position at the Sorbonne and his international career as a visiting professor at Columbia. His book, *Le Demon de la théorie* (1998), is an exercise in scepticism that aims to dissect, meticulously, the unspoken theoretical assumptions of the French academy and pit them against what he calls 'common sense', in a move that will be recognisable to those familiar with Valentine Cunningham's *Reading After Theory*. The quote chosen also suggests another interesting factor in the apparent precedence of methodology over Theory: the existence of a veritable 'industry' in textbooks, handbooks and coursebooks, geared to explaining how to succeed in the state exams, which may earn their authors a welcome celebrity among colleagues and students and even some royalties. They may not have the intellectual prestige of 'real' research, but they are nevertheless instruments of cultural power, 'normalising' and 'canonising' a certain type of knowledge, as Bourdieu (1984: p. 135) explains.

The ultimate aim of the cult of methodology is to transmit a foolproof system of literary analysis, a set of technical keys to open textual doors, as another handbook makes clear:

> modern rhetoric ... is not concerned with contents ('meaning' we would say these days); it is not a hermeneutics. ... our poetics is what a culture of the commentary can integrate under the guise of rhetoric. It presents itself as an efficient means of reading, when, in fact, it is an efficient means of production. The text is turned into a machine to be taken apart from the same angle that will allow it to be put together again subsequently, to be reproduced. (Ravoux Rallo 1999, p. 129)

The idea of reproducibility is important because it implies that the method adopted has to be strictly codified in order to be transmittable, and that this is the source of its success, as another commentator remarks: 'It is hardly surprising that formalist criticism has triumphed in higher, as well as secondary, education: contrary to interpretative criticism which is more totalising and differentiated, it is transmittable'

(Thumerel 2002, p. 168). Out of the numerous French textbooks I consulted when researching this essay, the majority called energetically for 'method', 'technique', a 'scientific approach', 'rigour', 'mastery' (a term repeated in the examples chosen above), either explicitly, or implicitly, harking back to Roland Barthes' call for a 'science of literature' in 1966, glossed by a professor of comparative literature as follows:

> What was known as *nouvelle critique* in the sixties and caused so much debate was in fact the affirmation of a return to the text. Thus was born what Michel Charles called 'speculative rhetoric', poetics, narratology, and all the critical approaches that tend to consider the text as a 'machine', the workings of which must be analysed, by creating instruments for the examination of those internal workings. ... It is not a question of commenting on the text, it is a question of describing the way it functions, by elaborating a literary terminology; it is a question of ordering it, of closing it off, of theorising it. (Ravoux Rallo 1999, p. 95)

The choice of the word 'poetics' is also highly significant, for, as another guide to criticism and literary theory points out, 'poetics is an internal approach towards literature ... it raises itself up against interpretation ... it is a refusal of history ... it turns away from author, environment and context generally' (Cabanès and Larroux 2005, pp. 342– 3).

In order to verify if this impression of methodological obsession were indeed general, I also set up a questionnaire for colleagues teaching literature at university level, in which I asked them to define their methods and then comment upon them. All claimed that they used a variety of approaches, but on closer examination, when asked to actually name those approaches, they invariably put Structuralism, Semiotics and Narratology at the top of the list, as in the following example:

> The study of literature for students preparing the competitive exams requires a very detailed knowledge of the context and the generic category of the work, and an in-depth analysis of the text. No particular critical approach is favoured, but all the conceptual and analytical tools that might help to elucidate the meaning of the text are welcome. My critical approach is at the crossroads between philology and literary criticism, drawing on the immense variety of methods and tools available to them. I favour, among others, structuralist, stylistic, narratological and semiological analysis.

Again it is worth noticing the repetition of the words 'tool' and 'analysis' and the insistence on 'detailed' and 'in-depth'. It is clear from these examples that the spectre haunting the French university system is not only that of the state exams, comprising the compulsory ritual of the 'essay' and the in-depth textual commentary, both elevated to canonical status, but also a seemingly inexorable formalism. The centrality given to the text, particularly to specific passages of texts, singled out for close analysis, is a key aspect which makes the teaching of literature in France from the *lycée* onwards very different from pedagogical practice in the English-speaking world. This is especially true now that New Criticism has been lost in the mists of time and replaced by a largely poststructuralist consensus, as Cunningham (2002: p. 71) would seem to imply, in his discussion of key elements of contemporary theoretical terminology:

> In Theory's view, the text is not all there. ... You get this kind of vision only by courtesy of many Theory assumptions ... via the post-Saussurean notion of perpetual difference, the alleged perpetual elusiveness of the signifying chain, the idea of the textual *mise en abyme* instead of the *mise-en-scène*, the ratting on the idea of presence, the interest in textual marginality and borders and decentrings, the push away from fullness, or *pleroma*, to its edgy, marginal, emptied, emptying opposite.

What Cunningham is describing here is at odds with what actually goes on in literature classes at a French university, for his *bête noire* seems to be mostly a Derridean poststructuralist mindset which would tend to go *against* the formalist dominant of an academy that strives consistently for closure and still sees Saussure as a contemporary coordinate, rather than as a stage on the way to the nirvana of 'an endless play of signifiers' (Cunningham 2002, p. 80).

It is obvious that close textual analysis works best on 'scientific' premises, as the New Critics themselves averred, and this is why it is almost exclusively of Formalist origin in France. For the over forty-fives, it will be largely influenced by the early Barthes, Structuralism, Semiotics and Russian Formalism via Jakobson, Propp and Greimas and, of course, by Saussure himself; for the under forty-fives it will bear the mark of Genettian narratology and the taxonomic tendency, evoked by Compagnon. For all categories, there will be a strong linguistic bias, latterly via Benveniste, involving a high level of linguistic expertise and technical vocabulary. Of course, the continuing success of Structuralism and its various avatars in France also has its roots in history, for, the Practical and New Critical schools of thought never having darkened its shores, Barthes' cry for a new form of criticism in the sixties was seen as a much-needed response to the bourgeois preciosity and pretention of academic erudition, represented by Gustave Lanson and his heirs:

> We can assert that the task of criticism is purely formal: ... it is not to discover in the author's work something 'sacred', something 'profound', something 'secret' which may have gone unnoticed hitherto ... but, like a good carpenter trying to fit together two parts of a complicated piece of furniture, simply to adapt the language available to us now, to the language, that is to say, to the formal system, elaborated by the author in his own time. (Barthes 1964, p. 256)

According to some, this was little short of a 'Copernican revolution' (Thumerel 2002, p. 83), to which many have continued to remain faithful, as a symbol of progressive, enlightened, and democratic thinking, as opposed to the forces of elitist obscurantism.

What is clear from this brief presentation is the centrality of the text as an object to be analysed, according to a fixed system, and the necessity of producing this analysis to the satisfaction of a rigid set of criteria. From first through to third year, literature classes are geared to this aim, as are some Masters seminars, which may espouse the format of what is required by the state examination papers in order to evaluate the students who sign up for them. Thus the student will furnish either a textual commentary, an essay, or an oral presentation on the model of the *leçon* at the *agrégation* (the most prestigious of the exams), which is in fact an oral version of the essay, in short a demonstration, ideally of implacable logic; it is not merely an exercise in rhetoric, but a quasi scientific argument, based on intellectual rigour and objectivity. All these factors help to explain why, in France, Theory, as understood elsewhere, has been institutionalised as Formalism. Poststructuralism is not considered useful as a method of textual analysis, precisely because it is simply NOT a method of textual analysis in the academic sense, but a philosophy, as Johannes Angermüller (2007: p. 28) so cogently remarks, in his comparative study of contemporary theory in France and Germany: 'The presence of Derrida in the German field of discourse analysis never fails to surprise French observers who are accustomed to rigid distinctions between different branches of academic learning like philosophy and the humanities, the latter having given rise to discourse analysis in France.' Although Derrida may be referred to in passing, he is largely irrelevant to the concerns of the average student and the Grand Narrative of Theory remains hidden behind a utilitarian and functional vision of literary analysis. The movement from text to discourse never really got off the ground in France, despite the presence of Derrida and Foucault, or only in the linguistic-orientated sense of discourse analysis, Benvenistean 'utterance' and thus, further technical precision rather than relativity, as Angermüller explains (2007: p. 24): 'In contrast to the word *text* ... the notion of *discourse* has always remained surrounded by a considerable terminological vagueness, which has created a gap between the *theories* of discourse, characterised by a strong intellectualism and the *analysis* of discourse as practised in France, which has had very few repercussions internationally (among a non-French readership).'

Poststructuralism, as understood by the English-speaking world, remains virtually invisible in the country which gave birth to it and indeed the label itself is rarely used, as one of its founding fathers himself explained in 1983 when asked to situate himself in relation to it: 'although I can see very clearly that the problem posed by what was called Structuralism was largely that of the subject and the refashioning of the subject, I fail to see what type of consideration could be a common concern of those who are being called Postmodernists and Poststructuralists' (Foucault 2001, p. 1266). This is perhaps not as paradoxical as one might at first suppose, if figures such as Derrida and Foucault are seen as philosophers, first and foremost, rather than as having much to do with literature per se. Thus the prolific progeny of the poststructuralist turn and its obsession with discourse, now frequently grouped under Cunningham's 'sheltering canopy of "Theory"' (18), and accommodating such offshoots as post-colonialism, Queer studies, New Historicism, to name but a few, have no hold and very little visibility within a system where the term 'Cultural Studies' does not even have an official translation and is virtually unknown. When analysing such approaches in front of a class, of which more later, one cannot but help be struck by their seeming irrelevance to the reality of literary studies in France. In the next section, I will attempt to explain how the French academy's rigid adherence to the models mentioned earlier is not mere critical gesturing or a supposedly neutral scientism, but a distinct ideological positioning with the dominant models seeking to suffocate rival models, which might undermine them and invade their territory, and sometimes causing violent clashes as a result.

Following which model? Turf wars and the usual suspects

'It is more of a business to interpret the interpretations than to interpret the texts' (Michel de Montaigne)

As an inexperienced postgraduate teaching assistant in the early nineties, struggling through a doctorate on contemporary British fiction, I was asked to take on a first-year tutorial on English literature as a complement to the lecture on the subject which was compulsory for all students. I was handed a booklet with definitions, examples, extracts and a large helping of stylistic and structuralist wisdom. Obviously, this presented no problem to one who was now schooled in such matters. However, the difficulties began when all the teachers of the module concerned, met to discuss the grading of the exam, a textual commentary. It soon became abundantly clear that the convenor of the module, one of my former teachers, had assumed a consensus that simply did not exist, and, to my horror, I discovered that some of the other teachers had not even been using the booklet! The meeting dragged on for hours, becoming increasingly heated, as it became increasingly obvious that we just could not agree on what was acceptable. Eventually, raised voices and slammed doors signalled the impossibility of continuing. A more experienced colleague, taking pity on the neophyte that I then was, dazed and confused by the virulence of the exchanges witnessed, explained to me that this was merely part of a long-standing feud between a Lacanian vanguard and what she called a 'rearguard action based on outmoded forms of Structuralism'. I blush now to think of my ignorance, but that ignorance had been fostered by the unspoken presuppositions blithely used to bolster up my own critical approach. I was well aware of what to do and how to do it, as well as what not to do, but was still not sure why I was actually doing it. Unfortunately, this is not just an isolated example of the ignorance of an innocent abroad, for the majority of French students writing their Masters dissertations today are equally unaware of the theoretical stance they unquestioningly espouse, whatever it may be.

This anecdote serves to illustrate some key points in the negotiation of a territory for theory in France. Even if overt claims to truth are not asserted, a method will stake its claim to fame on its validity, as the early Barthes (1964: p. 255) advised: 'the task of criticism is not to find "truth", but only "validity". In itself, a language is not true or false, it is either valid, or it is not'. One of the ways of vouchsafing such validity is articulating one's theory in an elaborately technical language which aspires to the scientific and thus requires a high level of competence to combat, as a former student, now turned critic and writer, explains: 'When I understood that ... the only business of the novel was to speak of the novel, literature seemed to me a universe as complete and as coherent as that of mathematics ... I understood that this form of criticism [Structuralism] was strong enough to be able to appropriate any text' (Darrieussecq 2005, pp. 19–21). The more scientific the model, the greater its claims to authenticity in a Cartesian universe where no empty spaces, let alone poststructrualist aporia, are allowed, as a literature professor at the Sorbonne explains:

> scientific criticism, that practised by 'professors' ... fulfils two essential functions: the first is to maintain the literary past present in our minds, the second is to furnish a description and an interpretation of this past which the recourse to other contemporaneous texts, but also to the humanities, renders more precise, more technical, more scientific. Even if the butterfly specialist is attracted to his objects of study because of his consciousness of their beauty, the description he gives of them ... has no need to be beautiful, simply exact and complete. (Tadié 1987, p. 13)

The last two adjectives used are significant for my discussion of theoretical dominance here. The idea of exactness suggests science of course, but also doctrinal certainty, and formalism is consistently keen to assert its superiority by comparing itself favourably with the less rigorous methods which it scorns: 'Where empiricism, impressionism, paraphrase, the separation of form and content once dominated, as well as overly realistic explanations which, by relying on sources, author and context, distorted the essence of the text, its substance, structuralism proposes a *method*, which is not only *rigorous*, but *universal*' (Rohou 1993, p. 94). The author's use of italics is telling, not to mention the inflated claim to universalism, and the ternary rhythm of the sentence gives an almost incantatory nature to his syntax, reminiscent of biblical revelation.

All the dominant theoretical models in France share the same totalising ambition and use methodological terrorism to bolster up their intellectual states within the academic state: 'Thus theory reacts against the practices that it judges atheoretcial or anti-theoretical. By doing so, it often turns them into scapegoats' (Compagnon 1998, p. 19). Scorn for rival churches, especially the antichrist of empiricism, is a way of securing hard-won territory, staking the claim to canonicity, as well as establishing an index of the forbidden. Gérard Genette, the high priest of narratology, recognises the possibly venal sins of his creation, 'an irritating aspect of soulless technicality', its 'pretension to be a ground-breaking science', while, in the same breath, proposing it as the antidote to interpretative criticism, that 'regrettable mixture of speculation and empiricism', and finally absolving it, in the name of its 'high degree of sophistication and methodological complexity', as well its respect for the 'mechanisms' of the text (see Genette 1983, p. 7). The myth of purity, the disappearance of the referent and the triumph of autotelism are among the articles of faith needed for the smuggling-in of a covert formalist ideology: 'Structural criticism is pure of all the transcendent reductions of Psychoanalysis, or Marxism, for example, but exerts in its own way, a sort of internal reduction, gliding over the substance of the work in order to reach the skeleton below' (Genette 1966, p. 158). The examination of the skull beneath the skin, however, suggests a critical fantasy of closure, accompanied, perhaps, by a whiff of immortality. If, as the historicist and hermeneuticist Jean Starobinski (1920 –) claims, 'Structuralism is a refutation of the easy dramaturgy of the absurd' (qtd. in Bergez *et al.* 1999, p. 188), then it may indeed be an aspiration to transcendence, camouflaged as immanence, keeping its metaphysics warm, thanks to a linguistic alibi.

As Compagnon rightly asserts, criticism and theory in France, are first and foremost, oppositional and polemical, and the eclecticism or '*de-facto* pluralism' so wittily described by Cunningham (p. 27) as characteristic of 'Theory's multiplex of approaches ... shop around; roll your own; pick' n' mix ... its espousal of multivalence and multiculturalism and its suspicion of canons and evaluation', is simply not possible in the sectarian climate of the French university. A choice has to be made, a creed espoused: 'The theory of literature, like any epistemology, is a school of relativism, not of pluralism, for it is not possible not to choose. In order to study literature, it is essential to take sides, to choose one route or another, for methods are not cumulative and eclecticism leads nowhere' (Compagnon 1998, p. 311). Such convinced monologism is typical of the French academy and opposed to the ideal of 'dialogic criticism', suggested by the former structuralist, Todorov, in his *Criticism of Literary Criticism* (1984), heavily influenced by his discovery of Bakhtin: 'Dialogical criticism does not speak of the work, but to the work — or rather: with the work; it refuses to eliminate either of the two voices present' (Todorov 1984, p. 186). The refuseniks and renegades from the dominant formalist and linguistic models, 'old' humanists such as Paul Benichou (1908–2001) and reformed apparatchiks like Todorov himself, have been busily lamenting the 'trauma' of the linguistic turn (see Todorov 1984, p. 163) for the last twenty years and have called incessantly for a new humanism: 'Literature is inextricably linked to our humanity, it is a discourse ... orientated towards truth and morals' (Todorov 1984, p. 188). However, such dissenters are still merely voices crying in the wilderness. Perhaps this is why Todorov has upped the ante in his latest work, significantly entitled *Literature in Peril* (2007), by acerbically assimilating formalism with nihilism and solipsism:

> Nihilism and solipsism reinforce the formalist mindset rather than refuting it: in each instance, but in different ways, it is the external world, the world common to the self and to others that is denied or depreciated. That is why, to a large extent, contemporary writing in French is inextricably bound up with the idea of literature that one finds at the heart of teaching and criticism, and a ridiculously absurd and impoverished idea it is. (p. 36)

Ironically, some of the accusations made by the early Structuralists against what they saw as a worn-out humanist tradition, characterised by authoritarianism and a certain moralism could now be levelled against their followers, responsible for the institutionalisation of theory in the academy. As Bourdieu explains (1984: p. 136), theories can be ruined by their widespread dissemination, and he describes the process by which original thought becomes assimilated into the institution, thanks to textbooks that are

> the natural extension of an impressive teaching machine based on the principle of reproduction, whose legitimising simplification of knowledge is supposed to inculcate in students what 'the consensus represented by the community of doctors' considers as understood and accepted and, thanks to this process, institutionalise it as officially certified knowledge, ratified and sanctioned academically and thus worthy of being taught and learned, rather than produce a new or heretical knowledge, or encourage the aptitude to produce such knowledge. (p. 136)

Compagnon (p. 9) shares this pessimism: 'Theory has become institutionalised, it has been transformed into a method, it has become just another teaching practice.'

However, the linguistic turn, which grew naturally out of Structuralism, not only maintains its tenacious hold on the hearts and minds of the representatives of the academy, but has been strengthened by recent interest in Benveniste's theories of discourse analysis. Any new preoccupation with the subject of discourse remains linguistic rather than social, therefore. Thus, the return to history, ushered in elsewhere by Cultural Studies, stands very little chance of getting a hearing, although it may manage to slip in unannounced on the back of the recent interest in

genetic criticism, which has turned to former traditions of erudite scholarship in its obsession with rediscovering old manuscripts as a means
of pursuing textual analysis. However much affirmative action bud-
ding Postcolonialists or Queer theorists may take, Lacan's ex-cathedra
pronouncements proclaiming the superiority of the signifier over the
signified, Benveniste's discussion of the categories of 'utterance' and
Genette's confidence in the text as a closed system – all remain unassail-
able in their different ways. Their complex practices take practice, they
cannot be improvised and cannot accommodate the approximative
translations of Poststructuralism, the notoriously erroneous 'freeplay of
the signifier', being a case in point. What is more, they are protected
by the precision tool of mathematics and its impressive axiomatic constructions. Lacan may misquote Descartes, as Cunningham gleefully
points out, but it is difficult to deconstruct his algorithms without tying
oneself up in knots. The generalisation of linguistic models of analysis
in all their varied complexity banishes to the limbo of unprofessional
naivety those within the system who betray ignorance of the requi-
site terminology and incompetence in using it. In this context, theoretical thought itself becomes a language, literature's double, one long
Saussurean sentence, functioning as a system of signs.

Thus, in the French debate on theory, it is easy to round up the usual
suspects and pick them out of the line-up: Formalism with a capital F
and its most successful avatars, that is to say, Structuralism, Linguistics
and Lacanian Psychoanalysis. If variants on these may skirmish on the
borders of theory's territory, jockeying for precedence in the academy, as I
tried to illustrate with the anecdote at the beginning of this section, these
nasty squabbles tend nevertheless to keep things in the formalist family.
One step forward for Lacanianism may be one step back for old-style
Structuralism, but it is certainly not a move in the direction of Historicism.
Even Alain Badiou, a contemporary philosopher, teacher and writer,
whom Angermüller tries to recruit into the ranks of Poststructuralism, is
still striving for the ultimate mathematical formula, the global theory of
everything: 'A STRUCTURE IS THE MODEL FOR A FORMAL THEORY, IF
ALL THE AXIOMS OF THE THEORY ARE VALID FOR THAT STRUCTURE'
(Badiou 2007, p. 107; capitals in the original). As Angermüller suggests,
one of the reasons that theory, as practised in France today, may be so
mystifying to the mindset of the outsider is because of its continuing
adherence to a fundamentally Marxist and/or psychoanalytical belief in
the possibility of a total and totalising explanation (see Foucault 2001, pp.
1252–4). While the supposedly liberationist theology of Poststructuralism
may, elsewhere, seemingly, have replaced such global theories, both are

very much alive in France and continue to kick in their various subtle incarnations. The French academy cannot be said to be post-Marxist or post-ideological and is certainly not post-theory or even post-Theory in the glib sense in which these labels are sometimes used. The fact that the ideology of a theoretical approach remains implicit rather than explicit, only makes its effect all the more insidious, or effective, depending on one's point of view. Subtly and surreptitiously it may take hold, imposing its 'truth', or rather, 'validity', under cover of method, tooling up with terminology for its conquest of unsuspecting minds.

Thus the theoretical 'reds' remain very much under, rather than in, the beds. Todorov sees this as the consequence of the unquestioning faith in a particular critical doctrine and the unwillingness to distance oneself from the practice of it: 'as long as one is part of a doctrine, one is incapable of grasping it as a whole; conversely, being able to do so, means that one is no longer part of it' (qtd. in Lazzarin 2007, p. 188). The inaudibility of its presuppositions confers on it the authority of unshakeable convictions without revealing its ideology in full view, as he (1984: p. 182) explains: 'What I had thought until then to be neutral instruments, purely descriptive concepts (mine), now seemed to me the consequences of specific historical choices – which could have been different and these choices had their corollary in "ideology", a fact that I was still not ready to deal with.' His antidote to the authoritarianism of the formalist framework, the overwhelming inevitability of which, tends to mean that 'the rest is silence', is discussion and debate with his readers, a communicative engagement. Rather than acting as a mole bent on the underhanded accumulation of proofs for a show trial marking the end of the structuralist revolution, it is to be hoped that a teacher who encourages critical distance from the dominant model may help to foster understanding and informed respect for that model, engaging it in an ongoing dialogue with other critical stances.

Losing my religion: the perils and payoffs of speaking up

'Is not love speaking up when one should be silent' (Charles Péguy)

In the mid-1990s, having obtained my French doctorate and secured a new job in another university, I was asked, as a specialist of literature, to take on a third-year lecture-course entitled 'Stylistics'. The former teacher of the course, on the point of retirement, told me that it was destined to give the students reliable critical tools and methods for the competitive exams which they would be taking in a year or two.

I could certainly see the sense in this and for the first two years made no attempt to question the implacable logic behind it, using extracts from the books on the syllabi of other literature classes to illustrate the method. Everybody seemed happy, the students and my colleagues, and, above all, teacher herself, secure in the knowledge that she was providing a useful service, as was indeed proved, when she met up later with some of her former students in classes preparing books for the *concours*. However, not long afterwards, I began writing a complex account of my pre- and post-doctoral research as part of the rite of passage in applying to become a full professor. This formal exercise in French demanded that I explain and justify my critical approach to literature throughout my whole career so far. Delving into my critical identity was a chastening and a traumatic experience, as I came to realise the extent to which I had espoused various theories and models without questioning them and how, unwittingly, I was a member of a vast consensus on how to analyse literature, a somewhat hermetic French model, very different to that of French Theory, bolstered up by an academic tradition wary of imported goods and secure in its theoretical certainties. Indeed, why look elsewhere when Roland Barthes or Gérard Genette have already provided such elegant and reliable solutions to the problem of literary analysis?

Needless to say, my self-examination soon became self-dissatisfaction and I began to revolt against the consensus I had so slavishly accepted in order to fit in. It was at this point that I also became increasingly frustrated with the students' anxious attachment to the models in which I was myself schooling them, and their fear of getting it wrong, so alien to my first experiences of being taught literature, back in the bad old days of the dreamy tutorials, when reading was fun. For most of them it seemed as if the books on the syllabus were abstract puzzles to be solved, with little, if any, bearing on their own experience. At this point, a course on literary theory, based on a vaguely Anglo-American model, began to seem an attractive prospect as a means of opening up the closed text of theory and fostering a new sense of intellectual possibility. The problem was, how to justify this within the rigid contours of the existing system. My answer, a somewhat incongruous one, it has to be admitted, was to maintain the title 'Stylistics' and devote several in-depth sessions to this, as well as focusing heavily on structuralist approaches, but to add a sub-title, 'An Introduction to Literary Theory', allowing me to throw in the 'rogue' elements of Feminism, Marxism, Postcolonialism and Ecocriticism to give us some time off from formalism. This may, indeed, appear bizarre to those habituated to a more Theory-friendly context, but it possessed the advantage of being reassuring and, above all, recognisable as useful, to both students and colleagues.

Thus the backbone was to consist in a detailed examination of Formalism in its many incarnations, a sort of 'how-to' guide, but this time, a conscious one. I decided to follow more or less the format suggested by most Theory coursebooks (see, for example, Barry 2002 or Selden 1989[5]), that is to say, an historical and theoretical introduction to each chapter and then a critical example or reading, using the method under discussion. This posed two sets of problems, firstly that of definition, the temptation of the dangerously reductive formula of 'Feminist criticism is...', especially when faced with all of two hours in which to finish the sentence, and secondly, the choice of texts to be studied. I soon realised that in order to tease out the presuppositions of a school of thought, define its methodology and evoke its possible limits, it would be necessary first to examine in detail examples of the theorists theorising, before attempting to apply their practices to the texts my students were studying in other classes. Unsurprisingly, this worked very well with Barthes and the five codes of *S/Z*, which were then easily transferred to almost any text, while extracts from Derrida's *L'écriture et la différence* and *La Dissémination* bemused students, despite the fact that they were able to read them in the original, and seemed to produce a constrained silence rather than a proliferation of interpretative possibilities. Even what I thought of as a successful attempt at a deconstructionist re-reading of an extract from Ford's *The Good Soldier*, based on the etymological possibilities of the word 'stirrup' and its hidden connotations, enabling me to read the text against the grain, failed to impress, as did the general philosophical presupposition behind it, of reality as an endless tissue of textuality.

I was keen for the approaches discussed not to remain vague and abstract to the students but to be seen in action in relation to our raw material of literature so their assessment was to be based on the examination of an extract, using one of the approaches discussed, but formulated in such a way as to avoid the temptation of producing the textual commentary usually expected from them. Thus the formulation chosen was: 'Imagine that you are a Feminist/Marxist/, etc. critic: what kind of elements would you choose to analyse this passage and why?' It soon became clear, when choosing extracts for class or homework, that some theories are better suited than others to certain kinds of texts. Thus the most successful classes were a Marxist reading of an extract from Fowles' *The French Lieutenant's Woman*, a feminist reading of Winterson's *Oranges Are Not the Only Fruit* and an Ecoreading of

McCarthy's *The Road*. Although at first suspicious and scared of the relativism I was encouraging in their textual practice, the students gradually gained the confidence to experiment and proved particularly receptive to the three approaches above, perceived as accessible, coherent and relevant to their experience, while Lacanian psychoanlaytical theory, Poststructuralism, Postcolonial and Queer, paradoxically, were felt to be reductive rather than productive, closing down, rather than opening up the texts. This is most probably due to the highly theoretical nature of such critical practices, their complex and unfamiliar terminology and a general vagueness surrounding some of their presuppositions, as well as the difficulty of their consistent practical application to texts. Of course it was also necessary to protect the students (and myself) by warning them to stick to a formalist model if they opted for the competitive exams and, as a question of etiquette, to avoid openly resisting another teacher's critical model, were they to identify it. This being said, once my colleagues understood that I was setting the students extra work on the books they were teaching, they welcomed the initiative, willingly showed me their course plans and were happy to explain what they were doing in class.

In answer to an interviewer's question as to whether theory can help people to enjoy literature, Compagnon replies categorically: 'No, I don't think so. Criticism, as I define it, is both an epistemology and an ethics ... I believe that what one does with literature represents an existential undertaking and that this existential undertaking is also a moral undertaking' (Prstojevic, no page numbers). On the surface, my class proposes a lighter, more recreational attitude to literary analysis than that usually favoured by an academy that takes its thinking very seriously. If I may be reproached with treating theory as a mere theme-park, it is to be hoped that the rides can be taken, not with a detached postmodern irony, but with an informed awareness of both epistemology and ethics, and that the final destination will not only be clarity and critical distance, but also a form of intellectual empowerment that will take in moral as well as existential considerations.

New critical identities

To my satisfaction, the course does indeed appear to have particularly liberating consequences for French students who, by and large, have been taught to read and analyse 'scientifically', following a particular method that they are supposed to pick up by copying, a model presented to them as having very high truth-value and which, if questioned, may result in their failure. The realisation that a particular theoretical stance is only one among many and can be espoused or abandoned without compromising proficiency and integrity, frees up their creative energies and enlivens their responses and reading. They are no longer constrained to 'get it right', but involved in a serious game of possibles that implicates them ideologically and thus contributes to their intellectual maturity. Instead of feeling excluded by the mysteries of the unspoken laws of the strand of theory to which they have been most exposed, but which they may not fully comprehend, they are able to identify the mechanisms of theory as a whole and use it performatively as a tool for testing varied responses to a text and literature in general, as well as a way of forging new critical identities. If they decide to conform to a model, they are now doing it willingly and knowingly, and must take responsibility for their stance. The payoff is both intellectual and existential, for such an approach fosters tolerance and discussion rather than sectarian solipsism. Sometimes, the view from elsewhere can help one feel more at home, even if it is only a series of momentary glimpses from the roller coaster of Theory as it attempts to negotiate the loops and inversions of complex critical thought.

Notes

1. The essay genre enjoys little respect in France as a vector for serious ideas, being frequently associated with amateurism and imprecision, as its etymology suggests. The French *dissertation* is distinctly 'Cartesian' in the French sense of the word, that is to say, rigorous and methodical, proceeding by logical deduction, adhering to a strict methodology and, above all, to rationality.
2. My intention in recycling the title of Cleanth Brook's seminal study is not necessarily to equate New Criticism and the practice of close textual criticism in France, although, as I will be explaining later, they do share some similarities.
3. When talking about theory from a French point of view, I will use a small 't', as opposed to the capital of the anglicised notion.
4. All translations are mine, unless otherwise stated.
5. Green and Le Bihan are voluntarily less historical in their approach in order to shy away from 'isms' (xv), but such de-historicisation can pose problems for students who are blank slates when it comes to Theory. Their glossary at the end of each section, however, and annotated bibliographies, were examples that I hastened to follow.

References

Angermüller, J. (June 2007) 'Qu'est-ce que le postructuralisme français? A propos de la notion de discours d'un pays à l'autre', *Langage et société*, no. 120, pp. 17–24.

Badiou, A. (2007) *The Century*. London, Polity.

Barry, P. (2002) *Beginning Theory: An Introduction to Literary and Cultural Theory*, Manchester, Manchester University Press.

Barthes, R. (1964) 'Qu'est-ce que la critique?' in *Essais critiques*, R. Barthes, Paris, Seuil, pp. 252–7.

Bergez, D., P. Barbéris., P-M de Biasi., M. Marinin and G. Valency. (1999) *Introduction aux méthodes critiques pour l'analyse littéraire*, Paris, Dunod.

Bourdieu, P. (1984) *Homo Academicus*, Paris, Minuit.

Cabanès, J-L., and G. Larroux (2005) *Critique et théorie littéraires en France (1800–2000)*, Paris, Belin.

Compagnon, A. (1998) *Le Démon de la théorie*, Paris, Seuil.

Cunningham, V. (2002) *Reading After Theory*, Oxford, Blackwell.

Darrieussecq, M. (2005) 'La critique: la lire, l'écrire, la subir ou en profiter?', in *La Critique, le critique*, ed. E. Baneth-Nouailhetas, Rennes, Presses Universitaires de Rennes, pp. 17–25.

Foucault, M. (2001) *Dits et écrits II; 1976–1988*, Paris, Gallimard.

Genette, G. (1966) *Figures I*, Paris, Seuil.

Genette, G. (1983) *Nouveau discours du récit*, Paris, Seuil.

Green K. and J. Le Bihan (1996) *Critical Theory and Practice: A Coursebook*, London and New York, Routledge.

Lazzarin, S. (2007) 'Sortir de la revolution structuraliste: le cas de Tzvetan Todorov', in *La critique littéraire du XXème siècle en France et en Italie*, eds S. Lazzarin and M. Colin, Caen, Presses universitares de Caen, pp. 181–97.

Lodge, D. (1986) *Working with Structuralism: Essays and Reviews on Nineteenth-and Twentieth-Century Literature*, London, Ark.

Prstojevic, A. 'Antoine Compagnon, Entretien', *Vox Poetica*, [Online] Available at: http://www.vox-poetica.org/entretiens/compagnon.htm (20 March 2009).

Ravoux Rallo, E. (1999) *Méthodes de critique littéraire*, Paris, Armand Colin.

Rohou, J. (1993) *Les Etudes littéraires: méthodes et perspectives*, Paris, Nathan.

Selden, R. (1989) *Practising Theory and Reading Literature: An Introduction*, Hemel Hempstead, Harvester Wheatsheaf.

Tadié, J-Y. (1987) *La Critique littéraire au xxème sicèle*, Paris, Belfond.

Thumerel, F. (2002) *La Critique littéraire*, Paris, Armand Colin.

Todorov, T. (1984) *Critique de la critique. Un roman d'apprentissage*, Paris, Seuil.

Todorov, T. (2007) *La Littérature en peril*, Paris, Flammarion.

9

Reading by Recipe: Postcolonial Theory and the Practice of Reading

Neil Murphy

The decision to apply a theoretical model to a work of literature represents the initiation of an analytical process that has several implications; firstly, it registers a critical attitude to the status of the literary text in the scholarly process, and signals the centrality or otherwise of the specificity of the text in the process of reading. Secondly, the decision to read in one way, as opposed to another, usually indicates an ethical, aesthetic, political, or formal position on the part of the reader and, in turn, the world of the text is filtered through this framing-position. One could argue that these positions are not necessarily, in principle, mutually-exclusive but in practice they are very often so. By extension, pedagogically speaking, when one formulates a university literature module, it is frequently with a theory (or theories) of reading in mind, the consequence of which is that one inevitably contextualizes the primary literary text by accommodating the model being endorsed. In some cases a theory of society, or history, or culture, is implicitly championed, and the text in question subsequently becomes a function of the theoretical process. This is what occurs, in general (though certainly there are many significant variations), when postcolonial literary analysis, is applied to works of literature and the present essay argues that this has a number of effects on the pedagogy of teaching literature in higher education, including the implicit choice of a socio-cultural frame within which the novel is situated, the acknowledgement of a particularized historical model, and the acceptance of a specific ethical position. In a practical (readerly) sense, these choices assume a series of recognizable analytical gestures, a discipline-specific terminology, a postcolonial canon of theorists, and a by-now predictable array of authors and modes of writing that fall within the limits of these theorists' remit. Thus, a cohesive body of ideas, language and scholarship has been developed, but a significant problem has however simultaneously emerged; to avail of Neil Lazarus's words, "a very restricted kind of reading', has grown to define the field (Lazarus 2005 424), a kind of sameness and a quality of repetition, to such a degree that it ends up having enormous implications for a nuanced, comprehensive and sophisticated mode of reading, the kind of reading one would hope is inculcated in students of literary texts, not to the exclusion of all else (or *anything* else in fact) but as a required basis that makes all else possible. With much of postcolonial analysis, the all else becomes less possible, and the reading, the fundamental process that defines the discipline above all else, is rendered deeply problematic. This essay will argue that postcolonial analyses frequently suffer from being too heavily constricted by their political (and thus theoretical) frames and thus produce readings whose first allegiances are to the world-view rather than to the text.

A postcolonial analysis typically proceeds as follows: with a healthy dose of alterity, and a pinch of its sister (or brother perhaps!) the sub-altern, a liberal mix of hybridity, blended with the multicultural, intercultural, transcultural and cross-cultural, heavily garnished with ethnicity, exile and exoticism, or its more authentic offspring, essentialism; and negritude is frequently a requirement, as is nationalist *bourgeoisie*, global capitalism, and the politics of power power power. The main actors in attendance are Bhabha, Said, Chakrabarty, Spivak, Fanon, Ashcroft, Griffiths, and Tiffin, although Achebe and Ngugi Wa Thiong'o too are crucial and, more recently, work by Robert Young, Achille Mbembe, Prem Poddar, Leela Gandhi has been added to required reading lists. One proceeds thereafter by embracing the familiar subjects like Rushdie, Coetzee, Walcott, and Achebe or, alternatively, by lining up the familiar targets *Heart of Darkness*, *The Tempest*, *Othello*, *Mansfield Park*, and *Jane Eyre*, although this list can be extended endlessly in any direction it appears, as exemplified by David Lloyd's reading of Samuel Beckett's "First Love', the narrator of which suffers from, Lloyd assures us, "equally the perpetual condition of the colonized: dominated, interpreted, mediated by another" (Lloyd 1993 54), and not existential grief after all, as might initially seem apparent to readers.

A little more seriously, the application of postcolonial theory to literature (as distinct from the study of postcoloniality *per se*) typically involves initially placing one's encounter with postcolonial theory very firmly in the space between reader and text before one begins the process of "unpacking" the text, that most unfortunate, utilitarian-sounding word. Inevitably, this not-so-liminal space will then be occupied (if I might temporarily borrow the word) by ethical considerations, usually offering extremely clear distinctions between victim and aggressor, and a persistent assertion of Foucauldian politics of power. Furthermore, because context is everything, even more than the text itself, the post-colonial reader, ideally, will also have a deep understanding of the historical frame into which the text in question is placed.

The title of this essay registers an impression of postcolonial theory as prescriptive, formulaic and reductive and this is part of the critical position upon which this essay is built but I am also aware that in recent years several postcolonial critics have themselves alluded to these very problems. For example, Neil Lazarus's desire to see a new formulation for postcolonial literary studies arises from his dissatisfaction with the quality of current scholarship in the field:

> To read across postcolonial literary studies is to find, to an extraordinary degree, the same questions asked, the same methods, techniques, and conventions used, the same concepts mobilized, the same conclusions drawn – about the work of a remarkably small number of writers (who are actually much more varied, even so, than one would ever discover from the existing critical discussion). For some scholars in the field, evidently, all that is required of the postcolonial literary texts evoked is that they permit – which is to say, not actively disallow – a certain, very specific and very restricted kind of reading to be staged through reference to them. (Lazarus, 2005,424)

Lazarus has written convincingly of the need to formulate "a new theory of postcolonial literature" (Lazarus 439), one that would effectively resuscitate the field, and it appears that this would involve an acknowledgement of the sheer multiplicity of authors, and their contexts, in the fullest sense possible" (435). It would also require a reconstitution of what he calls "a certain limited optic on the world, a selective tradition ... imagined as a universal" (434). In this Lazarus clearly registers a movement away from the reductionist position that proliferates the field but there are other, perhaps even more significant, reasons why reading by formula(e) is problematic for literary studies in general, and it is to this critical problem that this essay is addressed, both in the context of the consequences for the teaching of literature in higher education, and in terms of the implications for literary scholarship in general.

A fundamental condition of many postcolonial analyses is that the political frame often compromises the complexity of the text upon which it is brought to bear resulting in, at worst, the text being reconstituted into an expression of the mode of reading. This is, of course, a problem with all theories of reading but postcolonial analyses frequently exacerbate the problem by not attending to the formal and figurative signals associated with close reading in an effort to convey an often justified sense of grievance. Such readings frequently suffer from interpretative flaws based on a conflation of historical and literary texts, often to the detriment of the primary literary texts. The assumption is that the literary text becomes merely an aspect of a historical and/or cultural frame and its primary significance then is to the extra-literary. For example, when Seamus Deane, referring to what he names the Irish political crisis, concludes that "Field Day's analysis of the situation derives from the conviction that it is, above all, a colonial crisis" (Deane 1990, 6) it is assumed that the same is true of imaginative Irish literature. In fact, to Deane, it is the duty of the postcolonial critic to relocate the text to its proper (national) context after having been "(mis)read in the light of what was understood to be English or British literature, international modernism, the plight of humankind in the twentieth century" (Deane 1990, 11). Deane's solution is to localize Yeats and Joyce in the pursuit of historical accuracy and accountability.

Critical errata

Politically-motivated analyses are frequently characterized by two particular tendencies; flawed theoretical assumptions and highly selective reading practices. Weak theoretical assumptions are commonplace, like the dogma that all texts are essentially political or, a variation of that claim, that all relationships are defined by power struggles, an imperative that results in a rejection of anything apolitical as evasive or irresponsible, although it is also commonplace to suggest that being apolitical is also a political act. This position is compounded by the twin assumptions that, firstly, history is a fixed narrative entity and, secondly, that the value of a writer's work is deeply connected to our contemporary understanding of what is true and good. The second kind of weakness, the act of selective misreading, is even more injurious to the study of literature, because political readings frequently make few valid gestures towards close reading, apply deeply biased selectivity of textual exemplum and continually assign centrality to marginal or textually non-existent issues. The process of securely anchoring one's critical reflections to the literary text is then generally not a priority with the critical energies primarily driven by a desire to allow the contextualizing theory to contain and invent the text, rather than the reverse. Several of these tendencies are illustrated below.

In literary–critical discourse Foucault is the primary source of the theoretical prescription that power pervades all human action, and is "always already there" (Foucault 141), and one must always proceed with "a logic of the specificity of power relations and the struggles around them" (Foucault 1980145). This position, added to Jameson's insistence that "everything is 'in the last analysis' political" (Jameson 1981, 20), essentially precludes narrative being about anything other than political power struggles. This logic is responsible for a severe narrowing of the multiplicity that underpins complex literary texts and, as Kermode claims, results in "the reduction of criticism to a single quest for the defining political sense" (Kermode 1997 94); it also rarely deals with the fact that not all actions have the same degree of impact. The suggestion that power underpins everything is itself a questionable grand theoretical–narrative position from which to begin and extraordinary readings of literary texts are effected as a result of the view that every gesture, and every spoken word, inevitably are part of the substance of some wider political power-based construction. The irony here, of course, is that an insistence on the power-based model of existence results in a conviction that may in fact be anti-culture, anti-pluralist. For example, Ihab Hassan objects to Foucauldian logic in the following way: "Nor is knowledge tantamount to ideology, as Foucauldians cant. In fact, culture is what we have to resist the raw demands of power, self-interest, hype" (Hassan 1997, 191). Hence, for Hassan, the richness that politicized readings seek to delegitimize represents the very heart of culture and an insistence on ideological readings has the effect of undermining culture itself and results in "a logic of the specificity of power relations, but with a logic of little else. The consequences of this for the literary classroom are enormous because encouraging students to participate in an exclusively power-centric consciousness, à la Foucault, inevitably impacts upon the critical approach to such an extent that the student may choose (or be actively encouraged to choose, as is often the case) to focus on extra-literary conclusions rather than on what constitutes the text-in-itself. Frank Lentricchia, for example, recounts an incident from one of his graduate literature classes in which a student attacked DeLillo's *White Noise* for its insensitivity to the third world. Lentricchia in turn pointed out that there was no mention of the third world in the novel only for the said student to respond, "that's the problem. It's ethnocentric and elitist" (Lentricchia 64). The text is not allowed to be about anything other than the prescribed political directives. If a text is not overtly dominated by the political issues that are in vogue at any given time, then one either rails against it or focuses on its "shortcomings'. As a consequence, Lentricchia writes of having chosen to stop teaching graduate students believing that they had already been lost to the study of literature.

Despite the original pluralist intentions that underpinned the new historicism, the dominant expression of epistemological uncertainty in Modernism, and the intellectual implications of structuralism, post-structuralism and deconstruction, contemporary political readings of literature frequently present history as a fixed narrative entity and, as Graham Good has suggested, it is a particularly curious historical sense that dominates postcolonial studies:

> Postcolonialism's dependence on colonialism also leads to a lack of historical depth. Presentism conceals from view almost everything before the nineteenth century. Thus Roman imperialism is rarely discussed despite its importance. ... Negative Eurocentrism (seeing Europe as the only guilty party) conceals from view non-European examples of imperialism like the Islamic conquests in Africa and India, Japanese annexations of Korean and parts of China, the Chinese invasion of Tibet, or the Indonesian invasion of East Timor. (Good 2005 291)

This provokes, of course, a plethora of questions like, which history? And how far does one recede into the past? And what constitutes the colonial past? Are all expansionist moments colonial, if some form of governance is established, or is the key issue really capitalist expansionism? These questions are central to the process of applying postcolonial theory to literary texts and the answers that many analyses provide tend to reveal the specificity of the historical lens through which the analytical gaze is filtered. The allegiance then, one could argue, is less to history than to a particular kind of history that affords one the opportunity to repeatedly offer critical commentary on one specific colonial historical zone, as opposed to a deep historical analysis, or a broader historical comprehension.

While the historical, intellectual and other narrative representations of the colonial period were certainly laden with the often unpleasant assumptions of that period, one too could argue that in many respects the replacement narrative too has faltered into an intellectual fixity. Again, Seamus Deane implicitly endorses this critical position in his highly influential essay, "The Literary Myths of the Revival', in which Deane objects to the fact that Yeats "distorted history in the service of myth" (Deane 1985, 32). This observation reveals a lack of sympathy for the imaginative process, but it is also assumed that Yeats misread his history which presumes that one can locate a true history, something that Deane claims is "evident in the poetry of men such as Daithi O'Brudair and Aodagain O' Rathaille', and that if Yeats had known a "little more about the eighteenth century, he would have recognized that the Protestant Ascendancy was, then and since, a predominantly bourgeois social formation" (Deane 1985, 30). Deane concludes, at least in this respect, by suggesting that "we might finally decide to seek our intellectual allegiances and our understanding of our history elsewhere" (Deane 1985, 32). A truer, less contaminated history, he might have said, one that fits the socio-political construction of reality to which he ascribes.

This, of course, gives rise to a parallel difficulty: retrospective moralizing essentially infuses current intellectual perspectives with a superiority that simultaneously exhibits a misunderstanding of the past, something of which Sartre is keenly aware when he writes of the misapprehensions in which we live in any historical epoch:

> [T]he limits and the ignorance did not exist 'at the time'; no deficiency was seen; or rather the age was a constant surpassing of its limits towards a future which was its future and which died with it; it was this boldness, this rashness, this ignorance of its ignorance; to live is to foresee at short range and to manage with the means at hand…But the human condition requires us to choose in ignorance; it is ignorance which makes morality possible. (Sartre 2001 246–7)

Hence, in Sartre's model of historical analysis, Yeats's political insights, now interpreted as misguided in some quarters, are a necessary part of the becoming that is the mark of true development. Comprehension, rather that resentment would appear to be a more fruitful response. Instead, what one encounters is a privileging of the present intellectual context.

The rejection of the imaginative taking in to oneself that constitutes the poetic act, in favour of a reconstituted postcolonial official history, is embedded in postcolonial theory. Here is Edward Said in characteristic pose: "And it must also be noted that this Eurocentric culture relentlessly codified and observed everything about the Non-European or presumably peripheral world, in so thorough and detailed a manner as to leave no item untouched" (Said 1990, 72). True of course, at least in the sense that the construction of the Oriental, the Other, was a constituent part of the colonial imagination, just as one "constructs" images of all that lies outside of oneself, a literary–imaginative truism older than Homer. Essentially, Said transposes upon this human inevitability a political dimension, more specifically a dimension that is dominated by a legitimate sense of victimization. A significant problem with Said's historical vision is that it doesn't acknowledge that this is an extra-political tendency, or an extra-colonial quality. Another problem is that this version of history becomes, for Said and his legion of followers, the official history. Pluralism, multiplicity and diversity are the real victims of such logic. It appears that pluralism, or what Deane has disparagingly named "the postmodernist simulacrum of pluralism," is not to be trusted because it "supplants the search for a legitimating mode of nomination and origin" (Deane 1990, 18–19). The mode of nomination, it would appear, is synonymous with the true history that Deane desires of Yeats and the obvious irony in this is, as Ihab Hassan claims, that "the attack on pluralism ends as an attack on Otherness, a certain kind of Otherness" (1995, 246). Hence Said's objection to colonial invention is itself a kind of credo, thoroughly laced with a desire to (re)locate history, to (re)nominate a legitimate narrative of the past that engenders a kind of truth. The consequence of this appropriation is that history becomes a corrective discipline rather than a way of glimpsing multiplicities.

Another central characteristic of ideological theory has been the assault on Modernism (as opposed to Modernity). Frederic Jameson suggests that the apolitical character of Modernism, its supposed turning inward, away from "social materials" is simply a "commonly held stereotype', one which is no longer "adequate or persuasive" (1990, 45). The keen force of this critical judgement is further emphasized in his assertion that any "contemporary theory of the modern" will wish to "dismantle', the notion of modernist writing as being concerned with aesthetics, introspection and "psychologization" (45). This is not an expansion of the critical faculties, rather it is an act of dismantling, replacement. The political zeal is clearly antagonistic to other forms of reading, dismissive of theories of the modern that gain very solid currency from the briefest of readings of classical modernist texts. Jameson's logic is driven by the belief that the colonized space radically transforms the modernist project, a project that he conflates with imperialism, a peculiarity in itself considering that many of the high modernist writers emerged from a variety of cultures; Germany (Mann), Kakfa (Czechoslovakia), Poland (Conrad), Ireland (Yeats, Joyce and Beckett), The United States (Faulkner, Gertrude Stein), Russia (Mandelstam) to name but a few. Jameson's efforts to contextualize Joyce, in particular, force him to make some intriguing observations regarding literary modernism and, furthermore, dissatisfied with what he suggests is an "absolute category of the modern canon', "style" (61) he seeks to politicize Joyce's subversion of linguistic style by claiming, that Joyce's "enumeration of English styles" is an attempt to discredit "the styles of the imperial occupying armies" (62). Much of Jameson's critical perspective is driven by the belief that the underlying structure of Irish society is that of the "Third world or of colonized daily life" (60). Historically speaking, of course, Ireland was colonized and de-colonized, but a significant difficulty, from a literary–theoretical perspective, emerges when one assumes that this historical truism then dominates the creative process, unwittingly or otherwise, of all writers and artists from colonial and postcolonial times. Such assumptions, when brought to bear on complex works of literature force Jameson into performing intellectual high-jinks in order to justify his postcolonial critical model. Because Ireland was colonized, Joyce's transformation of style from a system of representation into the subject-matter of art itself evolves, ingeniously, in Jameson's logic, into discredited politicized battalions of British linguistic styles.

Reading by recipe

A consideration of the reading strategies brought to bear on any text helps to explain the apparent enforced gap between text and context. For example, it has been a commonplace in postcolonial literary studies to offer up readings of *Heart of Darkness*, like Achebe's seminal essay, "An Image of Africa: Racism in Conrad's *Heart of Darkness*", which has been effectively canonized to such a degree that most undergraduates now read *Heart of Darkness* as a straight racist text rather than as an exemplum of literary Modernism. This is no doubt connected to Achebe's analysis and, in turn, to his sense of grievance as an African. Throughout his essay, Achebe offers up examples of racism, of representations of Africa, and Africans, which have ultimately participated in the perpetuation, perhaps even the formulation, of racist stereotypes. What is also extraordinary from a literary–critical point of view is that Marlow is only mentioned on one page of the essay, and elsewhere we are told of Conrad's view, without acknowledgement that many of the views are actually Marlow's. No skilled undergraduate would conflate the narrator and author is such a casual manner. In fact, Achebe, on that same singular page, literally conflates narrator and author as "Marlow/Conrad" again assuming that the position held by both is the same. So all Shakespeare's characters too are Shakespeare, despite their multiple differences, and all writing is simply a kind of disguised personal self-expression! Indeed, the critical errata don't end there. For much of the second part of the essay, selections from a variety of sources unrelated to the novel are offered up as further evidence that *Heart of Darkness* is a racist novel. This represents an endorsement of critical views like it is possible to read one text by drawing attention to another, unrelated one, or that it is acceptable to read the testimony of an Art historian, Frank Willett, writing about Gauguin, and quoted favourably by Achebe, to emphasize the insistence that *Heart of Darkness* was racist. I am not essentially questioning Achebe's observations about Conrad, although I do feel there is ample evidence in the novel to suggest a much less critical reading; of greater concern from a pedagogical perspective, and a critical perspective, is that this essay, and many others derived from it, are now part of the critical canon of postcolonial literary studies, and as an example of literary scholarship it encourages very poor reading practices based on the principles that it is appropriate to offer highly selective textual material, it is acceptable to conflate narrator and author, it is permissible to ignore an enormous amount of material in the novel that might render one's argument altogether more sophisticated, and less linear, and it affirms without hesitation that the critical practice of reading one text by alluding to another is a logical, untroubling, critical proposition. While the implications for literary studies are clear, it is worth noting, too, that the implications for the process of constructing a logical argument, the process of making legitimate connections between disparate pieces of evidence and the offering up of resentment as a substitution for careful analysis are all practices that lend little to scholarship in general.

While some readings, like Achebe's, are clearly politically motivated and linked to the ways in which a colonial mindset is purported to interact with the colonized world, the centrality of the nation, and of national identity, also came to dominate the critical discourse of postcolonial countries, and the writings of postcolonial critics observing the former colonies. It is intriguing to see how easily the reading practices make implicit assumptions, legitimized by such modes of discourse. One of the more familiar critical observations that has been assimilated into critical studies of Joyce's *A Portrait of the Artist as a Young Man* is that the culmination of the novel, related via a series of diary entries, is testament to Stephen's as yet unfulfilled promise to "narrate the Irish nation," (Howes 2000 75) in the "smithy" of his soul. The standard nationalized perspective then is that on the point of winged departure Stephen assures us of his concern for Ireland after all and that he will thereafter endeavour to create what remains uncreated, an expression of Irish identity. Howes makes the following assertion based on the implicit assumption that Ireland, or Irishness, is Stephen's primary focus: 'Stephen's initial claim, "I fear him", and his conclusion that he means the old man "no harm," indicate that his famous resolution to narrate the Irish nation, to forge in the smithy of his soul the uncreated conscience of his race, must incorporate or acknowledge these contradictory elements' (Howes 2000 75). Similarly, Emer Nolan implicitly conflates the "People of Ireland" with Joyce's "race": "The latter provides a place where the people of Ireland might apprehend a negative image of themselves in Joyce's 'nicely polished looking glass', and an ultimately positive one in the artist's image of 'the uncreated conscience of the race'" (Nolan 1998, 46). Notwithstanding the literary–critical hazards of neglecting the almost-certain ironic overtones to Stephen's bombastic close, there are other implications embedded in his final diary entries that are rarely, if ever, offered consideration. For example, while the critical focus generally falls on the latter part of the all-important clause, "to forge in the smithy of my soul the uncreated conscience of my race', the significance of textual signals in the former part, "forge" and "smithy" are largely ignored, despite the enormous significance of Grecian craftsmanship in the text, the effect of which is to implicitly distract from the proclamation of artistic activity, which is where the emphasis lies in the sentence. More significant still is Stephen's preceding diary entry of 16 April, in which he dreams of "the white arms of roads, their promise of close embraces and the black arms of tall ships that stand against the moon, their tale of distant nations. They are held out to say: We are your kinsmen. And the air is thick with their company as they call me to them, their kinsman, making ready to go, shaking the wings of their exultant and terrible youth" (275). Stephen here associates himself with other "kinsmen', from "distant nations" immediately before he talks of forging the conscience of his race, and thus generates considerable doubt as to the precise meaning of the subject of his promise. It is more than a little hazardous to neglect the entry of 16 April and blithely assume that Steven's "race" in the next entry signifies the Irish. There is, at least, a strong possibility that the "race" to which he promises to attend in the future is associated with the "kinsmen" of "foreign shores', that he imagines he will encounter in the future and hence the narration of the 'nation' becomes a deeply problematic assumption, one that has formed one of the cornerstones of all attempts to insist on Joyce's Irishness. Furthermore, Stephen's meaning of race must also be qualified by the dense pattern of Greco-Christian allusions evident in the novel, of which we have just been reminded at the close of the 16 April entry in which Stephen *Dedalus* envisages his kinsmen "shaking the wings of their exultant and terrible youth" (275).

Stephen, Greco-Christian-aesthete-martyr, is a far more complex presence than any narrow understanding of the word Irish will allow. The weight of evidence in this instance insists that Stephen's construction of an uncreated conscience will be informed by the dominant twin prongs of European culture, the Greek and the Christian, to which Stephen's own name testifies, and which his exuberant imagination visualizes in his diary entry of 16 April. If *Ulysses* represents the fulfilled creative promise, then the marriage of the Judaic–Greco–Christian–Celtic (Leopold–Stephen–Molly) may well be closer to what Joyce means by his race than that which is usually assumed. That one can arrive at a narrower construction of the text is made possible only when the allusive framework, so central to Joyce from *A Portrait* onwards, is simply not attended to, just as the prioritizing of one diary entry over another, or indeed one clause over another, will inevitably result in curious readings. Ultimately though, the critical responses are initially formulated with a fixed sense of Joyce-as-Irish author in mind, which essentially stems from working within the general frame of Irish studies, but also from the auto-critical habit of desiring the decolonized a clear distinction from that which lies beyond

Conclusion

A curiously restrictive kind of utilitarian essentialism underwrites much of socio-political theory, resulting in an insistence that almost all literary texts, despite the overt textual signals, are actually textual spaces in which various kinds of political anxieties are expressed, or contained. All texts are apparently political – all texts constructed in postcolonial nations must somehow reflect the postcoloniality of the subject – even if the subject is a French-speaking émigré whose greatest literary gifts to the world were absurdist drama and early metafiction. The casualty is complexity and great literary texts are, almost by definition, complex. Purely historical analysis (irrespective of the specific nature of the "history" being employed) tends to flatten authentic aesthetic difference, generally offering no way to evaluate the respective differences between different texts and authors from the same period. Texts then can be viewed as receptacles for social or historical energies without any meaningful distinction made between their artistic merits. Bloom offers scathing commentary on this now common practice of reading in Shakespearean scholarship: 'Shakespeare criticism is in full flight from his aesthetic supremacy and works at reducing him to the "social energies" of the English Renaissance, as though there were no authentic difference in aesthetic merit between the creator of Lear, Hamlet, Iago, Falstaff and his disciples such as John Webster and Thomas Middleton' (Bloom 2000 3). Similarly, John Ellis, asks the apparently simple question, "Why must literature be about the same thing," or a variant of that, "How can we know what a book is about before reading it?" (Ellis 1997 34). Ellis asserts that socio-political criticism doesn't desire or need receptiveness to a text because the focus of attention has shifted from a spirit of exploration to one of imposition in which the dominant textual signals in any work are no longer of primary significance, and the politically or historically motivated context dominates the reading, as in Said's contrapuntal readings in which one reads a text "with an understanding of what is involved when an author shows, for instance, that a colonial sugar plantation is seen as important to the process of maintaining a particular style of life in England" (Said 1993, 66). While this sounds oddly plausible, it is also quite clear that we have lost something in the process. For Erin O'Connor, writing of the consequences of postcolonial readings for the Victorian novel, what is lost is the literary text itself, in its most sophisticated sense:

> My most basic contention is that the postcolonial narrative of literary history has largely overwritten the Victorian novel, that it has ignored – even at times denied – the genre's thematic subtleties, structural indeterminacies, and genuine intellectual rigour in order to make the novel into the means of establishing broadly applicable theoretical paradigms. The majestic generality of positions such as Spivak's and Said's is after all a generic one: the assumption that culture and imperialism can be adequately and responsibly thought through the novel is an assumption that takes the novel to be, in form and content, a categorical generalization of these otherwise bafflingly enormous categories." (O'Connor 2005 300)

Thus, the narrow paradigm replaces the subtlety and variousness of the literary text and the complex conversation that is literature is no longer heard beneath the clatter of the formulae that approaches the text. It is important to remember that theories of reading are not all of equal merit and, as Hassan reminds us, "Etymologically, theory derives from the Greek *theoria*, viewing or contemplation. But the intelligent eye also questions what it sees" (Hassan 1997, 195). The imposition of a political model without affording the text its inherent diversity, the construction of a *theoria* of reading that refuses contemplation in favour of recognition of the power credo is really not a theory of reading at all, at least in the truest sense. This is a crucial distinction.

The British novelist, A.S. Byatt, has complained of "the fatal family like-ness" that characterizes much of contemporary criticism (Byatt 2001 2). In a field that aspires to emulate, in some senses, the diversity of the creative work to which it apparently attends, this is an extraordinary situation. In writing of the European novel, Milan Kundera claimed that "the spirit of an age cannot be judged exclusively by its ideas, its theoretical concepts, without considering its art, and particularly the novel', a literary form whose genesis, he asserts, can be located "where the bridge between cause and effect has collapsed and thought wanders off" (Kundera 1988). The multiplicity of writing, the space in which thought wanders off, deserves a more nuanced response. Instead what one encounters all too frequently, as O' Connor indicates, is the tendency in postcolonial literary studies towards "simplifying and distorting ... reducing literature to formula'. She believes that if paradigmatic interpretations were to now stop, "literary criticism can begin to address the complexity that several decades of paradigmatic thinking have deliberately and devastatingly obscured" (O'Connor, 2005 308). Similarly, Reed Dasenbrock, writing of what he names *conventional-ism* in contemporary theory, claims that literary studies were "killed in the culture wars" and as a consequence there is very little debate within the academy any more –that there is a kind of orthodoxy that dominates all, an orthodoxy that he names the "new thematics" (Dasenbrock 2001 xvi), while Derek Attridge too has detected an orthodoxy, an "instrumental approach to literature," to which he objects:

Although the majority of recent studies claiming a political function for literature to have appeared in recent years have situated them-selves on the left, there is a sense in which many of them could be said to participate in an instrumentalized system of literary educa-tion, criticism, and publication. (Attridge 2004 9)

So whether, one speaks of paradigms, orthodoxy, or recipes, whether one sees conventionalism or instrumentalism, there appears to be a growing disenchantment with the state of postcolonial studies, and with literary studies in general, arising from the view that it has become rigidified and operates by codified moral, cultural and historical practices. This has given rise to what can almost be termed a new literary-critical *ism*, an -ism that encourages a return to nuanced, skilled reading, that can attend more comprehensively to postcolonial and other literatures. The aridity of existing theoretical formulations need re-imagining, because if one does not encounter sophisticated reading in departments of literature, one will surely not encounter it anywhere else; in addition, it is clear that the increasingly elaborate literary texts of postcoloniality deserve more daring, more skill, and a more committed acknowledgment of pluralism, in an intellectual sense, rather than in a purely political sense. There is ample evidence that a change of atmosphere is already underway in the scholarship of literature, in part by virtue of the diminishing of overt, acrimonious argument about the form/content debate of recent decades and also, as Denis Donoghue observes, there appears to be a sense that people have found their constituency, and a less energized state of provocation holds sway (Donoghue 2003 7–8). More significant is the avalanche of work published, in recent years, on the practice of reading, on reconsiderations of the significance of theory, and of the importance of Art and form to literature by authors as diverse as Donoghue, Bloom, John Ellis, Alsop and Walsh, Frank Lentricchia, Ihab Hassan, Frank Kermode, Robert Scholes, Elizabeth Freund, Stephen Tanner, Derek Attridge, Reed Dasenbrock, Daphne Patai, Graham Good, Erin O'Connor, Marjorie Perloff, Richard Levin, Jacques Barzun, and many, many others.

When Italo Calvino writes of the process of re-reading as offering "as much of a sense of discovery as the first reading" (Calvino 2000, 5), he acknowledges the richness, the multiplicity, the *centrality of ambiguity* that any major literary work embodies, and implicitly celebrates the essentially non-linear intellectual epistemology that is a work of Art. It is to that condition of plurality that theories of reading must aspire and to the ever-alert sense of reading as "unceasing acts of mediation" (Freund 1987 63). The postcolonial experience is a richly textured one, and one that necessitates our unceasing acts of mediation, both in terms of the multiplicity of experience and in terms of the complex forms that authors have woven to house that experience.

Works cited

Achebe, Chinua. 'An Image of Africa: Racism in Conrad's Heart of Darkness'. Reprinted in *Heart of Darkness*, ed. Robert Kimbrough. New York: W.W. Norton & Company, 1988: 251–62.

Attridge, Derek. *The Singularity of Literature*. London: Routledge, 2004.

Bloom, Harold. *How To Read, and Why*. New York: Scribner, 2000.

Byatt, A.S. *The Biographer's Tale*. New York: Knopf, 2001.

Calvino, Italo. *Why Read the Classics*. Transl. Martin McLaughlin. New York: Vintage 2000.

Dasenbrock, Reed Way. *Truth and Consequences: Intentions, Conventions, and the New Thematics*. University Park, Pa.: Pennsylvania State University Press, 2001.

Deane, Seamus. *Celtic Revivals*. London: Faber and Faber, 1985.

Deane, Seamus. 'Introduction'. *Nationalism, Colonialism and Literature: Essays by Terry Eagleton, Frederic Jameson, Edward Said*. University of Minnesota Press,1990.

Deane, Seamus. 'Heroic Styles: The Tradition of an Idea'. *Theorizing Ireland*. Ed. Clare Connolly. Palgrave Macmillan, 2003: 14–26.

Donoghue, Denis. *Speaking of Beauty*. New Haven & London: Yale University Press 2003.

Eagleton, Terry. Crazy John and the Bishop and Other Essays on Irish Culture. Notre Dame: University of Notre Dame Press in assoc. with Field Day, 1998.

Eagleton, Terry. 'Nationalism: Irony and Commitment'. In *Nationalism, Colonialism and Literature: Essays by Terry Eagleton, Frederic Jameson, Edward Said*, edited by Seamus Deane, 23–39. Minneapolis: University of Minnesota Press,1990.

Ellis, John M. *Literature Lost: Social Agendas and the Corruption of the Humanities*. New Haven & London: Yale University Press, 1997.

Freund, Elizabeth. *The Return of the Reader: Reader-Response Criticism*. London: Methuen, 1987.

Foucault, Michel. *Power/Knowledge: Selected Interviews and Other Writings 1972–7*. Edited by Colin Gordon. Trans. by Colin Gordon, Leo Marshall, John Mepham, Kate Soper. New York: Pantheon books: 1980.

Good, Graham. 'Presentism: Postmodernism, Poststructuralism, Postcolonialism', *Theory's Empire: An Anthology of Dissent*. Eds Daphne Patai and Will H. Corral. New York: Columbia University Press, 2005.

Hassan, Ihab. *Rumors of Change: Essays of Five Decades*.Tuscaloosa: University of Alabama Press, 1995.

Hassan, Ihab. '"Let the Fresh Air In: Graduate Studies in the Humanitie's. In *Beauty and the Critic: Aesthetics in an Age of Cultural Studies*, edited and Intro by James Soderholm, 190–207. Alabama: University Of Alabama Press,1997.

Herr, Cheryl. 'The Sermon as Mass product: "Grace" and A Portrait'. In *James Joyce: A Collection of Critical Essays*, edited by Mary T. Reynolds, (PAGES?). New Jersey: Prentice Hall, 1993.

Howes, Marjorie. '"Goodbye Ireland I'm going to Gort": geography, scale, and narrating the nation'. In *Semicolonial Joyce*, edited by Derek Attridge & Marjorie Howes, 58–77. Cambridge: Cambridge University Press, 2000.

Jameson, Frederic. 'Modernism and Imperialism'. In *Nationalism, Colonialism and Literature: Essays by Terry Eagleton, Frederic Jameson, Edward Said*, edited by Seamus Deane, 43–66. Minneapolis: University of Minnesota Press,1990.

Jameson, Frederic. *The Political Unconscious: Narrative as a Socially Symbolic Act*. New York: Ithaca, 1981.

Kermode, Frank. 'The Academy vs. the Humanities'. *The Atlantic Monthly* Vol. 280, No. 2 (1997): 93–6.

Kundera, Milan. *The Art of the Novel*. London: Faber, 1988.

Lazarus, Neil. 'The Politics of Postcolonial Postmodernism'. *Postcolonial Studies and Beyond*. Eds Ania Loomba, Suvir Kaul, Matti Bunzl, Antoinette Burton and Jed Esty. Durham: Duke University Press 2005.

Lentricchia, Frank. 'Last Will and Testament of an Ex-Literary Critic'. Lingua Franca (Sept./Oct. 1996): 59–67.

Lloyd, David. *Anomalous States: Irish Writing and the Post-Colonial Moment*. Durham: Duke University Press, 1993.

O'Connor, Erin. 'Preface for a Post-Postcolonial Criticism', *Theory's Empire: An Anthology of Dissent*. Eds Daphne Patai and Will H. Corral. Columbia University Press, New York, 2005.

Nolan, Emer. *James Joyce and Nationalism*. London: Routledge, 1998.

Said, Edward. *Culture and Imperialism*. London: Vintage, 1993

Said, Edward. 'Globalizing Literary Study'. *PMLA* 116, no.1 (2001): 64–8.

Said, Edward. 'Yeats and Decolonization'. In *Nationalism, Colonialism and Literature: Essays by Terry Eagleton, Frederic Jameson, Edward Said*, ed. Seamus Deane, 67–95. Minneapolis: University of Minnesota Press,1990.

Sartre, John Paul. *What is Literature?* London: Routledge Classics, 2001.

10
Do I Hate Theory?

Richard Bradford

The title of this chapter is potentially misleading because the 'I' is not necessarily its author. It would be better to treat this particular first person pronoun as a device, a conceit devised by myself – that is, the real myself – as an exercise in teaching Theory to undergraduates. More precisely, it is a polemic designed to provoke undergraduates into taking positions for or against aspects of Theory.

The opening paragraph of the piece below offers a brief but accurate account of my relationship with Theory over the past quarter century. On some occasions I have taught basic introductions to Theory in first year modules which deal also with the principal literary genres and with the vast undifferentiated territory of Practical Criticism. More satisfying and endurable have been specialised elective modules on Theory, in which second or third years are required to tackle directly the originating texts of more than a century of Theoretical discourse. Most undergraduates who have chosen to take these modules fall into the categories of the daring, the recklessly inquisitive or the confidently gifted and on rare but treasured occasions all three. Very few are completely ignorant of the complexities and challenges of Theory in that they will either have encountered it briefly in the first year modules mentioned above or come upon it tangentially in other specialised elective modules covering topics such as gender, race and post-colonialism. Third year Critical Theory students are, at least in my experience, intriguing specimens; generally more intellectually adventurous than those who, perhaps with wisdom, chose to avoid Theory for the sake of a more familiar, predictable encounter with the standard menu of texts, authors and movements. This statement should, however, be qualified by the observation that although they often prove capable of mastering the enormous breadth and diversity of Theory, even bravely reading the original texts of the most demanding

163

poststructuralist thinkers rather than relying upon guides and primers, they generally remain cautiously immune from one aspect of the history of Theory that is vital to a proper understanding of its nature and impact. I write here of the resistance to its arrival in the UK and US university systems. Certainly it is possible to flavour one's account of the history of Theory with anecdotes regarding alleged conspiracies to marginalize Theorists, and here Colin MacCabe is the obvious case, and discussions of books such as Brian Vickers' which involve lengthy systematic refutations of the claims of Theory to academic credibility or relevance. However, while third year students might well appreciate how and why conventional academics and advocates of Theory have engaged in conflicts they tend to be alienated from the debate itself. Understandably third year undergraduates are reluctant to allow their intellectual, temperamental or visceral affiliations to override their commitment simply to getting the highest mark possible. While they understand the nature of the controversies that surround the influx of Theory they do not on the whole take sides. I should here point out that I have for some time pondered the question of how the contentious status of Theory can be made available to students as the subject of their assignments and examinations. This is, in my view, a feature of Theory-based modules that differentiates them from the more conventional author and text-focused elements of the curriculum. Few, if any, Shakespeare, Wordsworth or Joyce specialists would invite their students to question the eminence or legitimacy of these figures as writers. Theory, however, carries with it still a sense of division and controversy. Theory has most certainly arrived and is implacably rooted in the discipline of English Studies, but the perceptions and approaches toward literature that it has supposedly replaced and which are antithetical to its fundamental precepts are still advocated by a considerable number of academics and are quietly present in the routine protocols of teaching and examining English.

The problem I faced was twofold. Firstly, how might I reassure students that by taking an informed opinion against specific Theorists on the curriculum they did not place themselves in severe danger of losing marks? It is difficult to convince even the most unorthodox, daring undergraduate that an attempt to undermine and question the validity of their 'Recommended Reading' does not amount to heresy. Secondly, even if such reassurance could be given, I still faced an apparently insurmountable practical problem: how would I provide them with the opportunity to voice their doubts or reservations on Theory?

Even though these were relatively mature, experienced students they could hardly be expected to acquire a breadth of knowledge comparable to pro- and anti- Theory academics and upon which these figures had founded their polemical theses. I toyed, very briefly, with the hypothesis of adapting the module to ancient rhetoric-based pedagogic practice; that is, offer students for and against submissions alongside impartial lectures on each stratum of Theory. This seemed wonderful in principle and absurd in practice. Three years rather than one or two semesters would be required for such an ambitious undertaking.

The third year module attracted a relatively small number of students, for obvious reasons: during the year in which much of their degree classification would be decided most chose to stay away from this recondite rather intimidating field. Consequently the three allotted hours per week could, given available space, be linked consecutively as one 'block' of contact time involving the entire group: half a day with Critical Theory. My lecture of approximately 1½ hours would be followed by questions and debate on the more contentious, complex or impenetrable aspects of the week's topic. It seemed to me that this would be an ideal forum for the introduction of a teaching stratagem that had been maturing for several years.

The module was examined in three parts: two written assignments and one two-hour class-test. The second assignment would be due for submission three weeks after the completion of our lengthy tour of Theory's expansive realm. By this point the students would have had the opportunity to encounter, albeit in a somewhat abbreviated form, everything on offer. I inserted into the recipe of written assignments a wild card, typically: 'Respond in an essay to the paper delivered by Professor Richard Bradford on (inserting the end-of-semester date), pointing out what in your view are its most pertinent and flawed characteristics.' The title of the paper would be withheld until a week prior to its delivery, in effect the penultimate week of teaching. The students would, therefore, have a flavour of what awaited them a week hence, though without any intimation of the exact nature of this anti-Theory peroration.

The title of the piece below was only used once, during my final lecture for this module in 2007, but it reflects the tone of its predecessors. My lecture would rely upon notes and be partly improvised, enabling me to present the piece as a candid polemic rather than a flat disinterested retinue of points. The 1½ hour period following the lecture would as usual be thrown open for discussion and responses, although I made it clear that since this was more a tendentious diatribe than a routine pedagogic delivery they were welcome, indeed encouraged, to be entirely uninhibited in their responses. Following my first experiment with this end-of-semester piece the most notable, and enthralling, aspect of the group's reaction was their request for more time to discuss what I had said. I had already made it clear that a typed version of my lecture would be made available after the session, a necessity given that those who elected to write the 'wild card' essay would need to refer to specific passages and even quote verbatim from the lecture. However, a considerable number of the group – average size 15–20 students – asked if another hour of consultation could be made available the following week, once they had had the chance to read and reflect upon the lecture. Thereafter this became a standard feature of the module timetable.

What you have below is a composite, summarised version of various anti-Theory papers that I have delivered to students in the Third-Year Critical Theory module, emphasising the points that have proved to be the most contentious and sometimes divisive.

Four particular issues engaged students' attention. Firstly, the paper enabled the more confident to confront an otherwise sacrosanct aspect of Theory; its, alleged, recondite and elitist character. A good deal of nodding and apparent amusement was prompted by my contention that some aspects of Theory are maintained in a precious inaccessible state in order to enhance the notion of intellectual superiority that surrounds academia . One student, memorably, pointed out to me that she could 'understand' most of the fiction and verse offered in other modules and that the recommended critical commentaries were useful but not necessary supplements to reading. With, say, Derrida, Lacan, and Foucoult, however, she felt that there was an 'irreconcilable disjunction' (her phrase) between what she found in the primary texts and in their explanatory supplements. The latter did not enhance her appreciation of the former; rather they confirmed her impression that the guides were offering a 'dumbed down' version of something that would, for her, remain largely inaccessible. She was not disdainful of the overall experience, indeed she felt it reaffirmed her respect for the strangeness of Theory (which, she explained, had caused her to enrol for the module in the first place).

Even more attention was given to my discussion of the difficulties involved in reconciling Theory with the rest of the university curriculum. Every student who addressed this topic felt that there was a contradiction between what they had been encouraged to read about Theory, and often found fascinating, and what they encountered as undergraduates in our middle-ranking but innovative university English Department. On the one hand Theory was supposed to have become embedded in the post-1970s academic fabric yet in their experience it was still a sequestered, slightly exotic option, something set apart from the text and author-based core modules which ran, chronologically, from the early Renaissance (2nd year) to the present day (end of 3rd year). In these, as one of them pointed out, the ascendency of the purely literary text had never been challenged by cultural materialism. Only exchange-students felt able to offer a different perspective on this, notably those who had come from German or French universities where, according to their accounts, internecine conflicts regularly occurred. Many academics were devoted to the theoretical framework or system that had been the backbone of their research and had become an endemic feature of their teaching, irrespective of the text or author; very frequently an Althusserian and a Bakhtinian teaching on the same course would come to resemble bickering adolescents.

I had in several of these lectures used my attack on the anti-aesthetic aspect of Theory as a segue to the far more contentious issue of social and political relativism, arguing that the former serves as an academically respectable foundation for a widespread and insidious political doctrine which informs the media and much of the political infrastructure. I expected this to spark fury, rebuke or even enthusiastic assent, especially since this university is situated in a region where there is a guarantee of at least two diametrically opposed versions of history, identity and cultural affiliation. ('Ulster', 'Northern Ireland', 'The North of Ireland', 'The North', 'The Six Counties' will resolve any doubts that 'the signifier' is indeed incessantly 'sliding'.) Curiously, however, third years were reluctant to trace possible connections between their academic environment – nearly all were reading Single Honours English – and the world that had formed their own, their parents' and their grandparents' lives. (On average, at least 80 per cent of our undergraduates in English come from Northern Ireland.) This reaction might seem, to some, insular and protective, but my experience of this area causes me to disagree. For the vast majority of academics in Great Britain and the USA who find parallels between literary and cultural studies and the more peremptory world of social disparity and global politics, all of these phenomena are inert textual playgrounds, matters they observe rather than experience. For my students, however, the world they had grown up in and returned to at weekends was not of any obvious relevance to their chosen field of study. They were, of course, fully aware the political and ideological resonances of much Irish Writing in English but for many of them being constantly reminded by their lecturers of how the bifurcated condition of Ireland featured in numerous authors from O'Casey and Yeats onwards was something to be borne with weary resignation. As one of them put it, very astutely, he had signed up to 'Study Literary Theory, not to be told again and again how it [literature] was a prism for deeper understanding of bloody Ireland'. And he was most certainly Irish.

The point which students found both magnetic and inhibiting was my contention that Theory had systematically overruled the visceral, individualistic procedure of evaluation: specifically, how do we reconcile what we feel about a text with a universal aesthetic involving high and low cultural values? On the one hand Theory had highlighted, and questioned, a key aspect of their educational experience. They had, since GCSE, been confronted by 'the canon' of major authors and texts but no-one had explained to them why or how these had attained their elevated status. Now, Theorists of various persuasions, notably Marxists, cultural materialists and reception theorists, were informing them that literature was one of many competing discourses, with no intrinsic right to aesthetic pre-eminence, and that its alleged superiority was a bourgeoise delusion. They felt at once fascinated and disappointed, and in this regard most agreed with what I stated in my lecture. They welcomed the opportunity to challenge the judgemental criteria that buttressed the conventional academic curriculum, but Theory had in their respect 'opened a door to a blind alley' (and here I quote directly from one of the disillusioned third years). What they wanted was the opportunity to discuss how and why impressionism could be articulated and defended. They were keen to examine the discordances between their private, elemental responses to some literary texts – everything from boredom, through alienation to the simple, some might say simplistic, experience of feeling a personal affinity with a character in a novel – and the impersonal demands of literary criticism. Though not necessarily agreeing with my opinions, several were engaged by my discussion of Modernism. During their three years they too had encountered texts they felt were arbitrarily inaccessible, pointless exercises in experiment which yielded to the reader nothing resembling enjoyment. They had not, of course, felt able to voice such opinions to their tutors, and certainly not in written assignments or examinations. Nonetheless they would have welcomed the chance to talk, perhaps even write, about the reasons why we do or do not enjoy or admire literary texts. Theory, they felt, broadened this possibility but then foreclosed it: evaluation, either in terms of aesthetic principles or personal registers, appeared anathema to all aspects of the theoretical agenda.

The issue of evaluation was pressed for discussion more than others in the extra seminar following my close-of-module paper. Some, for practical purposes, wanted to test their own thoughts on this before risking the wild-card essay but others seemed simply engrossed by the opportunity to talk openly about a topic that interested them, was indeed essential to their engagements with literature, but which seemed throughout the curriculum to be 'the thought that dare not speak its name'. We discussed an enormous variety of authors and problems but to prevent these exchanges becoming counterproductive – given that a thorough grounding in aesthetics and stylistics would involve another module – I asked them to perform a dry critical analysis on the type of costive and oblique Modernist 'poems' used by Fish, Culler and Eagleton to illustrate points on interpretive relativity , and I urged them to supplement this with comments on the quality of the work and their opinions on the accomplishments of the poet. I used early examples of the work of that acclaimed practitioner of the Westernised Haiku, E.J. Thribb, resident versifier of *Private Eye* (having checked in advance that none of the group were readers of *Private Eye* – a confirmation that saddened me greatly), a free verse piece enjambed and shaped by myself with the words borrowed from an article on truffles in a magazine belonging to my wife, and a classic early William Carlos William poem which, I surmised and hoped, none of them had previously encountered. We talked of how small temperamental fissures on the part of the poet could be discerned in their isolation of a phrase, of how the language shaped its own poetic province and its particular emotional domain: this bespoke something unique and special – a combination of the poet's private register with his consummate skill as an artist. I should add that this was the response to the poem by Williams. E.J. Thribb and the redistributed sentences from the article on truffles were dismissed as: 'crap', 'infantile', 'self caricature', and 'pitiably incompetent'.

I would not go as far as to argue that my students are intellectually superior to Fish's or the putative victims of Eagleton's and Culler's dogma but I would claim that Theory exercises a dreadful stranglehold upon English Studies. Being asked to evaluate literary art, to identify and estimate its qualities means that you are obliged to conduct a private exercise; self-scrutiny. If after hours of close reading you can recognise that one poet is a genius and another a buffoon then you can move to the next stage, take a step back and look at how such judgements are made. They are your judgements and estimations but will you stand by them, defend them against opposing views? If you can, you are on the way to achieving some kind of balance between the quixotic preserve of individuality and the forum of argument and debate where subjectivity must be balanced against a system governed by abstract rules and conventions. Distinguishing good writing from rubbish – an activity discouraged by Theory – is in truth the keystone to English Studies' claim upon relevance and it was this issue which predominated among these students' responses to my, deliberately provocative, diatribe against Theory. We had, I think, fixed upon an embarrassing deficiency which Theory, albeit obliquely, brought to the surface but which was endemic to English Studies as a whole, from school through university.

The most memorable exchange involved, initially, Shakespeare but it spread into a discussion on issues rarely canvassed in seminars, and which has been influential in my decision to include this paper as part of my contribution to *Teaching Theory*. One student, let us call her Eimer because that is her name, had ventured, daringly, that Shakespeare had always provoked in her a sense of hostility and dissatisfaction and she explained why. She had, like many of her adolescent peers, felt for the great man's compulsory texts nothing more than boredom and indifference. An erudite, amusing sixth form teacher had caused her to appreciate the formidable artistry and intellectual gravity of the plays studied – appreciate, she emphasised, but not enjoy. She was, she affirmed, enjoying the opportunity that our discussion on evaluation had provided and she went on to describe why Shakespeare was still a personal *bête noire*. She could, she explained, marvel at the complexity of his achievements and engage with them appropriately (a First in her Shakespeare module proved that) but she still did not enjoy or in a very personal sense respect his work. Why? We asked. Because he was simply too good, an improvement upon all of the imperfections of his near contemporaries, and too 'ostentatiously clever'. His conceits were limitlessly perfect and exemplary. He seemed, as she put it, 'abnormal'. So therefore she was alienated temperamentally from what she must pretend – in essays and exams – to treat both with admiration and oleaginous respect. And then she turned to Theory, stating that there were parallels between her problems with Shakespeare and her experiences in the Theory module. She found much of what the latter offered intellectually engaging, sometimes exciting, yet at the same time once she left the seminar room the difference between what she had just encountered and the world in which she lived seemed both ludicrous and slightly infuriating. While she disagreed with some aspects of my anti-Theory paper, indeed found them 'myopic' and 'reactionary', she revelled in the dynamic of the exercise. It provided a channel for an exchange, or more likely a 'collision', between the sequestered field of academic studies – which students were generally speaking not encouraged to violate with their actual opinions – and the world in which choice and volition were continuous features; tackling the question of why we think or chose to believe or act in this or that manner, irrespective of what we assume is expected in an essay or a seminar presentation.

I would recommend to all of those teaching modules involving Theory something comparable to my anti-Theory exercise. It provokes and brings to the surface issues that are otherwise marginalized. It is, in my experience, the most effective method of introducing undergraduates to what is almost fifty years of conflict and division in academia.

The most engrossing question was asked every year: 'Are you telling the truth about your feelings and opinions or are you simply playing devil's advocate?' That, dear reader, is my business. Here is a version of my paper, so judge for yourself.

The Paper

Why I hate theory

I have taught Theory for almost twenty-seven years and have on a number of occasions written about it. When I began, my views on its significance were impartial, though apathy and indifference would be more honest descriptions of how I felt. Teaching it was a condition of my job and in the 1980s jobs were scarce. My employer was an august old-fashioned institution, justly proud of its purblind antiquity, and my job – non-permanent – was created because my new colleagues in English had come to accept, reluctantly, that Critical Theory could no longer be kept out of the curriculum but not one of them wanted anything to do with it. 1985 was the year. Yes indeed; how late it was, how late – but in those days Trinity College, Dublin made Oxbridge look voguish.

Now, a generation later, I can state without reservation that Theory prompts in me a feeling of abiding contempt. Where should I begin? Why not with the uncrowned monarch of this ghastly realm, Jacques Derrida. As I need hardly explain to fellow toilers, teaching, indeed understanding, Derrida must involve a lengthy tour of the radical ideas on language and epistemology which precede him, beginning of course with those of Ferdinand de Saussure. You will remember this from week 4. Along the way one is required also to look at how these theories diverge from a progressive continuum of thought that endured largely unchallenged for around two millennia prior to the late 19th century. This has, I confess, sometimes been fun, of the most shamefully egotistical kind. How wonderful it is to suddenly confront you with a model of who and what you are that bears no resemblance to what you had hitherto taken for granted. I could operate with the deft agility of the magician – turn actuality into apparitions and vice versa – but console myself that this is not just theatre and effect; it is the shock of the real, or to be more accurate the incessantly relative. Gradually, however, one becomes aware of the fact that the thrill is indeed derived mainly from the performance, that the alleged substance is a husk. After about ten years of teaching Derrida it occurred to me that he had not told me anything that I did not already know. I had been brought up as a Roman Catholic so I was fully aware of how doctrinal imbecility could function as a substitute for thinking. At communion I would wonder, does God really taste like this? And won't eternity be boring? How can we enjoy timeless bliss when we have nothing to look forward to? Language, as I then intuited and later acknowledged, could close as many doors as it opened. I had, I realised, been a deconstructionist since adolescence. We lived in the country, my dog was my closest companion, I spent most of my time fishing, and signifiers did not occupy my conscious attention – things did. So when I found out that the differential structures of language underpinned what most clever but deluded people treated as reality I wasn't surprised. I'd always enjoyed life without words; the trout waiting patiently between the chalk stream weeds was perpetually there, but its actual presence seemed endlessly, infuriatingly elusive, irrespective of what you called it.

Intellectual challenge and exhibitionism are part of the menu of higher education, so Derrida has long enjoyed an emblematic status in the curriculum. But his legacy has brought with it consequences variously pitiable and laughable. First of all I have become aware that as I drag you and your predecessors through the unforgiving territories of structuralism, poststructuralism and eventually deconstruction most, though not all, of you have a reasonably clear idea of what I am talking about. I do not simplify or distort but I try my best to explain to you that Saussure's unorthodox conception of language had gestated into the even more riotous thesis that all fundamental ideas and presumptions were destined to dismantle themselves, that without the ephemeral, unreliable network of signs which guaranteed their existence they were dust in the wind. One of your predecessors once asked me 'If this is what Derrida is telling us, why is he incomprehensible?' Quite. As a linguistic philosopher he was a worthy successor to Saussure; he had something significant to say. The architecture of his thesis was complex, demanding, but it could with attention and patience be understood, even if something like faith or pure obtuseness might cause us to disagree with it. So why then is his writing impenetrable? If his ideas can be addressed in ordinary language why didn't Derrida do this and save us the bother of having to translate his works into accessible chunks that people can consume and debate without feeling like refugees from Babel?

Derrida is dead so it is impossible to enquire. I would however venture this explanation: intellectuals are, amongst other things, very often elitists, and this sense of educated alienation and superiority is particularly acute in university English Departments. English is and always has been a neurotic, self-contradictory subject. Its shambolic history, involving sometimes ridiculous attempts at self-definition and affirmation of purpose, has been well-documented, and it is difficult to avoid the conclusion that Theory became so fashionable with academics themselves because it offered respectable, if borrowed, lifebelts for a discipline about to drown in a sea of amateurish vagueness and delusion. However, the true cause of the problems endured by academic English is its undoubted but unacknowledged status as a pariah. No other field of study involves such an uncomfortable, incestuous relationship with its subject as does English (and here you may substitute French or Chinese, provided that the subject is literature). Historians and sociologists create narratives from all types of evidence – most of it is recorded in language but rarely if ever is it intended as art. Historians seek to disclose authenticity from the matter at hand; no more and no less. Aesthetics-focussed subjects such as art history or music involve themselves in the dangerously fickle activity of evaluation but crucially their medium of interpretation, language, is not the one they share with their subject. With English it is, and this is one of the reasons that Theory has taken an addictive hold upon the discipline. It is in its various manifestations an annexation of other fields – politics, sociology, ideology, linguistics, philosophy *et al.* – all of which allow their practitioners to treat their subjects with the condescending superiority of the anthropologist or the clinical indifference of the pure scientist. A number, notably Marxists and cultural materialists, have argued that the sacred grand aesthetic of literary writing should be exposed as a charade and literature treated as but one strand of a broader weave of discourses and socio-historical symptoms. Some of them are I suspect resolute and secure in their convictions – sad though this is – but most Theory advocates are in truth attracted to the separation of Theory from its subject because it secures them against a dreaded fear of embarrassment.

Amazingly, in the long, tortuous history of the academic study of English no one has reflected at length upon the fact that when you

write about writers you are, of necessity, entering the unforgiving competitive realm in which they have already achieved eminence. If their
work is good, perhaps spectacularly good – and why else would we be
writing about it – then it demands a correlative tribute in the quality of
the writing that attends it.

Some have risen to the challenge. Bradley and Saintsbury (albeit more
than a century ago) were erudite, fickle and amusing; more recently
figures such as Carey and Ricks have produced criticism that involves a
stylish exchange between the interpreter and the artist. But in the vast
majority of academic writing in English over the past three decades
isolationism and inwardness are buttressed by Theory.

Consider if you will, Modernism. Modernism has without doubt set
the standard as the most exclusive and unpopular of literary sub-genres.
Demographics and sales cannot of course be taken as a measure of quality but never before have so great a number of books with so much in
common been ignored by so many. It has been rescued, provided with
the cultural equivalent of a life-support machine, by academia. One
might argue, of course, that the preservation of important artefacts is the
duty of academics and point out that without the educational infrastructure the work of Chaucer, perhaps even of Wordsworth and Coleridge,
would now be out of print. Perhaps, but one might also contend – and
I do – that Modernism has been kept alive for other reasons. Most people
find the classics of the Modernist sub-canon perverse and inaccessible,
and by 'most people' I do not have in mind those lumpen proletarian
types who prefer 'popular culture' – Jeffrey Archer, 'Eastenders', GMTV
and so on – to high art, because such people exist only in the minds and
consciences of Marxists. No. I refer to those for whom enjoyment, entertainment and aesthetic quality are interwoven strands in the experience
of reading. For them, or as I should put it 'us', literary Modernism is an
indulgence, a curiosity, something which no doubt tested the intellectual ambitions of its agents and acolytes but whose resemblance, say, to
the impatiently awaited next part of a serialised novel by Dickens is tenuous to say the least. Which is why academics treasure it. By presenting
themselves as gatekeepers to its secrets and complexities they take a
step toward that long-sought ranking as members of a prestigious discipline, an escape from their classification as dilettantes and intellectual
lightweights. Academics love Modernism – and indeed Postmodernism,
whatever that means – because they can treat it as their precious com-
modity, the aesthetic correlative to their own intellectual hauteur.

I dwell upon Modernism because its adoption as a hedge against
literary academia's status as a discipline without intellectual backbone

has been mirrored and overtaken by the influx of Theory. The story should be familiar to you. Around the end of the 1960s a generation of academics, predominantly in the United States, suddenly became aware of a deposit of Continental European riches which they sensed would transform both their discipline and their individual reputations. They were enthused because despite the fact that all were well-established intellectual figures, their profession had reached a cul de sac. The New Critics, so called, and the few others in Anglo-American criticism who had stepped outside the commonplace routines of critical analysis to contemplate its purpose and status had run out of ideas. Now, a whole menu of exotic cross-disciplinary servings had become available. None was based purely on the study of literature and because of this each offered devotees an escape route from such persistent, unforgiving questions as: what is literature; why do we study and write about it and, worst of all: how can we distinguish important literature from everything else?

The following is an example of Theory in its heyday, deconstruction employed by one of its most esteemed evangelists, J. Hillis Miller.

It is possible to distinguish chains of connection which are material elements in the text, like the red things; or metaphors, like the figures of grafting or of writing; or covert, often etymological associations, like the connection of grafting with writing or cutting; or thematic elements like sexuality or murder; or conceptual elements, like the question of cause or the theory of history; or quasi-mythological elements, like the association of Tess with the harvest or the personification of the sun as a benign god. None of these chains has priority over the others as the true explanation of the meaning of the novel ... Taken together, the elements form a system of mutually defining motifs, each of which exists as it relation to the others. The reader must execute a lateral dance of interpretation to explicate any given passage, without ever reaching, in this sideways movement, a passage which is chief, original, or originating; a sovereign principle of explanation. The meaning, rather, is suspended within the interaction among the elements. It is immanent rather than transcendent. ... This does not exempt the reader from seeking answers to the question of why Tess is compelled to repeat herself and others and then suffer through those repetitions. The answers, rather, must lie in the sequence itself.

(Miller 1982: 126/7)

Commendably, Miller is rather light with the gibberish and abstruse vocabulary that has clogged most Theory-infused writing since the 1980s – perhaps an Ivy League background is difficult to shrug off – but nonetheless he is determined to discuss the dynamic of reading rather that say anything unequivocal about what the novel means. Deconstruction – God bless it – is the top of the range intellectual counterpart to fin de siècle cultural decadence: a licence to fondle ideas, enjoy their corrupt vacuousness and then lounge in dissipated contemplation of nothing very much. Which is fine, for those paid and disposed to enjoy such opportunities, but how exactly does one go about explaining, let alone justifying, this to you, the undergraduates? Explanation is hard work and time-consuming, and it raises far more questions than it addresses, let alone answers. It is possible, if one were to swamp you with 'hands-on' guides to how Theory works, to get you to perform acts of deconstruction on texts. But how do I answer your enquiries – and they have been forthcoming – as to why exactly you are doing this? The fact is that in all universities Theory is entrenched but by no means integrated. You, the student, can't realistically expect to make use of this new tool in your core module on Renaissance Drama or the Victorian Novel for the simple reason that it will not be of the remotest relevance to their essay topics or examination questions. I note nods of agreement here.

You, or at least the more reckless and daring amongst you, will be aware that deconstruction is by its nature not an option or a matter of preference, something that can be used when you feel it appropriate or if the situation seems to demand it. It is an endemic self-consuming suicide note attached to everything written or spoken. So why, you might ask, does it not feature anywhere, indeed everywhere, else in the degree? Informing you that not all people are deconstructionists collapses the edifice that I have spent weeks building. It is the equivalent of introducing a four-year-old to the doctrine of Christianity, or for that matter Scientology, as the all-embracing explanation for existence and then, perhaps five years later, informing them that, well, it's merely one of many.

I concede that deconstruction is something of a special case, given that there are more detectable if frequently threadbare alliances between other branches of Theory – Structuralism and Marxism for example – which allow for an occasional sense of community. Narrow your focus sufficiently and you might even persuade yourself that Saussure is the grandfather of this disparate lineage.

Although Theory has taken root in the University curriculum it seems as yet to have no clear or determinate function. Everyone knows, or at least begrudgingly accepts, that it has to be taught, if for no other reason to inform undergraduates, you lot, of what many prominent academics have been up to in print for more than a generation. Yet the relationship between the essentially orthodox structure of virtually all degrees, shaped around traditional stages in literary history and focussing on canonical authors and texts, and Theory remains unsettled and faintly ridiculous. Here, after the first year Theory tends to feature alongside yet separate from the core components of the old fashioned curriculum, sometimes in specialist elective modules; in more adventurous departments it is integrated as parallel compulsory strands. There are, however, at least as far as I am aware, no English Departments or faculties in which Theory has become comprehensively integrated with everything else. Consider the difficulties. A course on Shakespeare, 18th century verse or Romanticism has its own self-defining prerogatives and limitations as far as teaching and examining are concerned. Lectures and seminars attend to specific authors and texts with historical and cultural contexts featuring only as far as time and relevance allow, and these same permutations obtain regarding essay titles and examination questions. A given agenda as far as what can in practical terms be taught and examined over a one or two semester period prevails and governs the traditional structure of the vast majority of courses, though this is rarely acknowledged or addressed. The idea that Theory might come to inform let alone underpin this structure is absurd, as much for pragmatic as ideological reasons. Even if a lecturer were inclined to enrich their course on Renaissance Poetry or Modernism with an influx of Theory they would face several dilemmas. They might feel temperamentally or ideologically predisposed toward gender theories, but do they acknowledge that feminism or queer theory are but two selections from the burgeoning supermarket of big ideas, apply them to everything on the course and then forget the rest? Perhaps, but they would then have to acknowledge that the course was no longer history-focussed or based on genre, but upon a specific branch of Theory with a particular recipe of authors, texts and contexts, rolled in as targets for its exercises. A more equitable module offering an abundance of theoretical approaches to, say, the Renaissance lyric is again an unworkable hypothesis. In simple terms there would not be time and if by some miracle time were found then the vast majority of undergraduates would be either puzzled or frustrated by the plethora of competing and sometimes incompatible points of focus. 'This week we're concentrating on Marvell and Donne so please set aside for a moment what has already been established; that authors don't really exist, that they're strands of a discourse. These

two were men and they certainly existed, creating their characteristically bullying patriarchal texts.' How would you feel about that? This
spectrum of affiliations and emphases would prove chaotic enough in
teaching the course but would be impossible to implement in examinations. Would all questions be infused with a predictable Theoretical
subtext? (Which brings to mind the manner in which literature was
taught in the Soviet bloc.) Would some questions be neutral? (Most,
inclined to teach such modules would treat 'Non Theory' as a delusion
so that is unlikely.) Even worse, how could the standard agenda of texts,
genres and contexts be reconciled with the equally crowded platform of
Theories? What if, in preparing for the exam, you had given particular
emphasis to Shakespeare's History Plays and cultural materialism, in
the expectation that the two are mutually affiliated, and found in the
exam that the lecturer had reshuffled the pack? The permutations and
potentially disastrous practical consequences are limitless but more
significantly they point up an overweening and never acknowledged
fact. It is impossible to teach undergraduates about what literature is –
principally its intrinsic features and its history – while simultaneously
attempting to persuade them of the relevance to this of 'Theory'. The
two activities are antithetical and incompatible.

Theory is fed to you largely via a system of introductory guides.
Students with sufficient time and courage can be persuaded to sample
the core material – and I have attempted to do this – but your perception
of the broad panorama of Theory, its history and character, is shaped
by secondary material – a level of dependency which far outranks that
of the old fashioned relationship between the novel or poem and concomitant guidebooks. All of these introductions are partisan and biased –
some outspokenly, others only by implication – and the standard for
this process of proselytisation was set by Terry Eagleton's *Literary Theory*
(1983), now in print for a quarter of a century. Despite the book's apparent purpose as an impartial, explanatory guide Eagleton systematically
undermines the claims to validity of virtually every branch of theory,
with one notable exception. His objective is to advertise and promote his
own theoretical and ideological outlook, which is Marxist. Some studies treat the Formalists and the New Critics with apparent impartiality,
but grudging acknowledgements of their qualities are overridden by a
consensus that everything they attempted to do was shown by their suc-
cessors, the real Theoreticians, to be mere delusion and fantasy. They are
treated as curiosities, historical footnotes, because in their somewhat dis-
organised, idiosyncratic way they were pledged to a single objective, one
that is anathema to the doctrines of Theory that have prevailed for almost

forty years. They perceived literature as being characterised by intrinsic defining features, which set it apart from other linguistic practises and which made it art. It goes without saying that the various brands of post-Formalist, post New Critical thinking would not indulge such an outrage. Art is, depending on your branch of Theory, an assembly of bourgeois falsifications, a sign system no better or more significant than advertising, or a refuge for xenophobic bias or male exclusivity. Hence we begin to see why the integration of Theory with even the most liberal implementation of an intensive 3- or 4-year English degree course is an impossibility. The pragmatics of the curriculum, its architecture, inevitably involve the acknowledgement of distinct periods of literary history and a predominant canon of authors and texts, and this is predicated upon an acceptance that literature is different from everything else written or spoken and that some literary texts are, aesthetically, superior to others.

The Theory Wars are over, not because either faction has achieved supremacy or admitted defeat but because any subsequent exchanges will be familiar and predictable. There is nothing new to be said. The effect of this state of stagnation upon Theory in the undergraduate curriculum is, however, less straightforward. Whatever else might have occurred had Theory not emerged thirty years ago as the fashionable shibboleth for those of us looking for tenure and promotion is a matter for speculation. What has happened is that Theory has taken residence in universities and become an obligatory feature of virtually all that is published – particularly pedagogic pieces – but with no obvious focus or function. In doing so it has effectively suffocated the one opportunity that university English might have had to claim for itself an intrinsic sense of purpose and value. Theory has immunized criticism from that most contentious subjective feature of talking or writing about literature: an inclination to offer an opinion on whether or not the book or the author is any good. The reasons for this are many and various, but most obviously the Theoreticians' perception of the reader and author as the subjects or constructs of specific ideological conditions and discourses undermines the notion of being able to recognise aesthetic value or quality as intrinsic features of anything. This has, however, completely separated academic criticism – and by implication its reflection in teaching – from that broader fabric of exchanges involving, for example, newspaper critics and readers, or even two people enjoying a drink and talking about books, where evaluation – the recognition of what is or is not literature of quality – is the central issue.

I am not of the opinion that 'good taste' can be taught or that even if you were made aware of why and how you prefer one poem to another you, graduates in English, would be better people or more able to cope with the world beyond university. But if English and indeed other arts and humanities subjects can claim any sense of purpose or justification they must, I would aver, be able to offer students, you, a means of framing your instincts, and enable you to articulate them and to better examine their relationship with more fundamental systems or states of mind. A starting point for this, in the albeit rarefied sphere of literary aesthetics, is the confidence and ability to evaluate, judge and assess the quality of texts, and this over the past thirty years has been forbidden in a quietly Stalinesque manner by advocates of Theory.

In many of the early Theory guides of the 1980s a gesture surfaced so frequently that it bore an unnerving resemblance to a Masonic handshake. Eagleton (1983) and Culler (1975) used it, as did Fish in his hymn to cultural anarchy 'How to Recognise a Poem When You See One' (1980). Its purpose was to show how the structures and devices that were traditionally believed to be the building blocks of literary form had no immanent literary qualities at all, they could be found anywhere; that students, indeed critics, had deluded themselves into believing that identifying them, and judging how well the writer used them, allowed access to the exclusively literary qualities of the work.

Fish in his essay told of how when occupying a lecture room for his hour on the lyric he came upon a list of surnames on the blackboard left over from the previous class on linguistics – the names of significant but specialised linguists who he knew his arts-based students would not recognise – and decided to inform his group that they would not as scheduled be discussing the religious lyric but considering more recent, secular pieces, specifically the poem on the board which he asked them to analyse. He then offers a roughly 1000 word précis of their erudite insightful accounts of how this unnamed poet had coerced the cultural and pragmatic registers of each word/name into a chain of interactions, a Modernist version of how traditional line breaks inject a secondary current of meaning into the otherwise familiar routines of language. Culler played the same game by dividing up visually a tortuously mundane sentence by WVO Quine so that it looked like a piece of free verse and performing upon it the kind of analytical operation that has attended the work of William Carlos Williams. Eagleton appropriated a notice from the London Underground – 'Dogs Must Be Carried On the Escalator' – to show how those exclusively poetic devices, paradox and ambiguity, are available all over the place.

The premise upon which these exercises were based is now accepted dogma, rarely challenged. Fish comments that he has tried this same experiment in at least nine universities, with the same results from his Pavlovian charges. His point is that cultural registers per se are programmed by a collective consensus of expectations and have nothing to do with the intrinsic qualities of the object.

At the 2005 annual conference of the Modern Language Association of America, playwright and novelist Ariel Dorfman offered a beguiling paper, based, he claimed, on personal experience. He told of how CIA agents had recently detained him in a windowless room in Washington DC airport. One of his interrogators, the silent one, bore a disturbing resemblance to Trotsky, while the other, more loquacious, agent tortured him with endless questions and accusations designed to at once depress and unsettle him. Dorfman quoted from memory the interrogator's verbal assaults, comprising the kind of syntactic contusions and lexical hieroglyphics made fashionable by the likes of Derrida, Lacan, Lyotard, Foucault and so on and taken on as a routine critical dialect by many literary academics in the US and the UK. Disturbingly, most of Dorfman's audience failed to appreciate the joke and appeared confused by being offered a discourse that they recognized as their own within a most unusual context. The darkly comic image of intellectual inaccessibility allied with isolation from the world at large seemed beyond their comprehension.

Dorfman was not just playing games. His escape from Pinochet's Chile, under fear of imprisonment, and his grandparents' experience of the European pogroms testify to his commitment to the duty of writers as witnesses to the actualities of the world in which they live. What irritated him and prompted him to deliver his lecture was the apparent disjunction between the extensive fabric of what we might term literary culture – comprising writers, readers, publishers *et al.* – and the institutions, universities, wherein literature is studied intensively.

The lexicon, mannerisms and intellectual hauteur of literary theory are now endemic features of the critical writing of all but a small minority of academics. As a quasi-discipline in its own right Theory has much to recommend it – challenging as it does routine preconceptions regarding issues such as identity, language, race and gender – but at the same time its own preoccupations have effectively alienated it both form its alleged subject, literature, and the body of individuals who are that subject's lifeblood, intelligent ordinary readers.

Caught somewhere in the middle is you, the hapless undergraduate, often seduced by the thrills of Theory and its albeit somewhat shopsoiled reputation as a hive of radicalism – virtually all of it is now standardised and dogmatic – yet puzzled by what exactly it has to do with the rest of your degree, let alone your personal inclinations as readers and your prospects as graduates.

The most depressing aspect of the PMLA episode was its illustration of how ideologically inflexible Theory has become. Evidently no one was capable of accepting Dorfman's image of CIA foot soldiers – no doubt to a man agents of the neocon hegemony – using as blind noise a discourse that they recognised and had come to treat with intuitive sympathy; suddenly Derrida *et al.* were presented as architects of a dreadful species of torture in which the brain is bombarded by a string of limitless, densely packed units of gibberish. In truth – and this was Dorfman's shrewd subtext – there is and always has been a disturbing similarity between most Theory and those brands of thinking and writing that are in their manner elitist and impenetrable and in their character totalitarian. Certainly the history of Theory has seen occasional clashes between branches that might suggest a healthy indulgence of dissent. During the 1980s for example the deconstructive pursuits of the high-powered US Ivy League institutions had an amusing set-to with the emerging so-called New Historicists, who seemed to aver that literary works and their socio-historical contexts might, just, be discernable entities. But these were sideshows, distractions from an overarching unity of purpose that has suffocated all aberrations. I'll give this a name: cultural relativism. Irrespective of the seemingly inherent disparities within Theory – and the Queer theorists, the poststructuralists, the Feminists and the Marxists sometimes appear to have little in common – a single, common agenda unites it: an utter contempt for the idea that a particular piece of writing or a writer might be superior to others. This is a problem to be addressed by those heroic individuals who plan and rationalise the literature of degree courses. Beyond the pragmatics, however, there is the undeniable fact that the influence of Theory among academics themselves has destroyed, or at best shackled, any inclination to discuss with students matters such as value, skill, talent, beauty. Read reviews and review articles in the best broadsheets and weeklies and you will find writers who, when encountering something worthy of celebration or disdain will raise their game stylistically and intellectually, recognise that when making such judgements, criteria have to be both established and practised. The ultimate question, 'is this any good?', is attended by the correlative demand: I must show that I am good enough to make such an assessment. To indicate how far the universities have distanced themselves from the real world of books and readers try to find a similar ordinance of demands either acknowledged or practised in a piece of academic writing. You will not.

The New Critics plus a few of their less easily classifiable contemporaries, and the Formalists, are the poor relations of Theory; treated with varying degrees of condescension and indulgence but in general ostracised because they committed the cardinal offence of attempting to define literature, to specify how it differed from all other uses of languages and types of representation. This was unpardonable because once the rules of the game generally known as literary writing are established it might be possible to pass judgement on how well, or otherwise, it is played. And the idea of innate superiority or inadequacy was anathema, albeit for different ideological reasons, to all branches of post-1960s Theory.

An early example of how, at least in my opinion, this approach became unquestioned dogma can be found in Eagleton's *Literary Theory* (1982), particularly the final chapter 'Conclusion: Political Criticism'. In this Eagleton rehearses the timeworn mantra of the 'illusion that literature exists as a distinct, bounded object of knowledge', and goes on to proclaim 'that literary theory can handle Bob Dylan just as well as John Milton' (pp.204–5).

An empiricist even with no knowledge of Formalism might concede that they both invest ordinary language with rhythmic undertow but then point out that such a similarity seems absurdly marginal compared with their manifest differences. Certainly a folk-rock ballad which reminds us persistently that 'The times they are a' changin'' bespeaks something of its sociocultural context but can we be expected to take seriously the implied claim that it belongs within the same field of intellectual endeavour and stylistic craftsmanship as the 12 book epic, *Paradise Lost*? Certainly there is no legal or professional ordinance that prohibits academics from practising and teaching discriminatory aesthetics but a tacit embargo obtains. The connection between cultural relativism and the politics of post-1970s academia, particularly in the arts, is self-evident: the instinct and practice which prompts us to rank some literary works as superior to others corresponds with the dreadful ideologies of class, race and gender discrimination.

This fashion might almost be commendable were it not riddled with hypocrisy. Following the success of *Literary Theory* Eagleton was commissioned by Blackwell to edit a series of short studies which would demonstrate just how the radical new order would operate in practice. Each of those books commentated upon an author who commanded high rating in the traditional canon and in literary history. Bob Dylan did not feature, but Shakespeare did, in the volume written by the series editor. The editor and the publisher knew that irrespective of the radical posturing of the authors of these short books, the canon and the consensus on what deserved to be in it would still be the backbone of every degree course in English. All of this could of course be treated as typical of the self-obsessed preoccupations of English Studies, an amusingly Swiftian realm of egotism and irrelevance providing ample fodder for the fiction of Lodge, Bradbury and others, if it were not for the fact that cultural relativism has become embedded in virtually everything that we are now allowed to do or say.

In this regard Theory is not just self-indulgent gibberish; it is dangerous. Until we re-establish an agenda which acknowledges that literature is intrinsically different from pop music, soap opera and the sign-systems of advertising, recognise its cultural superiority and begin to apply judgemental criteria to different literary works, then English studies will continue to play its part in the maintenance of an all-encompassing inflexible dogma which forbids the affirmation that some cultures, beliefs, social systems are intrinsically preferable, superior, to others.

Theory only permits and indulges political opinion so long as it is firmly left-wing, including the guilt-stricken mantras of Postcolonial Theory and such inviolable concepts as The Other. Theory entraps; it claims to offer unfettered radicalism while chaining its converts to an inflexible regime of what can and cannot be thought and said. The intellectual mechanism which eradicates discernment and evaluation from our encounters with cultural objects is disturbingly similar to that which disallows moral judgement from terrorist atrocities. It is a short step from a system of thought which ranks aesthetic discrimination as the symptom of late-capitalist ideology to that which perceives the suicide bomber as a function of unequal global power relations, rather than a murderous zealot. Similarly, the mantra of relativism, an extension of the founding principles of Theory, causes many of us, in the West, to treat with respectful indulgence a regime which sentences women to death by stoning for alleged adultory; we should not assume moral superiority over the cultural, religious and legislative traditions of other 'civilisations'.

I doubt that my speech will have any effect upon the comfortable, shambolic state we are in: Theory will continue to be taught, and its absurdities and loathsome imbecilities largely overlooked in the interests either of ideological evangelism or Quality Assessment, Course Revalidation and other concessions to overwhelming bureaucracy. Are there others like me? Perhaps, but most have retired or found a way of avoiding contact with or having to think about Theory. In my view

Theory should be taught in the manner that an anthropologist would introduce students to some curious self-determined fetish. It is a fascinating, horrible spectacle but not something with which most sane persons would wish to involve themselves. Yes, it should be taught, but if it were taught properly – that is, giving informed but objective attention to its true nature - few would want anything to do with it thereafter.

Bibliography

Culler, Jonathan (1975), *Structuralist Poetics. Structuralism, Linguistics and the Study of literature*, London: Routledge.

Eagleton, Terry (1983), *Literary Theory. An Introduction*, Oxford: Blackwell.

Fish, Stanley (1980), *Is There a Text in this Class? The Authority of Interpretive Communities*, Cambridge Mass.: Harvard University Press.

Miller, J. Hillis (1982), *Fiction and Repetition: Seven English Novels*, Oxford: Blackwell.

Vickers, Brian (1993), *Appropriating Shakespeare. Contemporary Critical Quarrels*, New Haven CT: Yale University Press.

Recommended Further Reading

Abrams, M. H. and Harpham, Geoffrey Galt. *A Glossary of Literary Terms*. 9th edn. Belmont, CA: Wadsworth, 2008.

Alsop, Derek and Walsh, Chris. *The Practice of Reading: Interpreting the Novel*. London: Macmillan, 1999.

Alter, Robert. *Canon and Creativity: Modern Writing and the Authority of Scripture*. New Haven and London: Yale University Press, 2000.

Alter, Robert. *The Pleasures of Reading: In an Ideological Age*. New York: Simon & Schuster, 1990.

Anderson, Perry. *English Questions*. London: Verso, 1992.

Attridge, Derek. *The Singularity of Literature*. London: Routledge, 2004.

Ayers, David. *Literary Theory: A Reintroduction*. Malden, MA: Wiley–Blackwell, 2008.

Barry, Peter, *Beginning Theory: An Introduction to Literary and Cultural Theory*, Manchester: Manchester University Press, 1995.

Barton, Edwin and Hudson, Glenda . *A Contemporary Guide to Literary Terms*. 2nd edn. Urbana: University of Illinois Press, 2004.

Beckley, Bill and Shapiro, David, eds. *Uncontrollable Beauty: Toward a New Aesthetics*. New York: Allworth Press, 2002.

Batsleer, J., Davies, T., O'Rourke, R and Weedon, C. eds. *Rewriting English: Cultural Politics of Gender and Class*. London: Methuen, 1985.

Belsey, Catherine. 'Theory in Cardiff', *News From Nowhere*, 1990, 8, 75–80.

Bennett, Andrew and Royle, Nicholas. *An Introduction to Literature, Criticism and Theory*, Harlow: Pearson Education Limited, 2004.

Bergonzi, Bernard. *Explaining English : Criticism, Theory, Culture*. Oxford: Oxford University Press, 1990.

Berlin, Isaiah. *The Proper Study of Mankind*. New York: Farrar, Straus and Biroux, 1998.

Bertens, Hans. *Literary Theory: The Basics*, London: Routledge, 2001.

Birch, D. *Language, Literature and Critical Practice. Ways of Analysing Text*. London: Routledge, 1989.

Bloom, Harold. *A Map of Misreading*. Oxford: Oxford University Press, 2003.

Bloom, Harold. *How to Read, and Why*. New York: Scribner, 2000.

Booker, M. Keith. *A Practical Introduction to Literary Theory and Criticism*. New York: Longman, 1996.

Bradford, Richard, ed. *The State of Theory*. London: Routledge, 1993.

Bressler, Charles E. *Literary Criticism: An Introduction to Theory and Practice*. 4th edn. Upper Saddle River, NJ: Prentice Hall, 2006.

Burgess, Catherine, *Challenging Theory: Discipline After Deconstruction*, London: Ashgate, 1999.

Carter, David. *Literary Theory*. Harpenden, Hearts: Pocket Essentials, 2006.

Castle, Gregory. *Blackwell Guide to Literary Theory*. Malden, MA: Wiley–Blackwell, 2007.

Cohen, Ralph (ed.), *The Future of Literary Theory*. London: Routledge, 1989.

Collier, P and Geyer-Ryan, H. *Literary Theory Today*. London: Polity, 1992.

Collins, Sue. *Literary Criticism: An Introduction*. London: Hodder and Stoughton, 1992.

Croft, Steven and Cross, Helen *Literature, Criticism and Style*, Oxford: Oxford University Press, 1997.

Cuddon, J. A. and C. E. Preston, C. E. *A Dictionary of Literary Terms and Literary Theory*. 4th edn. Oxford: Blackwell, 2000.

Culler, Jonathan, *Literary Theory: A Very Short Introduction*. Oxford: Oxford University Press, 2000.

Culley, Margo and Portuges, Catherine. *Gendered Subjects: The Dynamics of Feminist Teaching*, London and Boston: Routledge Kegan Paul, 1985.

Cunningham, Valentine. *Reading After Theory*. Oxford: Blackwell, 2002.

Dasenbrock, Reed Way. *Truth and Consequences: Intentions, Conventions, and The New Thematics*. University Park, Pa.: Pennsylvania State University Press, 2001.

Davidson, Donald. *Inquiries into Truth and Interpretation*. Oxford: Oxford University Press, 2001.

de Grazia, Margreta *et al.*, eds. *Introduction to Subject and Object in Renaissance Culture*, 1–13 Cambridge: Cambridge University Press, 1996.

Deman, Paul. *The Resistance to Theory*. Manchester: Manchester University Press, 1986.

Delbanco, Andrew. 'The Decline and Fall of Literature', *New York Review of Books*, 4 Nov., 1999, 32–8.

Diane F. Sadoff and Cain, William, eds. *Teaching Contemporary Theory to Undergraduates*. New York: Modern Language Association, 1994.

Docherty, Thomas. *After Theory, Postmoderernism/Postmarxism*. Edinburgh: Edinburgh University Press, 1997.

Donoghue, Denis. *On Eloquence*. New Haven and London: Yale University Press, 1 May 2008.

Donoghue, Denis. *Speaking of Beauty*. New Haven and London: Yale University Press, May 1, 2003.

Donoghue, Denis. *Practice of Reading*. New Haven & London: Yale University Press, 1998.

Eaglestone, Robert. *Doing English: A Guide for Literature Students*. London: Routledge, 2000.

Eagleton, Mary. *Working with Feminist Criticism*. Oxford: Blackwell. 1996.

Eagleton, Terry. *After Theory*, New York: Basic Books, 2004.

Eagleton, Terry. *Literary Theory: An Introduction*. Oxford: Blackwell, 1996.

Eagleton, Terry. *The Function of Criticism*. London: Verso, 1984.

Eagleton, Terry. *Criticism and Ideology*. London: New Left Books, 1976.

Eakin, Emily. 'The Latest Theory Is That Theory Doesn't Matter', *New York Times*, 19 Apr. 2003: A17.

Ellis, John M. *Literature Lost: Social Agendas and the Corruption of the Humanities*. New Haven & London: Yale University Press, 1997.

Easthope, Anthony. *Literary into Cultural Studies*. London: Routledge, 1991.

Farrell, Frank B. *Why Does Literature Matter?* Cornell: Cornell University Press, 2004.

Farrell, Frank B. *Subjectivity, Realism, and Postmodernism : The Recovery of the World in Recent Philosophy*. Cambridge: Cambridge University Press, 1996.

Freund, Elizabeth. *The Return of the Reader: Reader-Response Criticism*. London: Methuen, 1987.

Fuller, David, Waugh, Patricia (eds) *The Arts and Sciences of Criticism*. Oxford: Oxford University Press, 1999.

Fuss, Diana. *Essentially Speaking: Feminism, Nature and Difference*. London: Routledge, 1990.

Good, Graham. 'Presentism: Postmodernism, Poststructuralism, Postcolonialism', *Theory's Empire: An Anthology of Dissent*. Eds Daphne Patai and Will H. Corral. Columbia University Press, New York, 2005.

Green, Keith and LeBihan, Jill. *Critical Theory and Practice: A Coursebook*, London: Routledge, 1996.

Groden, Michael, Kreiswirth, Martin and Szeman, Imre,eds. *The Johns Hopkins Guide to Literary Theory and Criticism*. 2nd edn. Baltimore: Johns Hopkins University Press, 2005.

Guerin, Wilfred L. *et al. A Handbook of Critical Approaches to Literature*. 5th edn. Oxford: Oxford University Press, 2005.

Hall, Donald E. *Literary and Cultural Theory: From Basic Principles to Advanced Applications*. Boston: Houghton Mifflin, 2001.

Harris, Wendell V. *A Dictionary of Concepts in Literary Criticism and Theory*. Westport, CT: Greenwood, 1992.

Harrison, Bernard. *Inconvenient Fictions: Literature and the Limits of Theory*. New Haven: Yale University Press, 1991.

Hartman, Geoffrey H. *The Fateful Question of Culture*. New York: Columbia University Press, 1997.

Hartman, Geoffrey H. and White, Hayden. *Criticism in the Wilderness: The Study of Literature Today*. New Haven: Yale University Press, 2007.

Hassan, Ihab. 'Let the Fresh Air In: Graduate Studies in the Humanities', *Beauty and the Critic: Aesthetics in an Age of Cultural Studies,* edited and Intro by James Soderholm. Alabama: University of Alabama Press, 1997: 190–207.

Hassan, Ihab. *Rumors of Change: Essays of Five Decades*. Tuscaloosa: University Of Alabama Press, 1995.

Heller, Scott. 'Wearying of Cultural Studies, Some Scholars Rediscover Beauty: Tentatively, They Seek Renewed Attention to Aesthetic Criteria in Criticism', *Chronicle of Higher Education*, December 4, 1998: A15–A16.

Holman, C. Hugh, and William Harmon. *A Handbook to Literature*. 11th edn. Upper Saddle River, NJ: Prentice Hall, 2008.

Hopkins, Chris. *Thinking About Texts*. London: Palgrave, 2001.

John, Eileen and McIver Lopes, Dominic, eds. *Philosophy of Literature: Contemporary and Classic Readings*. Oxford: Blackwell, 2004.

Kastan, David Scott. *Shakespeare after Theory*. New York: Routledge, 1999.

Kecht, Maria-Regina. *Pedagogy Is Politics. Literary Theory and Critical Teaching*. Indiana: University of Illinois press, 1992.

Kenneth Womack. 'Selected Bibliography of Theory and Criticism', *Norton Anthology of Theory and Criticism*, nd ed., gen. ed. Vincent B. Leitch. New York: W. W. Norton, 2010. 2655–88.

Kermode, Frank. "The Academy vs. the Humanities', *The Atlantic Monthly* Vol. 280, No. 2 (1997): 93–6.

Kermode, Frank 2001 "Art among the Ruins" (Review of Kastan's *Shakespeare after Theory* and Gallagher and Greenblatt's *Practicing New Historicism*), *New York Review of Books*, July 5, 59–63.

Kermode, Frank and Alter, Robert. *Pleasure, Change, and Canon* (The Berkeley Tanner Lectures). Oxford: Oxford University Press, 2004.

Kermode, Frank. *Pieces of My Mind : Essays and Criticism 1958–2002*. New York: Farrar, Straus and Giroux, 2003.

Kermode, Frank *Shakespeare's Language*. New York: Farrar Straus Giroux, 2000.

Kernan, Alvin. *The Death of Literature*. New Haven: Yale University Press, 1990.

Klarer, Mario. *An Introduction to Literary Studies*. 2nd edn. New York: Routledge, 2004.

Knight, Christopher J. *Uncommon Readers: Denis Donoghue, Frank Kermode, George Steiner, and the Tradition of the Common Reader*. Toronto, Ontario, Canada: University of Toronto Press, 2003.

Kundera, Milan. *Testaments Betrayed*. New York: Perennial, 2001.

Lather, Patti. *Feminist Research and Pedegogy with/in the Postmodern*. London: Routledge, 1991.

Lechte, John. *Fifty Key Contemporary Thinkers: From Structuralism to Postmodernity*. 2nd edn. New York: Routledge, 2007.

Lentricchia, Frank. *After The New Criticism*. Chicago: Chicago University Press, 1980.

Lentricchia, Frank and Thomas McLaughlin, eds. *Critical Terms for Literary Study*. 2nd edn. Chicago: U of Chicago P, 1995.

Lentricchia, Frank. "'Last Will and Testament of an Ex-Literary Critic'*, Lingua Franca* (Sept./Oct. 1996): 59–67.

Luke, Carmen and Gore, Jennifer. *Feminisms and Critical Pedagogy*. London: Routledge, 1992.

M. Keith Booker. *Teaching with THE NORTON ANTHOLOGY OF THEORY AND CRITICISM: A Guide for Instructors*. New York: W. W. Norton, 2001.

MacCabe, Colin. *Futures for English*. Manchester: Manchester University of Press, 1988.

Macquillan, Martin, MacDonald, Graeme, Purves, Robin and Thomson, Stephen. *Post-Theory: New Directions in Criticism*, Edinburgh: Edinburgh University Press, 1999.

Makaryk, Irena R., ed. *Encyclopedia of Contemporary Literary Theory: Approaches, Scholars, Terms*. Toronto: University of Toronto Press, 1993.

Malpas, Simon, and Wake, Paul, eds. *Routledge Companion to Critical Theory*. New York: Routledge, 2006.

Mitchell, W. J. T. "The Commitment to Form, or, Still Crazy after All These Years'*, PMLA, 2003*, 118: 321–5.

Nelson, Cary, ed. *Theory in the Classroom*. Urbana: University of Illinois Press, 1986.

O'Connor, Erin. "Preface for a Post-Postcolonial Criticism'*, Theory's Empire: An Anthology of Dissent*. Eds Daphne Patai and Will H. Corral. Columbia University Press, New York, 2005.

O'Dair, Sharon. *Class, Critics, and Shakespeare: Bottom Lines on the Culture Wars*. Ann Arbor: University of Michigan Press, 2000.

Parker, Patricia A *et al.*, eds. *Shakespeare and the Question of Theory*. New York: Methuen, 1985.

Parrinder, Patrick. *The Failure of Theory*. Brighton: Harvester Press, 1987.

Payne, Michael and Schad, John, eds. *Life After Theory: Jacques Derrida, Frank Kermode, Toril Moi, and Christopher Norris*. London: Continuum International Publishing Group, 2003.

Pope, Rob. *Textual Intervention: Critical and Creative Strategies for Literary Studies*, London: Routledge, 1995.

Posner, Richard A "Against Ethical Criticism: Part Two', *Philosophy and Literature* 22 (1998): 394–412.

Posner, Richard A. "Against Ethical Criticism', *Philosophy and Literature* 21 (1997): 1–27.

Rabinowitz, Peter and Smith, Michael W., eds. *Authorizing Readers: Resistance and Respect in the Teaching of Literature*. New York: Teachers College Press, 1998.

Richter, David H. and Graff, Gerald. *Falling into Theory: Conflicting Views on Reading Literature*. Boston: Bedford Books, 2000.

Robert Scholes. *Textual Power: Literary Theory and the Teaching of English*. New York: Yale University Press, 1985.

Ryan, Michael. *Literary Theory: A Practical Introduction*. 2nd edn. Cambridge: Blackwell, 2007.

Sartre, John Paul. *What Is Literature?* London: Routledge Classics, 2001.

Scarry, Elaine. *On Beauty and Being Just*. Princeton, NJ: Princeton University Press, 1999.

Schwan, Anne and Shapiro, Stephen. *How to Read Foucault's Discipline and Punish*. London: Pluto Press, 2011.

Schwartz, Richard B. *After the Death of Literature*. Carbondale and Edwardsville: Southern Illinois University Press, 1997.

Selden, Raman, Widdowson, Peter and Brooker, Peter. *A Reader's Guide to Contemporary Literary Theory*, Hemel Hempstead: Harvester Wheatsheaf, 1989.

Shaw, Peter. *Recovering American Literature*. Chicago: Ivan R. Dee, 1994.

Siebers, Tobin. *The Ethics of Criticism*. Ithaca: Cornell University Press, 1988.

Sim, Stuart and Van Loon, Borin. *Introducing Critical Theory*, Cambridge: Icon Books, 2005.

Soderholm, James, ed. *Beauty and the Critic: Aesthetics in an Age of Cultural Studies*. Tuscaloosa: University of Alabama Press, 1997.

Trilling, Lionel. *A Gathering of Fugitives. Uniform Edition*. New York: Harcourt Brace Jovanovich, [1956], 1978.

Trilling, Lionel. *The Liberal Imagination. Uniform Edition*. New York: Harcourt Brace Jovanovich, [1950], 1979.

Tyson, Lois. *Critical Theory Today: A User-Friendly Guide*. 2nd ed. London: Routledge, 2006.

Ulmer, Gregory L. *Applied Grammatology: Post(e) – Pedagogy from Jacques Derrida to Joseph Beuys*. Baltimore and London: Johns Hopkins University Press, 1985.

Waugh, Patricia, ed. *Literary Theory and Criticism: An Oxford Guide*. Oxford: Oxford University Press, 2006.

Widdowson, Peter. *A Practical Reader in Contemporary Literary Theory*, London: Prentice Hall/Harvester Wheatsheaf, 1996.

Wolfreys, Julian, ed. *Introducing Criticism at the Twenty-First Century*. Edinburgh: Edinburgh University Press, 2002.

Index